#1x12 46

Writing for College
A PRACTICAL APPROACH

Writing for College
A PRACTICAL APPROACH

ROBERT E. YARBER
San Diego Mesa College

SCOTT, FORESMAN AND COMPANY
Glenview, Illinois   London, England

An instructor's manual is available. It may be obtained through your
local Scott, Foresman representative or by writing to the English Editor,
College Division, Scott, Foresman and Company, 1900 East Lake
Avenue, Glenview, Illinois 60025.

Excerpt from *Anne Frank: The Diary of a Young Girl* by Anne Frank. Copyright 1952 by
Otto H. Frank. Reprinted by permission of Doubleday & Company, Inc. and
Vallentine, Mitchell & Co. Ltd.

From *Readers' Guide to Periodical Literature,* May 1983. Copyright © 1983 by H. W. Wilson
Company. Material reproduced by permission of the publishers.

Stanley Elkin, *The Franchiser,* Farrar, Straus, Giroux, 1976.

Dick Gregory, *Nigger,* E. P. Dutton, 1964.

Margaret Mead, *Coming of Age in Samoa,* William Morrow and Co., 1928.

Library of Congress Cataloging in Publication Data

Yarber, Robert E.
  Writing for college.

  Includes index.
    1. English language—Rhetoric.   2. Report writing.
I. Title.
PE1408.Y37   1985   808'.042   84–13875
ISBN 0–673–16639–2 (pbk.)

1 2 3 4 5 6 - KPF - 87 86 85 84

Preface

Writing for College: A Practical Approach is a process-oriented textbook for today's college freshmen. It presents a sound, workable, and contemporary approach to writing that blends a traditional approach in organization and terminology with the latest findings in composition.

Features

Instructors and students will find the following features:

- Writing is presented as a process broken up into a series of manageable steps that can be mastered by even the least confident student.
- *Writing for College* is written in a jargon-free style that is inviting and reassuring, rather than intimidating or threatening.
- Abundant exercises and writing assignments accompany each chapter, arranged in escalating difficulty to reinforce and strengthen the skills they accompany.
- A case history of a student-written essay—from the writer's first tentative notes to her final revised copy—provides a clear demonstration of writing as a process.
- Throughout the text, revising is stressed as an integral part of the writing process. Chapter 6, for example, offers detailed comments and analyses, taking the reader through the process of revising a student-written essay.

Writing for College is based on the conviction that the act of writing is a process that can be learned by anyone motivated enough to work at it. Students are introduced to the three stages of writing: prewriting, writing, and revising. Although these stages often overlap, each involves distinct activities. By analyzing what good writers do when they write; by considering the demands of the subject, audience, and purpose; and by approaching writing as a process to be mastered rather than as a product to be revered, even the most hesitant student can become a more effective and confident writer. This philosophy has determined the overall organization of *Writing for College*.

Organization of the Text

The steps in the writing process are presented sequentially in the first six chapters of *Writing for College*. The student is taken from the first attempts to find a subject to final editing and proofreading.

Chapter 1 establishes a sympathetic tone and encourages the student to begin writing immediately with success and confidence. Chapter 2 offers practical solutions to the two problems faced by every writer: coming up with ideas and getting started. Chapter 3 gives detailed suggestions for choosing and limiting a topic, determining purpose and audience, gathering material, and writing a thesis statement. Chapter 4 presents the most important organizational patterns available to the writer, as well as suggestions and models for writing outlines. Chapter 5 explains and illustrates the most helpful patterns for developing the expository essay. The importance of revision and editing is demonstrated in Chapter 6 by detailed comments and extensive analyses of two student-written essays.

Because much college writing requires that the writer persuade the reader to take a specific course of action or accept a particular point of view, Chapter 7 considers the problems unique to persuasive writing. Chapters 8, 9, and 10 move from the larger to the smaller units of discourse: the paragraph, the sentence, and the word. Chapter 11, based on the new MLA style, offers an innovative approach to the term paper by teaching the students a "search strategy," a step-by-step process of collecting and evaluating information on their topics. Since other important writing that students will do involves essay examinations and business letters and résumés, Chapter 12 provides practical and detailed suggestions for mastering these skills.

"A Handbook of Grammar and Graphics" is more than a compendium of rules. It tackles the most common errors in usage and explains how they may be avoided. Designed as a teaching and editing tool rather than as a sterile reference work, it contains copious exercises on sentence errors, punctuation, and capitalization. The appendixes contain two helpful writing aids: a glossary of usage, and a list of 250 writing topics for those inevitable times when students cannot think of anything to write about.

Exercises and Writing Assignments

The act of writing daunts many students. They believe that they have nothing to say; they do not know how or where to begin when faced with a writing task; and they ignore the process of writing, emphasizing instead only the finished product. The exercises and writing assignments in *Writing for College* are designed to respond to these situations. They enable the student to start writing with success immediately by beginning with manageable tasks and by developing meaningful ideas.

Most instructors will find more exercises and assignments in each chapter than can be satisfactorily used in a semester course in composition. Because classes vary in ability (and because instructors like to avoid the monotony of the same assignments semester after semester), users of *Writing for College* will be able to modify or vary the assignments in each class.

Acknowledgments

Every textbook is inevitably a collaboration, and *Writing for College* is no exception. It is a pleasure to cite my indebtedness to colleagues and friends who have provided inspiration, ideas, and valuable criticism.

This project began as a result of conversations with Christopher Jennison, a Scott, Foresman editor and longtime friend. James Burl Hogins, a distinguished colleague, author, and experienced classroom teacher at San Diego Mesa College, was a source of invaluable counsel and sage advice. Emil Hurtik, also of the Mesa College English department, helped clarify several concepts and ideas in Chapter 7. Virginia Tiefel, head of undergraduate libraries at The Ohio State University, generously supplied information about the search strategy explained in Chapter 11, and Jeanne Newhouse of the San Diego Mesa library cooperated with her customary cheerful patience.

Several instructors throughout the country commented on the manuscript and offered helpful suggestions. In particular, I would like to acknowledge the contributions of Charles T. Bunting, Santa Fe Community College; Michael Fuller, California State College-Stanislaus; C. Jeriel Howard, Northeastern Illinois University; Charlotte Koomjohn, Towson State University; Mary Mittler, Oakton Community College; Charles Moore, California State University-Sacramento; Mary Northcut, Richland College; David Skwire, Cuyahoga Community College; and George Welch, Miami-Dade Community College.

I would also like to record my gratitude to my students at San Diego Mesa College who used earlier versions of this book. Their candor and their suggestions for its improvement have helped immeasurably to make it a useful and practical textbook.

The debt that I owe Constance A. Rajala of Scott, Foresman goes beyond the usual obligation of an author to an editor. At every stage of the development of this manuscript she has given encouragement, sound advice, and helpful criticism. Her common sense, good humor, and classroom experience have combined to make her an editor *par excellence*. Patricia A. Rossi, also of the Scott, Foresman staff, has meticulously and judiciously edited the manuscript and saved me from several stylistic and chauvinistic lapses.

Finally, it is a pleasure to thank my wife Mary, who has listened, reacted, comforted, and inspired.

Robert E. Yarber

A Brief Table of Contents

Contents

CHAPTER 3 *Planning the Essay*   25

CHAPTER 7   *Writing the Persuasive Essay*   127

CHAPTER 8 *Writing Paragraphs*

CHAPTER 9   *Writing Effective Sentences*   *185*

C H A P T E R

1

On Writing: A Preview

Why Write?

You have probably been told by your high school and college instructors that writing is an important and practical skill. Nevertheless, you may not be convinced that the ability to write will be important in your own future. If so, you will be surprised at the results of a recent survey by the National Institute of Education. More than four thousand working men and women who had graduated fifteen years earlier were asked to name the courses they would have taken in college if they had known then what they know now. The designers of the survey expected people to name courses in computer science, mathematics, or business. But the courses most often mentioned by the respondents were courses in writing.

If you already have a job, you are probably not surprised at their answer. Many jobs require the ability to write. Corporate leaders agree that despite the increasing use of the telephone and the computer, much information must still be communicated in writing. Some ten million Americans—managers, engineers, sales representatives, and countless others—write regularly as part of their jobs. Summaries, reports, proposals, letters, and speeches are required in today's world of work. The ability to write, therefore, is a marketable skill, and the individual who is successful in his or her profession is almost always the one who can communicate successfully in writing.

Your success in college is also determined, to a great extent, by your ability to write. Almost every class requires writing of some kind; summaries, exams, reports, critiques, essays, and term papers are typical assignments. Regardless of the specific assignment, your instructors expect you to write clear, well-organized prose without too many gross mistakes. They want you to be able to develop an idea in a logical and convincing way without losing the reader in the process. They expect your writing to be interesting as well as coherent, and sincere as well as correct.

That is the kind of writing emphasized in this book, and those are the qualities your writing will acquire if you follow the suggestions of your instructor and this text this semester.

Writing communicates your thoughts and feelings to others; it also tells you something about yourself. It helps you know who you are, what you believe, and what your purposes are. Maybe this is what Eldridge Cleaver had in mind in his autobiography, *Soul on Ice:* "I started to write . . . to save myself . . . I had to seek out the truth and unravel the snarled web of my motivations. I had to find out who I am and what I wanted to be, what type of man I should be, and what I could do to become the best of which I was capable." By expressing your thoughts, feelings, and beliefs, you discover and learn more about yourself.

How Is Writing Different from Speaking?

As a speaker of English, you already have a grasp of the structure of the language. This knowledge of the way the language works will help you as you become a better writer. Of course, there are several differences between speaking and writing, and some of them are obvious.

When you speak, your audience is in front of you. As a result, you can rely heavily on gestures, facial expressions, and even body language to convey your meaning and to detect the reaction of your listener. You can take shortcuts like incomplete sentences, single words, and omissions without confusing your listeners. Depending on the audience, you can use specialized language, dialect, slang, or even profanity. You can repeat a word or an entire sentence if it is not understood, or you can pause dramatically, whisper, or shout to convey a particular impression or point. Finally, you don't have to rewrite or edit your words as you speak, and as a result your speech is usually more direct and simple than your writing.

You have few of these advantages when you write. Although you can revise or censor yourself before you write the words on paper (have you ever said something for which you were immediately sorry?), the lack of an immediate audience presents some challenges.

To begin with, your writing must be more organized than your speech, because when you talk, you can change the subject, repeat yourself, wander off to a different topic, and then finally return to the original idea. Instead of a gesture or an emphasis with your voice, you have to use punctuation, word choice, and sentence structure to convey shades of meaning. To avoid confusing your reader, you have to select your words carefully and arrange them in sentences that follow each other in a particular order. Instead of using slang or terms known only to a certain group, you have to use words that are understood by most readers. Instead of bits and pieces of sentences, you use complete sentences when writing to avoid distracting readers.

What Is Good Writing?

It would be impossible for everyone to agree exactly on a definition of good writing, just as it would be impossible to agree on the precise definition of a good film or a good song. The problem is complicated because you have to write for different situations, for various purposes, and for different audiences. Nevertheless, most effective writers would probably agree on the following description of good writing:

> Good writing, like a good film or song or friend, is not boring; it keeps your interest by what it says and how it says it.
>
> Good writing is easy to follow because it follows a plan. In the case of an essay, this means that it sticks to one dominant idea which is supported or developed by enough facts and details.
>
> Good writing presents ideas that are fresh and original, not hand-me-down, tired ideas borrowed from someone else. As a result, it sounds like its author rather than like everyone else.
>
> Good writing uses language that is right for the job—formal when required and informal when appropriate. The writer uses words that are precise and vivid and exact, avoiding wornout expressions and clichés.
>
> Good writing is free of serious mistakes in grammar, spelling, and punctuation because those errors get in the way of the writer's ideas and distract the reader.

What Do Good Writers Do?

If all of this sounds overwhelming and impossible to achieve, you should realize that all writers, even professionals, face the same problems: How do I get started? What can I write about? What is it I really want to say? How should I say it?

Good writers solve these problems in ways that are as different as their personalities. But despite their individual quirks and writing habits, they share several traits. Before they begin to write, they make certain that they understand the kind of writing called for. In college, this means understanding exactly what the assignment requires. Good writers probably spend more time on prewriting—thinking, dreaming, making lists, and so on—than they do on the actual writing. They decide who their audience is, the tone they will take, and the level of language they will use. Before beginning a first draft they often work on focusing what they want to say. They put their main or controlling idea into one sentence before they begin to write.

Many good writers have a plan or organization in mind before they write; others let the ideas take shape as they write, and rearrange after the first draft. In both cases they present their ideas in a pattern that will make sense to their readers. They often make changes in wording, in sentences and paragraphs, and in entire sections of their pages as they subtract, change, or add material. Finally, good writers respect their readers; they go over their work carefully and correct mistakes in grammar, punctuation, and spelling.

Writing: The Three Stages

In the chapters that follow in this book, you will be introduced to the three stages of writing: *prewriting, writing,* and *revising.* Although each stage involves certain distinct activities, you will find that the three stages often overlap. The first step often takes more time than the act of writing itself. **Prewriting** is a time in which you mull over past experiences, observe the world around you, interview others who can give you information and ideas, and read articles and books for additional background when necessary. During this stage you will make notes and tear them up, take more notes and rearrange them, and write an outline before finally trying a first draft of your composition. In the course of all of this chaos you will discover that you have more to write about than you originally thought you did.

The second stage of the composing process—**writing**—is sometimes indistinct from the prewriting stage or from the stage that follows. Most writers report that the writing stage goes rapidly if they have spent enough time on the prewriting or "hatching" stage. In other words, after you have decided the purpose of your paper, the audience you are writing for, the main point you want to make, and an organizational pattern that makes sense, the composition almost writes itself.

The final stage—**revising**—is one that many student writers neglect. They are satisfied with their first draft and turn it in to the instructor, only to be disappointed at the grade it receives. Very few (if any) professional writers are content with the first draft they write. The purpose of revising is to remove the warts and blemishes from the paper—to add more ideas, remove weak sentences or irrelevant details, correct misspellings and grammatical errors, rewrite confusing sentences, and so on. In other words, this stage is a time to examine the essay from the reader's point of view—to make sure that it is clear, interesting, well-organized, and free from errors that might confuse or irritate the reader.

By thinking of the process of writing as three manageable steps, you will become a more confident writer, and you (and your instructor) will notice an improvement in your writing.

Some Suggestions for This Semester

If you follow the suggestions in this book and those of your instructor, you will become a better writer this semester. Here are some tips for improving your writing that apply to all your writing, not just the assignments you complete for your writing courses.

Read

You must have something to write about. If you are a recent high-school graduate, your experiences have probably been limited to your family and friends. Your biases, opinions, and prejudices, and therefore your writing, reflect that limited background. What can you do about it? *Read.* Reading is a way to acquire information, experience, knowledge, and an appreciation for other points of view and other cultures. It is also a way to liberate yourself from those fallacies that get in the way of logical thinking and clear writing. Reading is the handiest, most convenient way to expand your mental and intellectual horizons and to stimulate your imagination. If you become an active reader, your writing will be more interesting and stimulating because *you* will be more interesting and stimulating. Equally important, you will see how professional writers put words together into sentences and paragraphs, and you will improve your vocabulary. In other words, you will develop your style.

What should you read? *Everything.* The sports page, the magazines in the dentist's reception room, biographies, history, science fiction, the editorial page, travel books, your textbooks, the cereal box on the breakfast table, anthropology, short stories, novels, scientific writing, poetry, detective thrillers. *Everything.*

If you believe that you need to improve your reading skills, ask your counsellor to set up an appointment for you with a reading-skills instructor on campus who can test your reading rate, vocabulary, and comprehension levels and make recommendations for improving your ability in those areas.

Visit your library on a regular basis to look over the magazines and newspapers. Know where the card catalogue is and learn how to use it. Locate the fiction section, the reference books, and the *Reader's Guide.* Tell your librarian what your interests are and ask him or her to recommend some books for you. If you find an author you like, read other things he or she has written.

Be Nosy About Words

Use your dictionary when you see or hear a word whose meaning you are uncertain of. Notice the situation in which it was used and the kind of company it keeps. In addition to learning its meaning, know how to pronounce and spell it. Make it stick in your mind by reading about its history, variations in its spelling, or other quirks that will give it a personality. Keep a list of the words you have learned and make a point to use them in your conversation and writing.

You should own an up-to-date college-level dictionary. It is a learning tool that you will use in your college classes and for the rest of your life. Among the recommended dictionaries are *The American Heritage Dictionary*, new college edition; *The Random House College Dictionary*, revised edition; *Webster's New Collegiate Dictionary*, 9th edition; and *Webster's New World Dictionary of the American Language*, 2nd college edition. A dictionary contains much more than definitions.

Take Responsibility for Your Assignments

Make certain that you understand exactly what is called for when you are given an assignment in any class. Instructors are more impressed by a student who asks for an explanation of the assignment than by a student who turns in the wrong assignment.

First impressions are often lasting impressions. This is true in the academic world as well as in the social world. Turn in your work on time and make each assignment represent the very best work you can produce. Even if it does not receive the highest grade, you will have the satisfaction of knowing that you set a standard for yourself that you fulfilled. Your essays should be neatly written and legible. If you type essays written out of class, double space your manuscript. Follow your instructor's guidelines with respect to the heading, margins, title, and manuscript appearance. Before submitting your papers, look them over carefully for mistakes in spelling, punctuation, capitalization, and usage. You will find suggestions for revising your papers in Chapter 6 and a handbook of common usage errors and a guide to punctuation and capitalization at the back of the text.

An Explanation of the Exercises in This Book

Throughout this book you will find a number of assignments called "Exercises." Some are placed within the various chapters, and some are at the end of the chapter. Most call for a written response, some for a discussion. Your instructor may assign some, many, or all of the Exercises. Exercise 1 for Chapter 1 contains a series of questions for discussion. Exercise 2 also invites a discussion. Exercise 3 calls for written responses.

E X E R C I S E 1

Discuss these questions with other students in your class.

1. What magazines do you read regularly? What books? If you had more time, what authors or books would you like to read?
2. If you have a job, explain the situations in which writing is important.
3. Describe the actual steps you take when you have to write an essay, a report, or a letter. Some students have to smoke a cigarette, sharpen pencils, clean the room, and so on. What ritual do you have?
4. What are your strengths as a writer? Try to be specific: mention ideas, vocabulary, organization, or any other aspect of your writing that does not present too many problems for you.
5. What are your weaknesses as a writer? Again, try to be specific: getting started, weak vocabulary, shortage of ideas, and so on.
6. Bring to class some of your own writing that you believe is good. Read it to the class (or have someone else read it) to get their reaction.
7. What is *your* definition of good writing? What is your definition of bad or weak writing?

E X E R C I S E 2

Here are two paragraphs by different authors. Which is better written? Why? Notice such matters as the picture that each writer creates, the kinds of words he or she uses, and the way the details are arranged.

1. At noon the entire village closes down and almost everyone goes indoors. The only people still out in the sun are some old women carrying baskets filled with laundry on their heads. They are going to the stream to wash their clothes. There are also some kids on the street corners waiting for tourists to come by so that they can sell them some trinkets. There is a place in the stream where the water is deep and some of the natives are swimming. As you look down the street you can see the stores and homes all boarded up as protection against the sun. It is so hot that you could cut the humidity with a knife. The heat lasts for about two hours in the afternoon, then the sun goes down and it gets a little cooler.

2. It is high noon. The sand burns the feet of the little children who leave their palm leaf balls and their pinwheels of frangipani blossoms to wither in the sun, as they creep into the

shade of the houses. The women who must go abroad carry great banana leaves as sun-shades or wind wet cloths about their heads. Lowering a few blinds against the slanting sun, all who are left in the village wrap their heads in sheets and go to sleep. Only a few adventurous children may slip away for a swim in the shadow of a high rock, some industrious woman continues with her weaving, or a close little group of women bend anxiously over a woman in labour. The village is dazzling and dead; any sound seems oddly loud and out of place. Words have to cut through the solid heat slowly. And then the sun gradually sinks over the sea.*

E X E R C I S E 3

This assignment calls for you to write one or two paragraphs on each of the following topics. In each case, your job is to make your paragraphs interesting by using vivid and fresh language, clear images, and exact details so that your reader can see your subject. *Remember:* You have no right to bore your reader.

1. Describe one of the following:
   Your favorite hideaway when you want to "get away from it all"
   Your impressions of a recent movie, concert, or television program
2. Tell what happened the last time you had an unpleasant encounter with a person in a position of authority. For example, it may have been an argument with a traffic cop, a dispute with your parents, a disagreement with an instructor, or a run-in with your boss.
3. Write one or two paragraphs explaining one of the following:
   How to plant a lawn
   How to train a dog
   How to rig a sailboat
   How to select ski boots
   How to avoid losing your temper
   How to refinish furniture
   How to study for a final exam
   How to build a bookcase
   How to complete your income-tax form
   How to plan a party

*One of the two paragraphs was written by Margaret Mead. Which one?

C H A P T E R

2

Generating Ideas and Getting Started

Coming up with ideas and finding the courage to write those first few words is probably the most common problem that writers face. No writer has ever lived who did not at some time or other find it either difficult to begin or impossible to continue. In one of his journals the American novelist John Steinbeck admits, "I suffer as always from the fear of putting down the first line."

Of course, there are quite a few good reasons for writer's block or for a shaky start. Sometimes a writer tries to write before he knows what he thinks; he ignores the prewriting stage described in Chapter 1 and jumps into the writing stage before he has thought through his ideas. It could be that she has been assigned a topic she does not know anything about or have any ideas on. Or perhaps he worries— particularly if he is a student—about the mistakes he will make, and about the red pen he imagines hovering over each line, waiting to pounce on every mistake in grammar or punctuation.

In this chapter you will be introduced to four forms of prewriting that will help you overcome writer's block and develop ideas: keeping a journal, free writing, brainstorming, and asking questions. In each of these activities you set down ideas and words without worrying about correctness or style. Instead, you put together ideas and relationships that may be valuable to you later. This way it will be easier for you to get started when faced with a writing assignment. Even more important, these techniques will help you to discover and to generate ideas that you can use in your essays, thereby making you a more confident writer.

Keeping a Journal

To be a good writer, you have to write often. Most good writers make it a point to write every day. They find that daily writing improves their writing just as daily practice improves an athlete's performance.

One of the most popular and effective ways to make yourself write every day is to keep a journal. Keeping a journal has many benefits. It gives you practice in observing and describing details in the world around you. Because you usually do not show it to other people, it creates confidence in your ability to record your impressions and ideas. Your journal can also be a sourcebook for ideas that can be used later in essays and stories. In fact, many famous poets, novelists, and biographers have kept journals in order to improve their writing, and later use ideas and impressions first recorded in their journals in published works.

One of the most famous journals ever written was kept by Anne Frank, a young Jewish girl who lived in hiding with her family in Holland for two years during the Nazi occupation. On her thirteenth birthday her father gave her a diary into which she poured the story of the hopes and fears of living under constant tension. Her family was finally discovered by the Nazis, and she died in a concentration camp in Germany at the age of fifteen, three weeks before British troops liberated the camp. The following excerpt illustrates how she used her journal to "support and comfort" herself during her family's exile:

I haven't written for a few days, because I wanted first of all to think about my diary. It's an odd idea for someone like me to keep a diary; not only because I have never done so before, but because it seems to me that neither I—nor for that matter anyone else—will be interested in the unbosomings of a thirteen-year-old schoolgirl. Still, does that matter? I want to write, but more than that, I want to bring out all kinds of things that lie buried deep in my heart.

There is a saying that "paper is more patient than man"; it came back to me on one of my slightly melancholy days. . . . Yes, there is no doubt that paper is patient and as I don't intend to show this cardboard-covered notebook . . . to anyone, unless I find a real friend, boy or girl, probably nobody cares. And now I come to the root of the matter, the reason for my diary: it is that I have no such real friend.

The Diary of Anne Frank. New York: Modern Library, 1952.

Here is a journal entry written by a community-college student in Southern California. Notice how she records specific details, as well as her impressions and feelings:

It's been four months now since Mom and I moved to San Diego, but I am still having trouble adjusting. I miss Dad very much, and especially Kenny. I miss the green hills that I took for granted, and the leafy trees that lined our street, and the friends that I grew up with. I don't think I'll get used to the students here. Everything about them is different: the way they dress, the things they talk about, their slang, even the things they laugh at.

I never dreamed that my parents would be getting divorced. That was something that happened to my friends' parents—not to my mother and father.

I went down to the beach last night to watch the sunset. The sun was like a bright orange ball slipping gradually into the water. I wish Kenny had been here. Tomorrow I have to look for a part-time job. Who knows; I may even look in the want-ads for a used surfboard.

In keeping a journal, there are a few things to remember. It should be more than a daily accounting of your activities. Nothing is duller than a record of day to day routine. ("I got up at eight o'clock this morning. I called Linda to see if she wanted to go skating. I had a hamburger and a Coke for lunch.") Instead, it should be used to record your opinions, your reflections, and your experiences and their meanings. In this sense, a journal is more than a diary.

There will be times when you will sit down to write in your journal and not have anything specific in mind. In such cases, you should feel free to ramble on. You will find that your mind will soon focus on something beneath your conscious level, and the words will begin to flow. The act of getting words down will help you to discover what it is you want to write about. And by not stopping to tidy up your grammar, spelling, or punctuation, you will overcome your fear of the blank page.

After you have become accustomed to writing regularly in your journal, you will notice that your writing is beginning to sound like *you*. Every writer has several "voices"; the voice you use depends on your audience. In writing or talking to your clergyman, you use certain words and avoid others; with your family, you use another "voice"; with your friends, still another, and so on. In some situations slang is appropriate; in others, a more formal and precise language is more effective. The point is that by writing freely and often, you will develop a variety of appropriate "voices," each fitting the situation, yet each sounding naturally like you.

Some Topics for Journal Entries

A journal entry should reflect *you* and your interests. Many students and other writers have found that topics like those on the following list are good "starters" for putting the first words down on paper. Look over the list if you need help in beginning your journal.

Summarize a lecture or a news report you heard.

Give your impressions of a recent concert you attended: the crowd, the performers, or the music that was played.

Describe some childhood memories. What is the earliest thing you can remember? Tell about the time you were spanked unfairly.

Copy a favorite piece of writing you have found—a poem, a paragraph, or only a few sentences. Try your hand at writing in the same style, but on another topic.

Write an imaginary conversation with a famous person you wish you knew.

Tell what happened the last time you cried.

Describe an incident in which you think you were treated
unfairly or were cheated.

Where are you now in your life? You might have an image in
mind; perhaps you see yourself in a bumpy airplane, or on a
roller-coaster, or on the beach in Hawaii. The important thing
is not to merely think about it; write it down.

Write a letter to the editor of a newspaper in reaction to an article
you read.

Explain why you disagree with an idea or belief that everyone
else seems to accept.

Freewriting

Freewriting can best be compared to the warmup exercises that a team
does when it comes onto the playing field. It is an activity that loosens
up your mind as well as your pen and gets you ready for a writing
assignment just as stretching and loosening up gets you ready for a
game or a marathon race.

When you freewrite, you force yourself to begin writing immediately. Set yourself a time limit; ten minutes will be long enough the
first few times, and you can expand to fifteen or twenty minutes as
you become accustomed to the technique. Begin writing on anything
and everything that occurs to you. If you can't think of anything to
write about, write "I can't think of anything to write about" until you
get bored and finally think of something to write about. There is only
one rule: *don't stop writing.* This means that you can't censor yourself or
erase, edit, correct, revise, or worry about the impression you're
making in someone else's eyes. If you can't continue a thought, abandon it and go on immediately to another. Occasionally sum up in a
sentence the main point of what you have written, and then start
freewriting again, using that sentence as your takeoff point. The
process is somewhat like the advice given to someone learning how to
ride a bicycle: Keep going! You'll have a chance later to repair, correct,
and expand any passages you like.

If you write long enough, a "center of gravity" will eventually
emerge. An underlying thought or concern troubling or perplexing
you as you write, or a question you have been grappling with, or a
subject that your mind is drawn to will become evident. This "center of
gravity" may develop and become the main point of your writing, or
even become the basis later of an essay or report. Although most of
what you write may not be very good, some of it will be salvageable,
and at times, even excellent. The process can be compared to fishing—
you can cast for hours and try to tempt the fish to the surface. In

freewriting you coax the ideas to the surface so that you may ultimately land them.

Freewriting often goes against everything you have been taught.
It forces you to be messy and to tolerate chaos. On the other hand, it
frees you to think about what you mean without worrying so much
about the way you are saying it. A couple of comparisons might help.
Convince yourself that you are working in clay, not marble. You are
free to shape and mold and adjust. You are free to make mistakes, look
silly, be foolish, and then to go off in another direction. You are
working on paper, not bronze, and your blunders are not eternal. No
one is waiting to seize your paper and print it as it stands.

As you can probably see by now, the benefits of freewriting are
many. Freewriting will not only help you overcome your fear of
writing, it will also help you discover what is on your mind. It will help
you overcome the hurdle of finding words and putting them down on
paper. Freewriting encourages you to get on with it. Don't worry
whether these are right or wrong words, but think, instead, of your
meaning. It helps to think about topics to write about; give your mind
free rein and let it take your pen wherever it leads. And finally,
freewriting is particularly helpful for developing ideas on topics you
have been assigned. As you write ideas as they come to you, other
ideas will come cascading forth. You will be able to select those that are
pertinent to your topic and develop them further.

E X E R C I S E 1

Write nonstop for at least ten minutes without interruption on
one of the following topics. After you have written as much as you
can, look over your writing and underline the ideas that could be
explored and developed into essays.

relatives	war
Hollywood	New York
hobbies	truck drivers
friends	high-school cliques
pollution	religion

Brainstorming

Brainstorming is a prewriting technique that is very helpful in gen-
erating ideas on a specific topic. When you are assigned a topic for an
essay, write down anything and everything that the topic brings to

mind. Write for at least fifteen minutes, putting down all of the words and phrases that come to mind. As in the case of freewriting, don't stop to correct your grammar and spelling—you are trying to get as many ideas down as quickly as possible. Unlike freewriting, however, brainstorming involves the listing of words and phrases rather than complete sentences.

Brainstorming is based on the psychological principle of free association; words and images trigger other words and images, and your mind is often led to surprising destinations. As you brainstorm, you will see divisions and aspects of the subject that you had not anticipated, and soon your paper will be filled with a list of ideas connected with your topic. Many of those ideas won't be usable, of course, but many will fit your needs. The point is to let your imagination race ahead unhampered and not worry about your thoughts being silly or irrelevant.

If you were assigned to write an essay on "The Influence of a Teacher on My Life," for example, you might, after a bit of brainstorming, come up with a list like the following:

Tenth grade geometry
Mr. Tillotson's class
Joyce Townsend - my big love
Teacher's jokes; corny
How to read a problem
Self-confidence
Constance R.: smartest girl in class
First answer not always right
Importance of proof.
Don't give up.
Fear of unknown; reputation of math
Test day; scared
Pi and radius and circumference
Still afraid of math

As you can see, this list is disorganized and haphazard. But that's not important at this stage; you can select and rearrange the ideas after listing the words and phrases that come to you as you brainstorm.

E X E R C I S E   2

Select one of the following words and, using the brainstorming techniques described above, list as rapidly as possible for fifteen minutes all of the words and phrases that the word triggers in your mind. When the time is up, look over your list and notice which words and phrases attract your attention. Try to make connections among them, noticing any patterns that emerge as you think about them.

television preachers	college athletics
diets	the library
unions	blind dates
hospitals	vacations
motorcycles	disco dancing

Asking Questions

Another technique used by writers to explore a topic is that of asking questions. The most frequently asked questions are the following: *who, what, why, where, when,* and *how.* By applying these questions to a topic you can generate material and develop ideas. Of course, not all six questions will apply to every topic, and there may be topics that will suggest additional questions.

By asking questions, you can approach a subject in a systematic way and "shake loose" any ideas that may have been entangled or snarled in the background. Asking questions also leads you to answers you had not considered and to see your topic in a new light.

Mary Laine, a freshman student, developed the following list of questions on the topic of "corruption in college sports":

Who? Who is to blame for the scandals in college athletics, including illegal recruiting, gambling, and cheating? Who are the real victims?

What? What forms do the scandals take? What are the motives? What is the payoff? What evidence is available? What steps are being taken to remedy the situation?

Why? Why are coaches and athletes jeopardizing their careers? Why have the colleges looked the other way? Why has the public tolerated it? Why is this a reoccurring event in college sports?

Where? Where is the corruption worst? In what part of the country? Where does the blame lie: with the public or the colleges?

How? How has the corruption been revealed? How was news of it accepted? How are games thrown? How are high-school athletes recruited illegally? How are transcripts altered and phony courses listed? How are payoffs made? How do coaches, players, and others involved justify these acts?

As you can see, by asking questions (and then trying to answer them), you can often develop a topic when you are uncertain where to start. In the series of questions that Mary Laine asked are the seeds of several essays.

In addition to the questions listed above, there are others that can be applied to topics in order to stimulate ideas for writing. Here are some of the most common; you can probably think of others.

What is happening?
When did it begin?
What is causing it to happen?
What does it do?
How is it being done?
Where is it being done?
Why is it happening?
What does it look like? (smell, feel, taste, sound)
What are its parts?
How many parts does it have?
How is it different from others in its class?
How is it similar to others in its class?
How does it work?
What are its features?
What are its effects?
What is it related to?

Narrative and Descriptive Writing

Now that you have learned some techniques for getting your ideas down on paper, you are ready to try your hand at narrative and descriptive writing.

Writing a Personal Narrative

Narrative writing is storytelling; a personal narrative is simply a story taken from your life. It is organized chronologically—that is, it moves along in time from one event to another as they happened. Whenever writers want to tell what happened they rely on narration, sometimes in combination with description and other kinds of writing.

A personal narrative is easy to write because it is about someone you are an authority on: yourself. A personal narrative has a beginning, a middle, and an end. If it is brief (and your first one will be only a couple of paragraphs long), it should be about *one main point* or incident. A personal narrative should give enough specific details and facts so that the reader can see and feel the experience, as well as read about it.

In the following personal narrative, Dick Gregory, the famed comedian and social activist, relates an incident which took place in a restaurant. Gregory was eating when a wino came in, sat down at the counter and ordered twenty-six cents' worth of food. When the owner asked him to pay the check, the old wino just said, "Don't have no money."

The owner yelled: "Why in hell you come in here and eat my food if you don't have no money? That food cost me money."

Mister Williams [the owner] jumped over the counter and knocked the wino off his stool and beat him over the head with a pop bottle. Then he stepped back and watched the wino bleed. Then he kicked him. And he kicked him again.

I looked at the wino with blood all over his face and I went over. "Leave him alone, Mister Williams. I'll pay the twenty-six cents."

The wino got up, slowly, pulling himself up to the stool, then up to the counter, holding on for a minute until his legs stopped shaking so bad. He looked at me with pure hate. "Keep your twenty-six cents. You don't have to pay, now. I just finished paying for it."

He started to walk out, and as he passed me, he reached down and touched my shoulder. "Thanks, sonny, but it's too late now. Why didn't you pay it before?"

I was pretty sick about that. I waited too long to help another man.

Nigger, Dick Gregory with Robert Lipsyte, New York:
E.P. Dutton, 1964.

Gregory narrates this incident chronologically—in the order in which it happened in time. It is a brief story (fewer than two hundred words long), yet it conveys the shame that Gregory felt and the lesson that he learned.

Here is another personal narrative, written by a student recounting an important event in his life. It, too, succeeds in conveying a strong emotion in relatively few words.

When I was sixteen, I overheard a conversation between my mother and father that changed my life. On this particular day I had stayed home from school because of an attack of asthma that I frequently suffered. While resting in my bedroom, I could overhear my parents discussing my illness.

"I wonder if asthma is inherited," my mother said. "No one in my family or in yours has ever had it. Tom must have inherited it from his mother and father."

"From <u>his mother and father!</u>" I couldn't believe my ears. Weren't those two people in the living room my mother and father? If they were not, then who were my parents? Suddenly I realized what they had meant. I was adopted.

That night I could hardly sleep, shaken by what I had heard. The next morning I confronted my parents with the words I had overheard and demanded to know the truth. They looked nervously at each other, trying to find the words to answer me. Finally, my mother told me the story. My real parents were unmarried, and I had been put up for adoption shortly after my birth. Their present whereabouts were unknown. My adoptive parents had been unable to have children of their own, and the adoption agency awarded me to them when I was two months old.

For a few weeks I was confused in my feelings. I wondered what my real mother and father looked like, what their occupations were, and even such little things as what they did for hobbies and entertainment. But little by little, my attitude and thoughts changed. I began to appreciate my parents in a new and powerful way. When I saw the ways in which they had to economize by skipping a vacation or driving an old car, I realized the sacrifices they had made for me.

The shock I experienced that night when I heard that conversation was soon replaced by an increased love and admiration for two important people in my life: my mother and dad.

E X E R C I S E 3

Write a personal narrative about an experience from your life that had a particular importance or meaning. Don't just *tell* the reader—let him or her see, feel, hear, and share the incident as it happened to you. This means that you will have to limit your paper to a single main event, and that you will have to provide enough details of the experience and arrange them in an order that makes sense to the reader. Don't wander off into unimportant digressions; stick to the main point. To generate ideas for your narrative, use some or all of the prewriting techniques you have practiced in this chapter.

REVISION CHECKLIST

Narrative Writing

After you write your personal narrative, answer the following questions:

1. *Did I select one main incident and stick to it? Or did I wander off into unimportant areas and bore my reader?*
2. *Did I arrange the events chronologically, in the order in which they happened? Or did I jump from the past to the present and back again, confusing my reader?*
3. *Did I build up to a certain point or idea? Or is my reader likely to put the paper down and ask, "What's the point?"*
4. *Did I give examples and details so that the reader could know what I had experienced? Or did I just make a series of vague statements, hoping that the reader could read my mind?*
5. *Did I check the dictionary when I wasn't sure how to spell a word, or did I just guess, hoping the reader would know the word I had in mind?*

Writing a Description

Descriptive writing can be compared to a good photograph: it presents a clear picture of an object, a person, or a scene. But good description goes a step further. It appeals to the reader's sense of sound, smell, touch, taste, and sight. It is filled with details that help to create a dominant impression; it has a focus.

Good description follows a plan. When you describe something, you supply details about it and arrange those details in a way that makes sense. Several kinds of plans are possible. For example, you can describe an object by starting with its most important feature and then describing other features of lesser importance. Or you can follow a spatial order, arranging the objects to be described in some systematic sequence in space. In describing your room, for instance, you can start at the left side and work toward the right, or work from the ceiling to the floor, or from a far wall to a near wall, and so on. The main point is that you must follow a plan or design. If your paper is nothing more than a hodge-podge of unrelated details, you will confuse or even lose your reader.

Equally important in description are specific details. Your reader must be able to see the object being described. This means that your description must be concrete—you have to supply your reader with specific images instead of vague or general statements.

One way to make your writing specific is to use precise diction. Use words that are sharp and clear. Instead of writing that a character "walked," for example, use a more exact word like "shuffled," "trudged," "strutted," or "strode."

In the paragraph below, written by the American novelist Stanley Elkin, notice how the author creates a dominant impression—darkness and mystery—by his word choice and the kinds of details he selects.

It was a hotel, dark except for the light from an open elevator and a floor lamp by one couch. The Oriental carpets, the furniture, the registration desk and shut shops—all seemed a mysterious, almost extinguished red in the enormous empty lobby. Even the elevator—one of four; he supposed the others weren't functioning—seemed set on low. He looked around for Mopiani but the man had remained at his post. He pressed the button and sensed himself sucked up through darkness, imagining, though it was day, the darkened mezzanine and black ballrooms, the dark lamps and dark flowers in their dark vases on the dark halved tables pressed against the dark walls of each dark floor, the dark silky stripes on the benches outside the elevators, the dark cigarette butts in the dark sand.

The Franchiser. Stanley Elkin. New York: Farrar, Straus & Giroux, 1976.

The following description, written by a student, describes a museum containing a replica of a street scene in the early 1930s. Notice how she supplies details that appeal to the various senses. Notice, too, her fresh word choice.

As you open the doors of the museum, you will think that you have stumbled onto the main street of a small Western town as it was in the early 1930s.

Hitched to a wagon immediately in front of you are four huge black mules, standing fetlock-deep in gray mud. The wagon is piled high with suitcases, children's toys, and mattresses. Through the open doors of a drugstore on your left come the big-band sounds of a Nickelodeon and the chatter of young people clustered around the soda fountain. The smell of licorice and other candy from the general store mingles with the scent of shaving lotion wafting from the barbershop. On the right a couple stands hand in hand gazing at a poster featuring a movie starring Myrna Loy and Gary Cooper. Inside the theater youngsters howl at a Marx Brothers movie. In the muddy street a Model A Ford chugs patiently, unable to move, its wheels stuck in the ooze. Suddenly the sky darkens, and lightning cracks the gathering clouds. Everyone stops and looks up, expecting another downpour that will turn the street into a river of mud.

E X E R C I S E 4

Write a description based on one of the following topics. Before you write, make a list of all the details you can think of. Then, decide on the plan or arrangement that is best for your description. Make certain that you have not included any details that are off the topic and likely to confuse or distract your reader.

To generate ideas for your description, review the prewriting techniques introduced in this chapter. You can also use a series of questions involving the senses: What do you see? What does the object or person look like? What does the object smell or taste like? What is on the left? The right? By asking questions on behalf of your reader, you will make your description more vivid and clear.

your neighborhood
a cluttered closet or toolshed
the layout of a golf course or a garden
your English class
a pet
a scene from your window
a place where you work
a tourist spot in your city

R E V I S I O N   C H E C K L I S T

Descriptive Writing

After you write your description, answer the following questions:

1. *Does my paper concentrate on describing one thing, scene, person, or object, or does it try to describe too much?*
2. *Does my paper have a plan, or does it jump around, confusing my reader?*

3. Have I given my reader specific details so that he or she can see what I am describing, or is my paper just a series of general and vague statements?
4. Are my words sharp and clear, or are they too general and vague?
5. Does my paper reflect the care I put into it, or is it filled with careless mistakes in spelling or other errors?

3

Planning
the Essay

An essay can be thought of as a series of paragraphs about one main idea. The main idea of the essay is usually expressed in a *thesis statement*, a sentence which tells the reader what the essay will cover. In other words, the thesis statement summarizes, usually in one sentence, the controlling or main idea of the essay. If there is no thesis statement, or if it is difficult to locate, the paper will probably be a collection of unrelated ideas without a focus. The result will be confusion for the reader and a low grade for the writer.

An Overview of the Essay

The typical essay contains three parts: an *introduction*, a *body*, and a *conclusion*. The *introduction* presents the thesis statement and catches the reader's interest so that he or she will read on. Introductions can vary in length, depending on the length of the essay. For a brief essay of 300 to 500 words, a paragraph will probably be enough. Longer essays sometimes contain introductions of two or more paragraphs.

The *body* is the longest part of the essay. It usually consists of several paragraphs, and its purpose is to develop and expand upon the thesis statement. Each paragraph in the body of the essay treats a different aspect or division of the thesis statement. An indentation in the first line of the new paragraph is a signal to the reader that a new thought is being introduced.

The *conclusion* of the essay is usually stated in the last paragraph, although, as in the case of introductions, it may consume several paragraphs in a long essay. The purpose of the conclusion is to signal that the essay is coming to an end. It reminds the reader of the major points, restates the thesis, or urges the reader to take a certain course of action.

The following diagram illustrates the main parts of the essay. Notice that the thesis statement is placed at the end of the introductory paragraph. Although it is acceptable to place it in other locations, many writers recommend that the thesis statement conclude the introductory paragraph so that it can lead in naturally to the body of the essay.

In your reading of magazines and books you will occasionally find an essay that departs slightly from this three-part structure. For example, an introduction may consist of only one sentence which is absorbed into the body of the essay, or it may run several paragraphs; the body may contain a dozen major points presented in a dozen paragraphs; and the conclusion may be a single sentence or several paragraphs. You may even find essays in which the thesis statement is strongly implied rather than directly stated. In any case, you will still be able to recognize the basic three-part structure in such essays.

TITLE

INTRODUCTION WITH THESIS STATEMENT

BODY

CONCLUSION

The following essay was written by a student. Notice the three-part structure: the first paragraph concludes with the *thesis statement*, the next three paragraphs comprise the *body* and support the thesis statement, and the *conclusion* ties the essay together.

How to Buy a Used Car

Introduction with Thesis Statement

Buying a used car can be a painful and expensive experience if you are not careful. Friends give conflicting advice on the best model to buy, the ads in the newspaper make every car sound like a "steal," and even a visit to the used-car lot can add to the confusion. But shopping for a used car does not have to be an unpleasant experience if you will follow a few simple steps.

You should decide on the kind of car you want before you begin to shop. Talk to friends who own similar models to learn of any problems they might have had with their cars. Study the "Blue Book" and read the newspaper ads in order to get a fairly accurate idea of how much you will have to pay. Decide in advance on the best method of financing your car if you do not intend to pay cash. By making these decisions before shopping, you can concentrate on finding the right car.

Body

Whether you buy from a private party or from a dealer, there are certain kinds of cars you should avoid. Be suspicious of a "good deal" on a very recent model. There is an excellent chance it is a "lemon," or has been wrecked. Resist the temptation to buy a sports car that has been modified. The odds are overwhelming that it has been driven fast and hard, and at today's 55-mile speed limit and in city traffic, it will not function efficiently. Don't buy a car that has been in a wreck. Even though it has been repainted and made like new, its steering mechanism and frame could be damaged. And unless you belong to a classic-car club, don't buy a model that is no longer made. Finding parts will be a headache, and finding a buyer for it when you are ready to sell it later may be difficult.

When you shop for a used car at a dealer's lot, there are several techniques that you should follow. Never confine your shopping to one lot; visit at least three dealers, and let each know you are looking around. This will keep them from being complacent and encourage them to give you the best deal. If you have a trade-in, park it out of sight. The reason for this is simple: the salesman will add the amount of the trade-in to the price of the car you want. In this way, he acquires your old car for nothing. The best time to talk trade-in is after you have found the car you want. Road-test the car that you like. This will give you a chance to test the steering, the suspension and the engine. After finding the car

Body   you want, offer the dealer your trade-in. Let him know you are familiar with the "Blue Book" price and point out why your trade-in is worth more. Finally, after agreeing on a price but before signing the contract, tell him you want to have your mechanic look at it. It may cost you a few dollars, but it will save you hundreds or possibly thousands if it keeps you from buying a car with hidden defects.

       It is human nature to be afraid of things we do not know much about. Buying a used car falls into that category for most of us. *Conclusion*   But if you follow these simple steps, you can make shopping for a used car a pleasant and profitable experience.

Starting the Essay

When faced with the problem of writing an essay, some students sit down and write a first sentence, then chew their pencils for a while, hoping that a second sentence will follow, and then a third, and so on. It is possible to write a paper like this, of course, but it is a painful method, and the results are usually dismal.

     Most experienced writers, on the other hand, realize that the act of writing follows a certain *process*, a series of steps that begins with a blank page and ends with an organized, unified, and coherent presentation of their ideas. The steps in the process of writing an essay, which will be explained in this and the following chapters, are:

1. *Choosing and Limiting a Topic*

2. *Determining Your Purpose and Audience*

3. *Gathering Material*

4. *Writing a Thesis Statement*

5. *Organizing and Outlining Your Essay*

6. *Writing the First Draft*

7. *Revising and Editing Your Essay*

     As you write your essays you will often find yourself repeating some of these steps. For example, after arranging your material into a pattern, you may decide that you need more ideas. Or you may find after outlining your paper that your subject is still too broad and that you will have to narrow it some more. Or you may complete the first draft only to realize that you have abandoned your thesis and actually developed another one. In any case, you will find that writing an essay consists of a series of continuous and overlapping actions and steps. By following the process, you will overcome your fear of writing and become a more confident and effective writer.

1. Choosing and Limiting a Topic

Many of the topics you will write about in college will be assigned by your instructors. In such cases, make certain that you know exactly what the subject or question demands. Many students' papers fail because their writers did not understand the assignment clearly. If your instructor asks for a paper explaining the functions of the Federal Reserve System, for example, he will not appreciate a paper defending the gold standard.

If you are allowed to choose the topic for your paper, the following section will help you avoid several pitfalls that students often fall into as they try to select a topic.

Choosing a Topic

When you have to choose a topic, your first reaction might be that you don't have anything interesting to say. This is not true, of course—you are a unique individual with unique experiences, interests, hobbies, opinions, and abilities. Therefore, the first step toward selecting a topic might be a self-inventory.

What experiences have you had that others would like to read about? Where did you grow up? Where did you go to school before attending college? Describe your family. What are your parents' occupations? What ethnic, religious, or cultural customs does your family observe? What languages are spoken at home? What kinds of work experience have you had? What was the worst job you ever had? The best? What are your plans for a job and family? Who has influenced you? What subjects would you like to learn about?

The point is clear: one of the best sources for an essay topic is yourself. You are a treasure-house of ideas that others would like to read about.

In addition to the inventory described above, use the prewriting techniques suggested in Chapter 2 to play with potential topics. By freewriting, brainstorming, asking questions, and referring to your journal, you will make the pleasant discovery that as you write, you will have many things to write about that others will want to read.

If you are allowed to choose your topic, keep these guidelines in mind:

Choose a topic that interests you and about which you either have some knowledge or can acquire it without much trouble.

Choose a topic which is small enough to handle in the usual essay of 500 to 750 words. Broad topics like "love," "war," "happiness," and "religion" would have to be narrowed and restricted to be discussed adequately in a theme of this length.

Choose a topic which will be interesting to your readers. An elaborate description of your dog, while fascinating to you, might not hold your readers' attention.

Try to avoid topics that have been written to death: arguments for and against capital punishment, the legalization of marijuana, abortion, and so on. Write on them if you have something fresh and new to say; it is unlikely, however, that you can add anything interesting to the millions of words that your instructor has had to read on these topics.

E X E R C I S E 1

Now it is *your* turn to select a subject that you could develop into an essay of 500 to 750 words. Using the suggestions in the preceding pages and in Chapter 2, choose a subject that you are interested in and know something about. If you need help in triggering ideas for possible topics, look at the list below; if you still don't see a suitable topic, turn to the list in Appendix B ("250 Writing Topics"). Select your topic carefully because you will be asked to develop it into a complete essay.

The marathon craze
Junk food and nutrition
Stereotypes that are true
Illegal aliens
Changing attitudes toward marriage
Life in a dorm
Punk rock
The minimum-wage law
Body language
Reincarnation

Sharks
Electronic games
Being an only child
Credit cards
Soap operas
Jealousy

Limiting the Topic

After you have decided on a subject, your next job is to trim it to manageable proportions. A helpful comparison is to think of your subject as a pie: you are going to offer your reader one narrow slice. Many beginning writers make the mistake of being too vague or general; they offer their reader the whole pie. They confuse the *subject* with a *specific topic*. A few examples will illustrate the difference.

"Education" is too broad a topic to be treated adequately in a typical college essay, but "The importance of a knowledge of computers for liberal arts majors" is a topic that could be handled in a relatively short paper. Likewise, "automobiles" is beyond the ability of any writer to discuss in a few pages, but "How the diesel engine differs from the gasoline engine" is narrow enough to be covered in 750 words. Similarly, "jogging" is too shadowy and vague as a topic; "the mental and physical benefits of jogging," however, could be treated in an essay.

The subjects in the left column are general; the narrowed topics in the right column are more specific and therefore more manageable for a short essay.

Subject	Narrowed Topic
History	The first white man in Oklahoma
Death	The first death in our family
Literature	Science-fiction writers as prophets
Television	A defense of soaps
Food	Fast food: The view from the other side
Morals	Why I know some things are wrong

Subject	Narrowed Topic
Education	Who says everyone should study computers?
Religion	Television preachers and electronic religion
Cheating	Why some students cheat
Holidays	Celebrating the Vietnamese New Year in an Anglo neighborhood

E X E R C I S E   2

In Exercise 1 you were asked to choose a subject that you could develop into an essay of approximately 500 to 750 words. Using the techniques of freewriting, brainstorming, and asking questions, narrow your subject until you are certain that you could adequately cover it in the prescribed limit. Your instructor may ask you to discuss your topic with other students in your class to help you focus it.

2. Determining Your Purpose and Audience

After you have narrowed your subject, your next job is to decide your purpose and to identify your intended audience. Every piece of writing has a purpose and an audience. You may be writing to borrow money (purpose) from your parents (audience). You may wish to get a change in the physical education requirements at your college (purpose) by writing a letter to the dean (audience). Or you may simply wish to send birthday greetings (purpose) to a friend (audience). In each case, knowing your purpose and your audience will help you devise a plan for making your meaning clear and put you firmly in control of your letter or essay from the start.

Purpose

In a sense, every kind of writing has a purpose, even if it is to express the writer's emotions as he or she writes a private diary entry. But most teachers of composition agree that the purposes of writing for others can be reduced to these three: (1) to *entertain or please* the reader by making the subject enjoyable (the *aesthetic aim*); (2) to *inform or instruct* the reader by conveying or explaining the meaning of certain information (the *informative aim*); (3) to *persuade* the reader by convincing him or her to follow a certain course of action (the *persuasive aim*).

Scientists and engineers who write on the job are aware of the importance of determining the purpose of a particular piece of writing. When they write proposals and recommendations to a client, their purpose is largely persuasive; when they write technical memos and progress reports, their purpose is largely informative. In many cases they have to juggle or combine purposes; a persuasive recommendation report might have sections that inform, and a proposal whose larger purpose is to persuade will also try to please its reader.

In your own writing, both in and out of class, you will find that these purposes often overlap, with the result that you will sometimes entertain your reader as you inform, or inform as you try to persuade. Nevertheless, each piece of effective writing has a *main* or *dominant* purpose. If it does not, it will be like a boat without a rudder, drifting without direction.

As you get ready to write, you must decide on your purpose. Suppose that you have to write an essay on nuclear energy. As you acquire information about the topic, you are faced with a decision:

Do you want to explain to your readers how nuclear fission reactors work?

Do you want to convince your readers that nuclear plants are safe? Or unsafe?

Do you want to convince your readers that they should work to ban the disposal of radioactive wastes in their community?

Do you want to inform your readers of the benefits of nuclear fuels as compared to fossil fuels?

Each of these purposes is related to the topic, yet each differs from the others. If you decide that your purpose is to write an informative essay in which you explain how nuclear fission reactors work, you will have to forego any lengthy development of the topics suggested by the other questions. If, on the other hand, you decide that the purpose of your paper is to persuade readers that nuclear plants are safe, you would probably need to include information about the workings of nuclear fission reactors. In this case your overall purpose is to *persuade*, but to support your argument you will find it necessary to *inform*. If, however, you write an essay that wavers between explaining how reactors work and urging your readers to ban the disposal of radioactive wastes, it is doubtful that you will either inform or persuade them. A paper that shifts its purpose succeeds only in losing readers.

Writing a Statement of Purpose

The best way to avoid confusion of purpose is to formulate a *statement of purpose* before writing. This is a sentence that states your purpose in relation to your audience and your subject. It helps you keep in mind your central idea and the response you want from your reader.

Imagine that you want to convince your city council that all restaurants in your city should have "No Smoking" areas. Keeping in mind your purpose, your subject, and your audience, you would write a statement of purpose like this:

> My purpose is to convince the city council that the restaurants in this city should designate "No Smoking" areas.

Writing a statement of purpose will help you keep your audience and purpose in sight. As you will see in Chapter 5, it will also help you select the most effective strategies for developing your ideas. Here are some examples of statements of purpose. Notice that they connect the subject, the purpose, and the reader.

> My purpose is to help the reader understand the difference between analog and digital computers.
>
> My purpose is to persuade our Student Senate to select me as its delegate to the national convention in Chicago.
>
> My purpose is to help my classmates understand the symbolism of the Japanese tea ceremony.
>
> My purpose is to get my little brother to appreciate the song lyrics of Stevie Wonder.

E X E R C I S E 3

Reread several essays or papers that you have written this or last semester. For each one, formulate a statement of purpose. Here is an example: "My purpose was to explain to the reader the difference between whole-life and term insurance."

E X E R C I S E 4

Write a statement of purpose for the topic that you selected in Exercise 1. Be sure that it combines the subject and your purpose.

Audience

As noted above, every piece of writing—unless it is a private diary—is intended for an audience. If the writing is a college essay, the audience is the writer's instructor and fellow students. If it is an application for a job, it is the prospective employer; if it is a request for a raise or promotion, the audience is the writer's supervisor. Unless the words have the right effect on the audience, the writer won't get the grade, the job, or the raise.

We have all heard about the professor who knew his subject but could not explain it to his students. He, too, had a problem with his audience. Knowing the audience that you are writing for is important because that knowledge determines, to a great extent, *what* you say, *how* you say it, and the tone or approach you take to the subject and to your reader. After all, what works with one group of readers will not necessarily work with another.

The following letters demonstrate that their writer is aware of this principle. In the first letter, Chris is writing to tell his buddy that he has the opportunity to travel with a rock group as a bass player for four weeks during the summer. In the second letter, he is writing to his parents who had expected him to come home during the summer and work in the family grocery. Notice that although both letters convey essentially the same information and discuss the same subject, their language, tone, purpose, details, and attitude of the writer toward the reader differ greatly.

Dear Mike,

What a blast! I just got a call from Joe Brady, the leader of the Ratchets, and they want me to play a couple of gigs with them this summer. Do you know what that <u>means,</u> man? It means that I'm playing ax with the hottest group making the rounds. Me—little ol' me! Just last week I was getting ready to pack my rags and head for home and stacking grocery shelves all summer—what a bummer! Now it looks like I'll be "On the Road Again" signing autographs and fighting off women. And maybe making a few bucks for tuition next year. I haven't told my old man yet. He was counting on me working in the store, but I can't let a chance like this get past me. Doc Miller told me that I flunked his bio class 'cuz I cut too many classes. I tried to tell him how I had to rehearse with the Ratchets, but he couldn't make the connection. I haven't told my folks about it yet, 'cuz I want to hit them up for some bread. Take care—and eat your heart out.

Have a good one,
Chris

Dear Dad and Mom,

I think you both know how much I've been looking forward to coming home this summer to work in the store. However, I have just been offered an opportunity to perform with a local musical group this summer while they tour the state. I will have a chance to make new friends as we travel from city to city, and I believe the experience will be very educational. I realize that this last-minute decision will cause you some hardship, but I believe the advantages far outweigh any inconvenience. The school year has just concluded, and I have decided not to major in biology because of a personality clash with my professor, who happens to be the chairman of the department. Incidentally, my expenses have been somewhat larger than anticipated. Would it be possible for you to send me fifty dollars by wire as soon as possible? When I receive my first paycheck, I'll repay you.

Love from your son,

Chris

You probably noticed several differences between these letters by Chris. His letter to his friend Mike is full of slang and colloquialisms: "What a blast!" "a couple of gigs," "playing ax," "hit them up for some bread," and so on. This informality is intensified by the kinds of allusions he makes to the prospects of playing with a musical group instead of working in his parents' store. The overall impression is of a young man who is looking forward to the excitement of playing with a musical group and not too troubled at having failed his biology class. He apparently dreads having to confront his parents with all of this news. Note that his second letter is deferential and more formal than his letter to Mike. He chooses formal words that make the tour sound like an educational experience. He avoids slang, and his sentences are longer and more complex. Note, too, how his explanation for failing biology differs from that he confided to his friend. All in all, the two letters show clearly that Chris had each reader in mind and that he adjusted his purpose, content, and language accordingly.

E X E R C I S E 5

Each of the following passages was written with a particular audience in mind. Who is the audience in each case? Describe the intended reader as clearly as you can. Are you included in that audience? Why or why not?

1. Drugs combine reversibly with receptors at a macromolecular level and bind to them by means of ionic bonds and hydrogen bonds. It is possible that the formation of these different types of bonds produces a stable drug receptor complex which leads to the pharmacological effects and these interactions are reversible.
2. This music will really blow you away, Man!
3. The intermodulation distortion is less than 0.25 for any combination of frequencies from 30Hz to 20Hz if instantaneous peak power is 80 watts per channel or less into 4 or 8 ohm loads and 60 watts per channel or less into 16 ohm loads with both channels operating.
4. Mommy and daddy are very proud of you.
5. It's your Second Chance at Love . . . and this time, there is no holding back. Here are sensual, fulfilling stories that go beyond most other romances, to share every moment of mature, passionate, experienced love. Love that reaches the highest joy and pleasure . . . because it has known the deepest pain.
6. I have been a healer and advisor for the past 50 years. Are you sick? Need help? Got bad luck? Lost your job? I can help you no matter what your problem is. I can cure you! I can help you! Let me remove all evil shadows and spells from you and your home. I use love potions, spells, dolls, herbs, oils, and candles in my work to remove or place a voodoo. I can advise you in love, marriage, business, luck, happiness, health, and money. Call me and be helped.
7. Hay una variedad de países que componen el mundo hispánico y existen diferencias entre ellos. La naturaleza en España y especialmente en Hispanoamérica es muy variada. Las diferencias y los contrastes entre las ciudades y los pueblos son enormes. Existen varias razas y grupos étnicos en el mundo hispánico.
8. Thank you very much for your kind invitation to dinner next Saturday, but I must regretfully decline. My aunt from Cleveland will be arriving, and I must make extensive preparations for her arrival.

Identifying Your Audience

As you get ready to write, you must ask yourself several questions about your audience:

Who is going to read this?
    What do I know about my readers? What is their age, sex, educational background, and occupation? What are their attitudes, values, beliefs, and prejudices?

How much do my readers already know about the subject?
Are they experts on it? Reasonably informed? Or is my subject likely to be completely unfamiliar to them? Can I assume they understand the basic concepts of my subject, or should I explain them?
How can I keep my readers' attention and make them want to read?
If they already know much about my subject, what can I do to make it interesting to them? If they are hostile toward the subject, how can I make sure that they will read the paper with an open mind? Do my readers expect to be entertained, informed, or persuaded?
What can I do to help my readers understand my writing?
What will be the best way to organize and develop my ideas? What kinds of examples should I use? Is a formal, reserved style better, or should I use a more relaxed, personal style?

When you have answered these questions and identified your audience, you will be better able to choose the kinds of information—the facts, arguments, and examples—that will work best for your purpose and audience. You will also be able to select the appropriate tone and level of language and the best way to organize your material. In short, by picturing your audience in your mind before you write, you will determine the best way to satisfy their expectations.

E X E R C I S E 6

One of the best ways to study the importance of audience is to examine several magazines. If the following magazines are available on your local magazine racks or in your college library, study their contents and advertisements. Notice the subjects of the articles; the level of the vocabulary; and the point of view, approach, and tone of the articles. Then try to describe the audience or reader that the publishers and advertisers had in mind for that particular magazine.

Rolling Stone	*Playgirl*
True Romance	*Ebony*
Glamour	*Forbes*
The Village Voice	*Foreign Affairs*
Playboy	*Popular Mechanics*

In a sense there is no such thing as *the* audience—there are only *audiences*. A stockbroker who owns a motorcycle might be an avid reader of *Motorcycle World,* and a surgeon who surfs might subscribe to *Surfer.* In fact, all of us change our "masks" or identities as we go from one magazine or article to another. We are a baseball fan as we read the sports page, an amateur gourmet when we read the food section, and a movie critic as we compare our reactions to a film with those of a reviewer.

In the light of these audiences, then, what are you to do? Simply this: recognize that your reader exists only as long as he or she reads your essay. That is, you should avoid falsely stereotyping any social, economic, political, or religious group by assuming that they all share the same reading tastes. The readers you are writing for often share only one thing: an interest in your subject. If you are enthusiastic, knowledgeable, and interesting, you will capture your readers.

But what about the audience for your essays in college? For such an audience, a natural, informal tone is most effective. You can assume that you are writing for readers who are educated, intelligent, and curious about the world. They have a variety of backgrounds and interests, and they are serious and thoughtful. They want to read an essay that is interesting, clear, and informative. If you meet their expectations, you can count on their attention.

E X E R C I S E 7

Imagine that you are the manager of a large apartment complex that has just opened. In order to encourage prospective tenants, write two letters: one to young married couples, and another to senior citizens. In each letter point out the advantages to that group of moving to an apartment in your building.

E X E R C I S E 8

Imagine that your younger brother is a freshman at your college and wants to drop his required physical education class. Write a letter to him encouraging him to remain in the class. Then write a letter to the dean or president of the college asking that the requirement be abolished.

3. Gathering Material

Having selected a topic, determined your purpose, and identified your audience, you are now ready to take the next step in the process of writing your essay: gathering material.

To develop your topic, you need to gather ideas, facts, examples, and details. If your topic is based on a personal experience, the ideas will probably come tumbling forth. But if your topic is on a subject other than yourself, you will have to set aside time for acquiring material to support your topic.

"Gathering material" does not necessarily mean a trip to the library. You have several techniques for collecting ideas about a topic at your command. You can begin by brainstorming and freewriting. Jot the ideas down as they come to you, without worrying about their order or relationship to each other. List anything about the topic that comes to mind; eventually you will find a focus or central point for your essay.

By asking questions, a technique discussed in Chapter 2, you can shake loose many additional ideas. Many writers base their questions on the six journalistic questions: *who, what, when, why, where,* and *how.* By asking *who* is connected with your topic, *what* it means, *why* it is important, and so on, you will generate more ideas than you thought were possible.

If you are having trouble coming up with ideas, talk to someone knowledgeable about the topic. Friends, relatives, and faculty members are often able to give additional ideas or leads. If you have been assigned a topic that you don't know anything about, read some articles about it. Look in the *Reader's Guide* in your college library for articles that might contain helpful information. If you quote directly from an article, consult with your English instructor or look on pages 254–56 for the correct way to acknowledge your sources.

Students who complain that they can't think of anything to write about usually wait until the last minute before they begin the assignment. By giving yourself enough time to consider the topic and think it through, you will soon accumulate a list of ideas. Then you will be ready for the next step: developing your thesis statement.

4. Writing a Thesis Statement

After looking over your list of ideas, ask yourself what you want to say about them. What are you really trying to tell your reader about the topic? The answer to that question is expressed in the *thesis statement*, a sentence containing the main idea and purpose of the essay.

The thesis statement contains two parts: the *topic* and your *assertion* or view of the topic—what you intend to say *about* the topic. Thus, "skiing" is a *topic*; "Cross-country skiing is the best way to enjoy the outdoors" is a *thesis statement*. "The college cafeteria" is a *topic*; "Although many students complain, the college cafeteria serves food that is tasty, nutritious, and economical" is a *thesis statement*. A paper about "skiing" or "the college cafeteria" would be a rambling, directionless collection of ideas. But with a specific thesis statement as a guideline, an organized and coherent essay could be written about either topic.

Below are several topics with sample thesis statements based on them:

Topic:	the effect of the new freeway on my hometown
Thesis statement:	The new freeway running through my hometown has transformed a sleepy little community.
Topic:	country-western music
Thesis statement:	Country-western music, once limited to older, rural audiences, is now booming, thanks to the influence of Elvis Presley and rock-a-billy.
Topic:	American heroes
Thesis statement:	Americans choose their heroes on the basis of accomplishment, fame, wealth, and a certain sense of glamour.
Topic:	returning to college in midlife
Thesis statement:	Older students usually do well in college because they are often more motivated, disciplined, and eager to learn.
Topic:	dating customs
Thesis statement:	Nowhere can the changes in social customs be seen as clearly as in dating patterns on my campus.

A well-stated thesis gives your paper a sense of purpose and direction. It answers the reader's question, "What's the point?" In a very real sense, a thesis statement is a commitment or promise by the writer to the reader. It tells the reader what to expect, and it offers a hint of the overall plan of the paper.

When should you develop your thesis statement? Should it be immediately after you have worked out your specific topic, or after you have accumulated your ideas and thought about them? Most experienced writers would probably agree that there is no magic moment for hatching the thesis statement. At times, you will know your purpose and main idea early in the writing process. At other times, you may find that you have started to write with one thesis statement in mind only to discover as you write that you actually were committed to another statement. The best advice, then, is that working out your thesis statement early gives you a plan and a goal and will keep you from expending wasted effort.

At the beginning of this chapter you were told that many writers prefer to place the thesis statement at the end of the first paragraph in a short article or essay before proceeding to develop and support it in the following paragraphs. For longer essays with introductions consisting of several paragraphs, the thesis statement can be placed at the beginning or at the end of the introduction. Your thesis statement might even be found in the concluding paragraph of the essay; this is effective in essays presenting arguments for and against a proposition, culminating in your own view at the end of the essay. The *exact* location is not the important point. What you should be certain to do is formulate a statement that clearly and succinctly announces to your reader the main or controlling idea that you intend to present.

Some Reminders When Writing Your Thesis Statement

A thesis statement should be stated in the form of a *sentence*. If it is not, it is just a topic. "Public television" is a *topic*, but "Public television offers programming that might not survive on commercial networks" is a *thesis statement*. Incidentally, longer papers sometimes require more than one sentence to express the thesis statement.

The thesis statement should not be expressed as a question. "Has tourism destroyed Hawaii's charms?" fails to state clearly the writer's position on the topic. "Tourism has created more problems for Hawaii than it has solved" is a thesis statement because it presents the writer's point of view.

Don't state the obvious as your thesis statement. "Alaska is the largest state in the Union" is a fact, but it is not a thesis statement because it leaves you no room for developing an essay. Similarly, "Divorce is one of the major threats to the family" is so obvious that your reader may yawn, "So what else is new?"

Your thesis statement should be manageable enough for the typical college essay of 500 to 750 words. "The effects of the Vietnam war can be seen in all aspects of our society" is worthy of a book, or at least a long chapter. "The reception given to the Vietnam veteran was different from that given the G.I. after World War II" is better but would still require extensive development. "The reception I received from my friends after coming back from Vietnam was different from that my father got after World War II" is much more limited and could be developed adequately in an essay.

Your thesis statement should not be too narrow. A paper that proposed to explain how to tie a tie, for example, would be too limited and boring. A paper claiming that the choice of a tie is often a clue to the wearer's personality, however, would be substantial and interesting.

E X E R C I S E 9

Read the following thesis statements and decide whether each is specific and narrow enough. Rewrite any that are not.

1. Many people attack television, but it can be educational.
2. Many people who retire are not prepared for the changes in their lives.
3. The labor unions in this country are too powerful.
4. Truck drivers are more considerate than other drivers.
5. The letters-to-the-editor page of our newspaper is a sanctuary for cranks and oddballs.
6. Students are encouraged to take liberal arts courses in college, but liberal arts graduates have a hard time getting a job.
7. Intelligence tests are not a reliable way of predicting a person's success.
8. Chivalry is dying.
9. My city changes its personality completely at night.
10. The desert has its own unique beauty.

E X E R C I S E 10

Write an original thesis statement for the following subjects. Each statement should express the purpose stated in parentheses.

1. meeting the parents of your boyfriend or girlfriend *(expressing yourself)*
2. the advantages of the community college *(persuasion)*
3. how to take notes for a lecture *(informing)*
4. the worst job I ever had *(expressing yourself* or *entertaining)*
5. why the administration should (or should not) be allowed to control the campus newspaper *(persuasion)*
6. pet peeves *(entertaining)*

7. a law that does not work *(informing* or *persuading)*
8. why otherwise intelligent people believe in astrology *(informing)*
9. why people lie *(informing)*
10. why love and sex are sometimes confused *(informing)*

E X E R C I S E   11

Now it is time to write a thesis statement for the topic you selected in Exercise 1. Look over the ideas you have collected and ask yourself, "What is the point? What do I want to tell my reader?" The answer to those questions will be your thesis statement. Don't try to cover too much ground, but don't be too narrow or obvious. Your thesis statement should be stated as a sentence. And remember: It is a promise to your reader.

4

Shaping the Essay:

Organizing

Your Ideas

5. Organizing and Outlining Your Essay

Organizing and arranging your ideas in an essay is like pushing furniture around in a new apartment. You try to achieve the most logical and attractive effect, yet you must recognize the boundaries you have to work within. The most interesting and exciting ideas in the world will not be worth much in an essay if your reader can't follow them. This means that all of your facts, details, impressions, and examples have to be organized in a plan that makes sense to your reader.

Organizing Your Essay

The nature of some topics suggests the best organizational pattern. For example, narratives that relate events which occurred in a particular time sequence are organized most effectively in *chronological order*, and descriptions of objects and people usually lend themselves to *spatial ordering*. Some topics, however, cannot be organized in a time or space order. Instead, the writer has to impose an order on them and create a pattern of organization that will make sense to the reader. The most effective orders to impose are *in order of importance, from general to specific, and from specific to general.*

The first step toward organizing your essay is to make a list of all your ideas. Do not worry if there does not seem to be a connection between them; your task now is to list all the main and less important ideas that you believe should go into the essay.

Outlining Your Essay

An outline is a plan for your essay, and it is a helpful tool for organizing and shaping your ideas. Preparing an outline will help you test your essay for *unity* and *coherence*. Although both of these qualities of good writing are discussed at greater length in Chapter 7, we should consider them briefly now.

Your essay has *unity* when all of its ideas support the thesis statement. When you finish your outline, check it to be sure that each major section relates to the thesis statement. Within each major section, make certain that each example and supporting detail supports the main idea of that section. In particular, check to see that you have not retained ideas that are unrelated to your thesis statement and its major subdivisions. Chapter 7 presents several ways to test your writing for unity.

Your essay has *coherence* if there is a connection between your ideas. You must move logically and orderly from one sentence to another and from one paragraph to another. If you detect abrupt shifts and gaps in your ideas, be sure that those ideas are in the right place in your paper. One way of showing the relationship between ideas is to use expressions like *furthermore, however, although,* and *in addition* to connect sentences and paragraphs. Chapter 7 offers other methods for making your writing coherent.

Keep in mind that the outline is a tool for organizing your essay—it is never the end product. It is not a sacred document that should never be changed. But whether it is a rough outline like those in this chapter or a formal outline like the one on page 56, outlines are invaluable for giving your essay direction—they help you see the structure of your essay at a glance.

Chronological Order

Margaret Casey, a freshman, was assigned to write an essay in which she narrated an incident. Here is a list of ideas that she prepared after she had thought about learning to ski. Notice that she has placed her thesis statement at the top of the list to remind herself of her purpose and controlling idea.

Thesis statement: "Learning to ski at 50 proves you can teach an old dog new tricks

1. strange feeling standing on skis
2. couldn't walk without falling
3. first run down hill; fell four times
4. I'm anxious to go again
5. cross-country, slalom are other types
6. skiing: not expensive if you have equipment; best to rent at first
7. instructor confident, good skier
8. showed us how to put skis on
9. skied down easy hill; snowplowing
10. followed teacher like ants
11. lunchtime: exhausted, hungry
12. rental of equipment; boots strange

13. Fell in morning lesson, couldn't get up
14. patient teacher
15. wanted to stop and rest; teacher made me return to lift
16. downhill over and over; down without falling finally
17. walked; how to fall and get up
18. easy hill first; snow-plowing to control speed
19. fell getting off ski lift; embarrassed
20. I was oldest of beginners
21. beautiful scenery in Utah
22. Mormons settled state
23. can't wait to return; teach my son
24. Sense of accomplisment

    As you can see, Margaret's thesis suggests that she wants to write an essay in which she conveys to her reader her sense of accomplishment at having learned to ski at the age of fifty. Her list of ideas is filled with incidents and impressions from her skiing trip to Utah. However, she has two problems: several ideas on the list are not related to her thesis, and those that are on the subject are not in the order in which they happened. Her job now is to look over her list and decide what should be cut and how to arrange the surviving ideas.

    The ideas numbered 5, 6, 21, and 22 do not have anything to do with her purpose or thesis. Idea 5 deals with other types of skiing, and 6 would send Margaret off on a discussion of the expense of skiing, so she cuts both ideas from the list. Items 21 and 22 are related to each other, but have nothing to do with the first time she skied, so she deletes those as well.

    Having removed the irrelevant items, she puts the remaining ideas in the order in which they happened, or *chronological order*. Here is her reorganized list; you will notice that she has renumbered them and changed the wording of a few.

    1. Rent skis, poles, and boots; boots feel strange
    2. Met other beginners in class
    3. I was oldest in class

4. Instructor was good skier, helpful
5. Showed us how to put skis on
6. I couldn't walk without falling
7. Fell, couldn't get up; felt embarrassed
8. Teacher was patient
9. Learned how to walk, fall, and get up without help
10. Class tried easy hill first
11. Learned to snow-plow to control speed and turn
12. Followed teacher up and down hills all morning
13. By lunch time, I was exhausted
14. After lunch, learned how to get on and off ski lifts
15. Fell out of chair getting off; operator had to stop lift
16. First run down hill: fell four times; children didn't fall
17. Wanted to rest; had to get back in lift line
18. Went down hill over and over; finally got down without falling
19. Sense of accomplishment
20. Anxious to go again, teach my son

This list is much easier to follow; the reader gets the overall plan of the proposed essay, and senses the general direction of the thought. But a problem still remains before Margaret can use her list as a guide to the writing of her essay: the list presents all of the ideas as if they were coordinate, or equal in importance. As we look at her list, we are not sure which incidents are important and which are less important—there is no subordination or grouping of ideas according to their importance.

Margaret now takes the final step in organizing her essay. She decides which ideas are important and therefore deserve a separate paragraph, and which are less important, and will serve as supporting details. She puts her less important ideas under the main ones, continuing to cross out, change, narrow, and expand her ideas as she revises and rearranges.

Here is Margaret's scratch outline, based on her revised list:

Thesis: "Learning to ski at fifty proves that you can teach an old dog new tricks."
1. Getting ready to ski
   renting equipment
   getting adjusted to strange feeling of ski boots, skis
2. Meeting the class
   helpful instructor
   I was oldest in class
3. First lesson: fundamentals

     learning to walk in skis
     learning to fall and get up without help
4. Skiing on gentle hill first time
     snow-plowing
     following instructor in procession
     going up and down hill million times
     lunch time: exhausted, hungry
5. Second lesson: ski lift
     falling out of chair; stopped lift
     wanting to quit; had to continue
     finally went down without falling
6. End of day
     sense of accomplishment
     wanted to return, take more lessons
     will teach my son, who said I was too old to learn

Margaret's outline suggests that her essay will have six paragraphs and that each will present, in chronological order, the sequence of events that happened on the day she learned to ski. Every detail that will be in her essay is not included in her outline. Nevertheless, by making an outline she has given herself a compass to follow as she begins to write.

Notice that her outline is not polished, and that it consists, for the most part, only of phrases. This kind of outline (a "scratch" or rough outline) is satisfactory for a short essay, but for longer papers you will want to write a more detailed outline like the one on page 56.

Spatial Order

As Margaret's outline demonstrates, a thesis statement will often suggest the best way to organize an essay. Her paper followed chronological order. But if your essay is primarily a description of someone or something rather than a narration, *spatial order* is probably the best pattern to follow.

Spatial order is based on the order in which our eyes see and movie cameras move: from top to bottom, left to right, near to far, and so on. A description of a scene from the top of a tall building would be based on the selection of details that would help the reader visualize the scene. But instead of flinging the details at the reader in random order, we have to present those details in a pattern that will make sense to the reader.

Here are some notes written by Jenny Diaz for an essay in which she described the pyramids of San Juan Teotihuacan outside Mexico City.

Thesis statement: "The pyramids of San Juan Teotihuacan are breathtaking in their grandeur."

1. Pyramid to the Sun: bigger than pyramids in Egypt
2. Large quadrangular court with minor pyramids
3. Beyond the temple—museum
4. Large avenue in front of Pyramid of Sun: Avenue of the Dead
5. Largest artificial mounds on the American continent
6. 35 miles north of Mexico City
7. Pyramid to the Sun—over 200 feet high, 700 feet at base
8. Surrounding area once had numerous buildings, thousands of inhabitants
9. Aztecs mistook mounds on either side of Avenue of Dead for burial mounds
10. Impressive view as you get out of parking lot; pyramids directly ahead
11. Pyramid to Moon directly behind Pyramid to Sun
12. Next to Pyramid to the Moon: Temple of Butterflies
13. Return to parking lot to see directly in front: Temple of Gods
14. Steps leading to top of Pyramid to Sun
15. Rear of courtyard: path leading to stairway behind
16. On all sides, view of valley—view from top
17. Stairway leading down to carvings, sculpture
18. To left, Pyramid to Moon
19. Around the pyramids now: farms
20. Over 2000 years old
21. Entire area: once extensive city
22. Still being excavated

Jenny has jotted her ideas in a dizzying blur. Now she has to put them in order so that they make sense to her reader. Because she wants the reader to *see* the pyramids of San Juan Teotihuacan, she knows that she will have to arrange her details in a *spatial order,* moving from left to right, near to far, and so on, just as the tourist would when first visiting the pyramids.

Jenny decides that she will begin her paper with an overall view, introducing the scene of the pyramids on the horizon as they would be encountered by the approaching tourist as he or she arrives at the parking lot. Then she will describe the most striking pyramid directly in front of the visitor, the Pyramid to the Sun. She will then describe the surrounding area as seen from the top of the Pyramid to the Sun, to give her reader an overall perspective of the scene. The rest of her essay, she decides, will describe the other buildings and temples as she moves methodically past them, returning finally to the visitors' parking lot.

Arranging her notes, she eliminates those details that seem trivial or unrelated to her thesis statement. She groups ideas according to their relative importance so that each main idea is followed by its supporting details. Because she wants to emphasize the antiquity of the pyramids rather than their beauty, she changes her thesis statement. Her outline, like Margaret Casey's, does not contain every detail that will eventually find its way into her essay, but at least it is adequate enough to keep her on course. Now that she has imposed some order on her material, she is ready to write.

> *Thesis statement:* "The pyramids of San Juan Teotihuacan are silent survivors of an ancient age."
> 1. Background information
>   35 miles north of Mexico City
>   site of ancient Toltec civilization
>   over 2000 years old
>   religious, business center
> 2. View from visitors' parking lot
>   Pyramid to the Sun directly ahead
>   over 200 feet high, 700 at base
>   larger than pyramids in Egypt
>   Pyramid to the Moon: directly behind Sun
>   almost as tall and wide
>   not completely restored
> 3. View from top of Pyramid to the Sun
>   steps leading to top
>   surrounding countryside
>   quiet farms, small homes
>   Avenue of the Dead
>   Aztecs mistook mounds for tombs
> 4. Return to base of pyramid for walk back to museum;
>   artifacts
>   restaurant: clashes with ancient ruins
> 5. Conclusion: Silent reminders of ancient glory; surrounded by silent fields, shiny new restaurant

Margaret Casey's essay narrating her first ski trip followed chronological order, and Jenny Diaz' description of the pyramids of San Juan Teotihuacan was arranged in spatial order. But effective writing often combines both patterns. If you were writing about the first fish you ever caught, you might tell, in chronological order, the steps you took on that unforgettable day: picking up your fishing buddy, selecting a fly rod, driving to the lake, learning to bait a hook, and finally, after hours of frustration, catching a bass. But while relating these incidents chronologically, you might also include some details organized spatially: the description of the beautiful sunrise as you left your home, the calm surface of the lake, and flash of the fish as it leaped above the water, for example. Good writing, then, can often use elements of both patterns.

Logical Order

Some topics cannot be arranged in a time or space order. Instead, the writer has to impose a logical order on them, creating a pattern or order that will make the most sense to the reader. Several possibilities exist for this kind of order.

Order of Importance. One of the effective systems of arrangement is *in order of importance*. Essays arranged in this pattern usually begin with the *least* important ideas and build up to the *most* important or dramatic ideas. If done well, it creates mounting interest and suspense.

Larry Raeber wrote the following preliminary list of ideas for an essay explaining why he is attending his local community college.

> *Thesis statement:* "I am attending St. Clair Community College because it offers several advantages."
> 1. With my high school buddies
> 2. Need review of math before taking calculus and trig
> 3. Not sure of my major
> 4. Able to keep my job
> 5. Save money
> 6. Interested in data processing and accounting
> 7. Girl friend attends same college
> 8. College only three miles from home; convenient
> 9. No tuition
> 10. Uncertain about my future
> 11. Can adjust my classes around my job
> 12. Afraid of big state university
> 13. Can save money while going to community college
> 14. Good counselors; can help me decide after first year
> 15. May enter service; not sure I want to go four years
> 16. Governor of state graduated from this community college

As you notice, Larry's ideas are not in any particular sequence or order. Because they are not connected in a time sequence and do not describe anything, he cannot use a chronological or spatial order.

After studying his list, he decides to present his ideas *in their order of importance*, beginning with the least important and building up to the most important. His most important reason for attending his local community college, he decided, was for the academic advantages. Therefore, he saves that for the end of his paper. The *least* important reasons are social, so he presents those first. If you attend a community college, you may disagree with his thinking. In that case, your outline would be different from his.

Here is Larry's scratch outline. Notice that he has combined items 10 and 15, 4 and 11, and 5 and 13 because they repeat essentially the same idea. He has deleted item 16 because it is not pertinent to his thesis statement. His outline is not elaborate or formal, but it is adequate to serve as a guide for an essay of 500 to 750 words.

> *Thesis statement:* "I am attending St. Clair Community College because it offers several advantages."
> 1. Social and personal reasons
>   with my buddies from high school
>   girl friend also attends
>   campus only three miles from home; carpool
> 2. Financial advantages
>   able to keep my job
>   save money by living at home
>   no tuition
> 3. Academic advantages
>   afraid of big state university
>   need review of math before taking advanced courses
>   excellent data processing courses
>   not sure about my major
>   not sure I want to go four years
>   excellent counselors: can help me decide after first year

From General to Specific and From Specific to General.   Two other patterns often used for arranging ideas in expository and persuasive writing are moving *from general to specific* and *from specific to general.* When you arrange your ideas from the general to the specific, you introduce your reader first to the "big picture": you begin with a generalization or overall view of your topic which is then clarified or substantiated in the body of the essay by a series of specific examples.

Suppose you were writing about the effect of diet on longevity and overall health. You might begin with a generalization: societies whose members live the longest avoid those foods most likely to block arteries or contribute to high blood pressure and strokes. The rest of your paper would examine, in a series of specific instances, the typical diets of those groups or cultures whose members are known for their long lives. Additional details on the findings of physicians and scientists on the effects of popular American foods like french fries and Twinkies would serve to support the opening generalization.

A paper on the same topic moving from the specific to the general might begin with an examination of specific foods and their effect on cholesterol, blood pressure, and heart disease. You might then examine the diets of several societies known for their longevity and show that they avoid harmful foods. After accumulating and presenting a series of specific instances, you would conclude with a generalization: societies whose members live the longest avoid those foods most likely to clog arteries or contribute to high blood pressure and strokes.

Here is an outline for an essay on another topic that moves from the *general to the specific*. Notice that the writer begins with a generalization in the first section and then illustrates it with specific details.

Opening generalization: Life on earth will be much different in the twenty-first century because of the "greenhouse effect."

I. Overall changes on earth in the twenty-first century
   A. Shortage of food
   B. Reduced water supply
   C. Warmer temperatures in most parts of earth
II. "Greenhouse effect" on food
   A. Shorter growing season
   B. Difficulty irrigating
   C. Frosts in food-producing sections of earth
III. "Greenhouse effect" on water
   A. Droughts
   B. Higher coastal waters
   C. Danger of living in low-lying areas near coasts
IV. "Greenhouse effect" on temperature
   A. Increased amounts of carbon dioxide in air
   B. Annual increase in average temperature
   C. Warming trend extended

The same ideas could be arranged in the *specific to general pattern*. Notice that the following outline begins with a series of particulars that lead to the generalization.

I. "Greenhouse effect" on atmosphere
   A. Annual increase in amount of carbon dioxide in air
   B. Annual increase in temperature
   C. Warming trend extended
II. "Greenhouse effect" on water
   A. Droughts
   B. Higher coastal waters
   C. Danger of living in low-lying areas near coasts
III. "Greenhouse effect" on food
   A. Shorter growing season

B. Difficulty irrigating
C. Frosts in food-producing sections of earth
IV. Overall changes on earth in the twenty-first century
A. Warmer temperatures in most parts of earth
B. Reduced water supply
C. Shortage of food

Concluding generalization: Life on earth will be much different in the twenty-first century because of the "greenhouse effect."

Which organization pattern—from general to specific or from specific to general—should you use? The choice depends to a great extent on your topic and your thesis statement. If your thesis is likely to meet resistance, you might first offer a series of particulars and specific examples which lead to your generalization or thesis. On the other hand, the advantage of leading with the generalization is that the reader knows exactly where you are going; you have told him what you want to convey, and the reader fills in the argument with the details you supply. These patterns, often called *deductive* and *inductive*, will be discussed in greater detail in Chapter 7 ("Writing the Persuasive Essay").

A Review of Steps to Follow in Organizing and Outlining Your Essay

Jot down all of the ideas that you can think of that might belong in your essay: statistics, examples, facts, details, reasons. Do not worry about their order; you will take care of that later. Test each idea on your list in terms of your thesis statement: does it belong in your essay, or is it off the subject? If it is irrelevant, cut it. Be ruthless!

Look over your topic and thesis statement again to see if their wording suggests the best way to organize your essay. For instance, an essay that explains how to do something is best arranged *chronologically,* and a topic that implies a visual impression would normally require a *spatial order.* On the other hand, content that does not lend itself to either a time or space pattern could be arranged in a *logical* order: *in order of importance, from general to specific,* or *from specific to general.* The ideas on your list will often trigger a suitable arrangement.

Group related ideas. Make separate "stacks" or "piles" of ideas, either on the paper or in your head. In each group, select the main idea that includes all the others. Arrange the major groups according to the pattern that you have selected. Make a scratch outline and order these groups, testing each item for its relevance to your thesis statement.

E X E R C I S E 1

List at least five main ideas to support five of the topics below. Arrange the ideas in the organizational pattern specified in parentheses.

The benefits of general education courses *(general to specific)*
An interesting person you work with *(general to specific)*
A classmate *(spatial)*
The reasons for attending college *(order of importance)*
A favorite scene *(spatial)*
Your first impressions of your boy friend or girl friend *(specific to general)*
How students prepare for final exams *(specific to general)*
Why I am (or am not) a church-goer *(order of importance)*
How to do one of the following: barter in a foreign city, change spark plugs in a car, make bread, shingle a roof, train a pet, prepare for a long trip *(chronological)*
Why computers are popular *(general to specific)*

E X E R C I S E 2

List the ideas for the thesis statement that you wrote (page 35) for your essay and then apply the steps discussed on page 57. After selecting the organizational pattern most suitable for your essay, write a scratch outline

5

Drafting the Essay:

Six Patterns

6. *Writing the First Draft*

Writing an essay forces you to make a number of decisions. You must select a topic, formulate a thesis statement, identify your purpose and audience, and determine the organizational plan you will follow. One of the most essential steps as you prepare to write your first draft is to select the most suitable mode or pattern for developing your essay.

Selecting a Pattern

The pattern that you will use depends on your purpose and your thesis statement. Several patterns are available. If you want to show your reader how something works or how it came about, you would trace a *process*. If you want your reader to see the similarities or differences between two things or ideas, you would use *comparison and contrast*. And if you are trying to show your reader what something is by giving illustrations, you would develop your essay by *exemplification*.

The wording of your thesis statement will also nudge you toward the most appropriate pattern of development. For instance, "There are three kinds of people who drive sports cars" suggests an essay developed by *classification*. "Most hunting accidents are caused by carelessness" will probably be developed by *cause and effect*. " 'Feminism' is a concept that has several meanings, depending on the person or group that uses it" will probably require an extended *definition*. By carefully considering your thesis statement, you will usually have little trouble selecting the right pattern.

Although your purpose and thesis statement will largely determine the method of development you use, your paper will probably not be restricted to *one* method. Instead, you will often combine methods: *comparison and contrast* with *exemplification*, *definition* with *exemplification* or *classification*, and so on. Nevertheless, each essay will be developed chiefly by one method. By doing this, you are providing a plan for your paper so that the reader can follow your thought.

Fortunately, the patterns used to develop an essay are similar to our normal thought processes. We tend to think of examples to illustrate a point, we classify and divide groups into categories, we compare and contrast things and ideas, we determine how things work and what they are made of, we look for the causes of events and their effects, and we try to explain what things are. By using these patterns in your writing, then, you are following paths that are familiar to your reader.

Although there are several patterns of development, here are the most common:

Exemplification
Division and Classification
Comparison and Contrast
Process and Analysis
Cause and Effect
Definition

To select the best pattern, ask yourself the questions your reader might ask. The kinds of questions you ask will suggest the method best suited for developing the thesis statement, as the examples below demonstrate.

Thesis statement:	The public behavior of some sports figures is a poor example for our youth.
Questions:	Why do you say that? What is your evidence? Name some examples to prove your point.
Method:	Exemplification

Thesis statement:	My city is actually comprised of a group of distinct communities.
Questions:	What are the various groups or categories that make up your city?
Method:	Division and classification

Thesis statement:	The music that my generation dances to is different from that of my parents.
Questions:	What was their music like? What is your music like? How are they different?
Method:	Comparison and contrast

Thesis statement:	Radiocarbon dating is a very exact way to date organic objects up to 75,000 years old.
Questions:	How is it done? What are the steps?
Method:	Process and analysis

Thesis statement:	Many college athletes graduate as functional illiterates.
Questions:	Why are they allowed to graduate? Who is to blame? Who's putting the pressure on the colleges to graduate them? How successful will they be in life?
Method:	Cause and effect

Thesis statement:	*Machismo* is an ancient concept that still affects male-female relationships in many Latin American cultures.
Questions:	What is *machismo*? What is it *not*? What are its characteristics? What are the origins of the term?
Method:	Definition

E X E R C I S E 1

For each of the following thesis statements, list the *questions* likely to be asked by the reader. Then select the *method of development* most appropriate for answering the questions.

1. "You don't have to be an electric genius to install a C.B. radio."
2. "The Library of Congress System is superior to the Dewey Decimal System."
3. "The withholding tax on tips has caused many hardships for waiters."
4. "My daughter has many opportunities available to her that were denied my mother."
5. "Scientists claim that most men are either Type A or Type B in terms of personality traits."
6. "Puppy love can be very painful for those who experience it."
7. "Study habits and attitudes toward school are often determined by one's cultural background."
8. "The kinds of cars that faculty members drive reveal much about them."
9. "American education in recent years has come under criticism from the public."
10. "Within the last two years the ranks of the permanently unemployed have increased dramatically."

Developing an Essay by Exemplification

Many of the papers you write in college will be developed by exemplification. For making a statement clear and supporting a generalization, examples are powerful tools. If you give your reader examples, he or she has a good idea of your point. If you do not supply them, he or she will probably have only a hazy notion of what you are trying to say.

Even individual paragraphs suffer when they consist only of general statements:

> The behavior of my coworkers makes me frustrated. They are not considerate in their behavior, and they interfere with my ability to perform my assignments. Their actions at times are immature, and at other times are selfish. It is often impossible for me to complete my duties.

This paragraph is vague—do you have any idea exactly what the writer's coworkers do that bothers him? All we have is a series of unsupported general statements that leave us with unanswered questions: What kind of behavior is he complaining about? How are the writer's coworkers inconsiderate? How do they interfere with his work? What are his assignments?

In the revision below, notice how much more specific the paragraph becomes, chiefly because the writer has added examples:

> The behavior of my coworkers makes me frustrated. They spend hours each day at the water cooler, laughing and joking so loudly that I can hardly concentrate. They pretend they don't hear the telephone ringing, so I have to take all of the calls. Some of them chew gum loudly; others insist on smoking foul cigars, polluting the air so badly that I become nauseated. They interrupt me while I'm transcribing letters, or borrow my stapler and scotch tape, failing to return them so I have to hound them for them later. Because of their distractions and interruptions, I'm rarely able to type my daily quota of letters and reports.

Organizing the Essay Developed by Exemplification

After you have listed examples that illustrate and clarify your thesis statement, you are faced with a question: In what order should you present your examples? If the examples occur chronologically, the obvious arrangement is in the order in which they happened. But if they do not have a sequential relationship, the best arrangement is usually *in their order of importance*, beginning with the least important and ending with the example with the most dramatic impact. In this way, you conclude your essay forcefully.

The organization of an essay developed by example is relatively straightforward. Your introduction usually contains your thesis statement, and the body of the essay presents a series of examples to support it. The conclusion reinforces the thesis. A typical essay would look like this:

Paragraph 1:   *Introduction* (with thesis statement)
Paragraph 2:   *First example*
Paragraph 3:   *Second example*
Paragraph 4:   *Third example*
Paragraph 5:   *Conclusion*

(*Note:* The outlines in this chapter illustrating the organization of essays are usually comprised of five or six paragraphs. This structure is for *illustrative purposes only;* as noted in Chapter 3, an introduction may consist of several paragraphs, the body might include a dozen or more paragraphs, and some conclusions are comprised of several paragraphs.)

This five-paragraph pattern could be used for developing the following thesis statement: "Much of what we think true—scientific 'facts,' episodes in history, anecdotes about famous people—turns out to be false." An outline for an essay developing this thesis statement might look like this:

Paragraph 1:   *Introduction,* with thesis statement: "Much of what we think true—scientific 'facts,' episodes in history, anecdotes about famous people—turns out to be false."

Paragraph 2:   Examples of myths and mistaken scientific notions about physical phenomena and occurrences

Paragraph 3:   Examples of commonly confused events (battles, elections, geographical discoveries)

Paragraph 4:   Examples of legends, mistaken accomplishments and identities, exaggerated reputations

Paragraph 5:   *Conclusion*

An alternate organizational pattern for the essay developed by exemplification is sometimes effective. In this method the writer begins his essay with one or more startling examples to catch his reader's interest, thereby delaying the introduction of his thesis statement, which is then presented in the second paragraph. The rest of the paper presents more examples to support the thesis. A typical paper arranged in this pattern would look like this:

Paragraph 1:   *One or more startling examples*

Paragraph 2:   *Introduction* (with thesis statement)

Paragraph 3:   *Second example*

Paragraph 4:   *Third example*

Paragraph 5:   *Fourth example*

Paragraph 6:   *Conclusion*

An outline of an essay that follows this pattern based on the above thesis statement might look like this:

Paragraph 1:   Series of surprising "facts" (Columbus did not discover America; Leif Ericson did. A compass doesn't point to the North magnetic pole *or* to the North geographic pole. The Declaration of Independence wasn't signed on July 4th, etc.)

Paragraph 2:   Delayed introduction, with thesis statement: "Much of what we think true—scientific 'facts,' episodes in history, anecdotes about famous people—turns out to be false."

Paragraph 3:   Examples of myths and mistaken scientific notions about physical phenomena and occurrences

Paragraph 4:   Examples of commonly confused events (battles, elections, geographical discoveries)

Paragraph 5:   Examples of legends, mistaken accomplishments and identities, exaggerated reputations

Paragraph 6:   *Conclusion*

Guidelines for Writing an Essay Developed by Exemplification

An essay developed by exemplification may be based on one detailed example, or it may be developed by a series of examples that support the thesis statement. In either case, the writer must follow certain guidelines:

Examples should be related to the point being made, and they should be typical and representative of the type under discussion.   This means that you should not cite exceptions or rare instances as examples to prove your point. A thesis that claims that formal education in our society is not necessary for success would not be convincing just because Jesus Christ, Abraham Lincoln, and Socrates were cited as examples of those who did not graduate from college.

The best examples are often taken from your own experience.   Personal examples are not always available, of course, but when they are, they have an impact. They have the ring of truth and conviction about them, and as a result are usually convincing. An essay which argues that a vegetarian diet leads to improved health and peace of mind would be much more convincing if you gave examples from your own life instead of anecdotes you have read.

Don't present your examples in a haphazard, random order.   Follow a plan.

A Student-Written Essay Developed by Exemplification

Here is a student-written essay developed by exemplification. Notice how it is organized: The introductory paragraph presents the thesis statement in its last sentence, and the body of the essay (paragraphs two through six) presents a series of examples, all illustrative of the thesis statement. The conclusion wraps up the paper by relating the examples to the thesis statement; as a result, we have a sense of closure or completion as we finish the paper.

Coping Devices: Everyone's Safety Valves

Everyone suffers from tension in our society. For students, the tension could be caused by the pressure of school work. For workers, it may be the deadlines and daily requirements of the job. Some individuals can stand much more tension than others, but each person has a limit. When the tension reaches this limit, it must be relieved in some satisfying way. In order to obtain relief from tension, people use many types of behavior which are called "coping devices."

Eating and smoking are two of the most common examples of coping devices. Many people eat when they are frustrated or angry or unhappy. Many smokers do not actually enjoy their cigarette, but use it as a means of relieving their tension.

Laughing, crying, and swearing are common expressions of tension that can be very helpful in relieving that tension. Laughing and crying, in particular, serve as outlets, and act as a kind of catharsis. Swearing for some people has the same function, but it carries a social stigma.

Talking out a problem can greatly relieve tension. Discussing one's problems with a trusted friend or advisor can be helpful, even if the person does no more than listen. It reduces the sense of loneliness, even if the listener is a perfect stranger. Passengers on airplanes often become compulsive talkers because of their nervousness or tension, and will volunteer information to the stranger sitting next to them that they would not ordinarily tell close friends.

Another coping device is physical exercise. A number of books on jogging claim that joggers become more relaxed and experience a number of other psychological improvements as a result of running. In fact, a regular program of physical exercise is often recommended by therapists for working off tension.

Two of the most widely used coping devices are also potentially the most dangerous, both for the individual who uses them and for society in general. Alcohol and drugs are among the most common outlets for tension. They work by dulling or altering one's perception, and they are among the least desirable coping devices. Many workers who have jobs that create tension have a martini or other drink with their lunch, followed at home by several more, in an effort to reduce the tensions of their work. Drugs, including cocaine and marijuana, are often used by those in desperate situations such as unemployment or poverty, in order to reduce the stress of their lives.

The purpose of these coping devices is to reduce tension and eliminate the possibility of a nervous breakdown. If abused, they can destroy the physical or mental well-being of the individual who uses them. If properly used, they serve a useful purpose in maintaining the mental health of those who practice them.

E X E R C I S E 2

After reading the essay carefully, answer the following questions.

1. What is the thesis statement of this essay? Why is it best developed by examples?
2. How are paragraphs two through six related? What is their function?
3. How are the examples arranged? Is there any order or plan in the sequence, or is it merely random?
4. How does the last paragraph "tie up" the preceding examples in the essay?

E X E R C I S E 3

Make a list of examples that illustrate one of the following thesis statements. Your examples may come from your reading, your conversations with friends, personal experience, or from current events. Next, arrange the examples in the most effective order, following the suggestions in this section. Then write an essay developing the thesis statement with your examples.

1. Movies are better than ever.
2. Many big oil corporations are trying to overcome their unfavorable image with the public.
3. A hobby can turn into a profitable business.
4. Some laws are unfair.
5. Appearances are sometimes deceiving.
6. Old age is not a barrier to accomplishment.
7. Experience is the best teacher.
8. Automobiles often reflect the personalities of their owners.
9. Many people turn to "inspiration" books to solve their problems.
10. Corporations should be required to share their profits with their workers.

Developing an Essay by Division and Classification

Division and classification are useful patterns for developing essays that present complex ideas or information. Although the terms are often used interchangeably, each implies important differences. *To divide* is to break a thing down into its parts; *to classify* is to show how those parts relate to the whole. We use both processes every day. If you set aside one drawer in your dresser for underwear, another for socks, and another for shirts, you are *dividing*. When you arrange your stack of laundry into separate piles of underwear, socks, and shirts, you are *classifying*. So, too, in other areas: you are constantly putting people, objects, and ideas into larger categories, and breaking down concepts and larger units into smaller, manageable components.

An essay developed by *division* answers the question, "What are its parts?" In breaking a large or abstract subject into its components, you have created a structure for making it easier to explain. You can explain or describe each part in detail, or show how each part functions, or how it contributes to the overall category.

If you were writing a paper for a business class in which you analyze a corporation's structure, you might proceed by dividing it into its individual parts: the sales division, the manufacturing division, the financial division, and so on. You could then explain the function of each section, its responsibilities, and how it contributes to the overall working of the company.

Not all topics are as complicated, of course. You could write an essay describing a typical day in your week by dividing it according to time, such as morning, afternoon, and evening. Or it could be divided according to another principle, such as various activities connected with school or work or social obligations.

Classification is a method you may use for developing a subject when you wish to sort things or ideas according to similar characteristics. It provides one way of answering the question "What (or who) is it and where does it belong?" If you wish to classify a given subject the simplest scheme of classification is to split your subject into a two-part system. Here is an example using campus organizations as the topic:

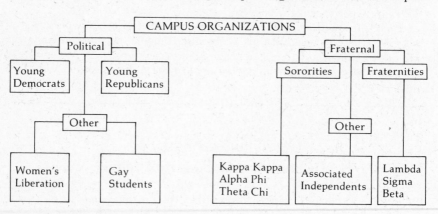

These classifications are not exhaustive. They may need to be explained or analyzed in further detail, but by using a simple system of division into categories, you can provide a working outline for yourself before you begin to write your essay.

Classification usually proceeds from the general to the specific, major to minor, or from categories that include the most of some characteristics to those that include the least. How could you classify "Campus Organizations" further? You could determine which ones are composed mostly of men and which of women; which have members predominantly in the 18–21 age group; which have most of their members in the over–25 age group; and which ones are politically active and which are not. Finally, you can determine the relation between a campus chapter and its national affiliate.

When you are classifying you must remember to take care that your subclasses are of the same rank. In the "Campus Organization" chart, you would not equate the classes Fraternal, Young Republicans, and Theta Chi. They are different levels. However, you *can* discuss two fraternities in equal terms: you may evaluate the service projects of the two groups, for instance, or compare the financial cost of joining these two organizations, or discuss the relative effects they might have upon the student government.

If classification is to serve as a useful tool for you in organizing your subject, you can approach it in two ways: horizontally or vertically. All of the major divisions may be discussed together and then the subcategories considered. This would be a horizontal organization. Or one major division at a time may be taken and all of its subdivisions discussed before considering the next major division. This would be vertical organization.

Classification should be simple for you as long as you remember to put like things in like classes.

Division and classification work well together in developing essays that clarify or explain. In writing a paper about soap operas, for example, a writer might begin by breaking up a typical "soap" into its parts in terms of the people involved: the producer, director, writer, and the actors, explaining the responsibilities and contributions of each to the show. The writer could then develop his paper by putting the audience into categories: women who work at home, senior citizens, college students, and the unemployed, for instance, and explain the interest and motivation each group has for viewing the programs. Or the writer might classify the soap operas on the basis of their main characters, the villains and heroes, the crises, and the similarities and differences among the plots.

Organizing the Division and Classification Essay

Division and classification essays are organized in similar ways. The introduction normally states the thesis and lets the reader know the categories or classes by which the subject is divided or classified. The paragraphs comprising the body of the essay present each category or class in turn, and the conclusion reinforces the thesis statement.

Here is an outline for such a paper:

Paragraph 1: Introduction with thesis statement indicating basis of classification or division
Paragraph 2: First category or division
Paragraph 3: Second category or division
Paragraph 4: Third category or division
Paragraph 5: Conclusion

An outline for an essay developed by *classification* might look like the following:

Paragraph 1: *Introduction with thesis statement:* "Many people speak of pollution as if there were only one type, but the alarming fact is that there is water, air, and soil pollution."
Paragraph 2: Water pollution; sewage, industrial wastes, fertilizer contamination.
Paragraph 3: Air pollution; electrical power plants and motor vehicles, smoke and exhausts.
Paragraph 4: Soil pollution; hazardous waste sites; city dumps.
Paragraph 5: *Conclusion*

Guidelines for Writing an Essay Developed by Division and Classification

When using the pattern of division and classification, you should follow some important guidelines:

There must be a unifying principle or purpose for your division and classification. Merely to list parts and objects is not enough. Explain to your reader in your introduction why you are breaking things down into their parts (division) or placing objects into various categories (classification). For example, an essay that merely divided the colleges and universities in your state into two- and four-year institutions would have little point. But an essay which pointed out the advantages and disadvantages, the available majors, and the expenses for attending each kind of college would have a direction and purpose.

Be certain that your categories are logical and do not overlap. To divide the student body into "men, women, and athletes," for instance, would be inaccurate because "athletes" obviously includes individuals from the first two groups.

When dividing, be certain that your parts account for all elements of the object. To divide the federal government into the judicial and legislative branches would be incomplete because the executive branch is omitted.

When classifying, make certain that every item fits into a category and that there are no items left over.

E X E R C I S E 4

1. Using *division*, select one of the following subjects and break it into its parts or components:

   Mexican cooking   The human eye
   An athletic team   Student government
   Your church or synagogue   An office
   A textbook

2. Using *classification*, place the following items into categories or logical groups. Be ready to explain the basis of your classification. You should be able to discover at least three categories.

   Toyotas   Delivery vans
   Pickup trucks   Datsuns
   Lincolns   Ford compacts
   Volkswagens   Chevettes
   Tractors   Cadillacs
   Porsches   Moving vans

A Student-Written Essay Developed by
Division and Classification

Here is a student-written essay that combines division and classification in its approach to the subject of food. Notice that the writer first *classifies* the six chemical classes of nutrients; next, she *divides* each class of nutrient into its parts.

What Is Food?

The typical American eats a variety of food every day: hamburgers, salads, ice cream, apples, and so on. Although they appear different and taste different, the nourishing materials they provide fall into only six chemical classes of nutrients.

The carbohydrates consist of sugars and starches. About half of all the total calories consumed in the United States come from carbohydrates, and they are the most important source of energy. Carbohydrates consist of one or more of the following simple sugar units: dextrose, fructose, sucrose, maltose, and lactose. Carbohydrates consisting of long chains of simple sugar units are called starches. Typical foods containing carbohydrates include rice, corn, grains, potatoes, sugar products, many fruits and honey, and milk.

Fat is another nutrient found in our food. It stores the body's energy in addition to being a high calorie source. A fat is made up of one glycerol molecule connected to three fatty-acid molecules. Some fats are designated as "saturated" and others as "unsaturated," according to the amounts of hydrogen in the molecule—the more hydrogen, the more saturated the fat. Typical foods containing fatty acid include meat, whole milk, cheese, nuts, olives, fish, butter, oils, and shortenings.

Proteins are made up of pure nitrogen and amino acids. Some of the essential amino acids can be found only in the proteins consumed in food. Typical foods containing proteins are meats, whole grains, beans, peas, peanuts, rice, and corn. Because amino acids are not stored in the cells, a person needs a daily supply of protein in the diet.

Mineral elements such as calcium, phosphorus, sodium, potassium, copper, zinc, chlorine, and phosphorus perform essential functions in the body. They make up vital parts of cells, bones, teeth, and blood. They may occur as simple compounds or be incorporated into very complex materials. They are found particularly in fresh vegetables.

Vitamins are another class of nutrients found in food, although in very small proportions. They are needed along with enzymes to carry out very important chemical reactions in the body. They act by helping a reaction take place. Except for vitamins D and K, vitamins cannot be synthesized directly in the body; they must be obtained from the diet. The fat-soluble vitamins (those stored in the body) are found in cheese, vegetables, eggs, milk, fish, beef, spinach, and tomatoes. The water-soluble vitamins (those that are not stored in the body and should be taken every day) are found in meat, whole grains, nuts, eggs, soybeans, potatoes, and citrus fruits.

Finally, the most important class of nutrient—water—is found in all foods. No material serves the body in as many vital functions as water. The body is over fifty percent water, and many of the tissues of the body are as much as ninety percent water. Digestion, absorption, and the secretion of materials must take place in water. Water loss can be replenished by liquids and foods of all kinds.

These are the nutrients that are found in food. They are important for growth and replacement of worn or damaged cells, as well as for the manufacture of cellular products such as enzymes and hormones. Other chemicals are needed in very small amounts so that various functions of the body can take place, but none are as important as the nutrients found in our food.

E X E R C I S E 5

After reading the above essay carefully, answer the following questions.

1. How does the writer's first paragraph suggest the method of development and organization that she will follow?
2. What is the basis of the division in this essay—what is being divided?
3. What are the divisions or categories listed by the writer? In what paragraphs?
4. How are paragraphs two through seven developed? What other method of development is used?
5. How does the last paragraph reinforce the thesis of the essay?

E X E R C I S E 6

Using division and classification as your basic method of development, select one of the following topics and sort it into categories. Write an essay developing your categories, making certain that you explain to your reader your purpose in classifying the thing, and the basis or plan for your classification.

1. Part-time jobs
2. Methods of studying for tests
3. Popular music
4. Bores
5. Ways to attract the opposite sex
6. Roommates
7. Methods of child-rearing
8. Stock-car drivers
9. Recreational vehicles
10. Newspapers

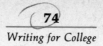

Developing an Essay by Comparison and Contrast

One of the most common kinds of writing assignments in college is the paper organized by comparison and contrast. Its popularity derives, in part, from the fact that it is one of the most common ways our minds organize information. We spend much of our day comparing and contrasting: selecting clothes to wear to school and work, deciding what to order from a menu, examining cuts of meat at the store, choosing a television program to watch, or picking a book to read. In our college assignments we are often asked to point out the similarities and differences between forms of government, between characters in a novel, between theories on the origin of the earth.

In each of these instances we are analyzing two or more items and noting their similarities *(comparisons)* and differences *(contrasts).* Technically speaking, comparisons reveal similarities *and* differences, and contrasts are concerned only with differences. In practice, however, comparisons suggest likenesses, and contrasts point out differences.

The purpose of comparison and contrast essays is to explain and to evaluate. We can explain something as exotic as the marriage customs of the Bushmen of the Kalahari by contrasting them with the marriage customs of Americans, or we can explain something as commonplace as a favorite pen by comparing it with one that is familiar to our reader. Usually, however, we compare and contrast for the purpose of evaluating: we want to show that one book or movie is superior to another, or that a particular instructor or make of car is better than another.

When organized and developed carefully, a comparison and contrast essay has a unity and logic that helps the reader understand our ideas. But if an essay is only a series of scrambled likenesses or differences that lead nowhere, the result will be chaos. To be certain that your comparison and contrast essays have clarity and coherence, read the guidelines on page 78 carefully.

Organizing the Essay Developed by Comparison and Contrast

Your first job in organizing your comparison and contrast essay is to decide what you intend to emphasize: the differences or the similarities between the two subjects. This can best be done by making two lists—one for the differences, and the other for the similarities—and choosing the angle most appropriate.

Your next job is to list the differences or similarities in their order of importance, beginning with the least significant and building up to the most dramatic and important.

The organizational patterns most often used for developing a comparison and contrast essay are *object-by-object* and *point-by-point*. Each has its own strengths as well as weaknesses; the complexity of your material and the length of your paper will determine the method better suited for you.

An essay using the *object-by-object* pattern of organization first presents all of the relevant details or aspects of one object, and then all of the corresponding qualities of the other. A concluding paragraph usually follows, summarizing the likenesses or differences or expressing an opinion. If you wished to contrast city living with country life using this pattern, you might first list all of the advantages of city living, then present the advantages of living in the country. A concluding paragraph would then express a preference based on the differences enumerated.

Because your reader might have a short memory, you should use the object-by-object pattern only when there are few points to be cited. Further, you must be certain that you do not allow digressions to destroy the design of your paper. Be sure, for example, that you give the same treatment to both items being compared or contrasted.

The *point-by-point* pattern is particularly helpful for complex comparisons and for longer papers. An essay using this plan alternates the points of comparison between two objects. In a detailed comparison of American and English high schools, for instance, you might explain how the American school is organized, and do the same for the English school; a discussion of graduation requirements for the typical American school might be followed by the same information for the English school. An analogy with a ping-pong game might be made with respect to the organization of such a paper, as the differences or similarities of each object are presented in turn.

Because it helps the reader keep in mind the two things being compared or contrasted by their being frequently mentioned, the point-by-point approach gives unity and coherence to complex topics. An entire essay developed in this pattern often profits by a closing paragraph that presents a conclusion based on the differences or likenesses established.

Here is an outline for a paper following the *object-by-object* pattern. Notice that it is organized an object at a time: the first paragraph contains the introduction and thesis statement, and the second paragraph discusses only Object A. The next paragraph is devoted only to Object B, and the last paragraph serves as a conclusion.

Paragraph 1:   Introduction and thesis statement

Paragraph 2:   Object A
            —Point 1
            —Point 2
            —Point 3
Paragraph 3:   Object B
            —Point 1
            —Point 2
            —Point 3
Paragraph 4:   Conclusion

Here is an outline for a paper following the *point-by-point* pattern. Notice that unlike the object-by-object pattern, this method organizes the paper around points: either similarities or differences. Each paragraph or section of the paper discusses a single point shared by both objects.

Paragraph 1:   Introduction and thesis statement
Paragraph 2:   Point 1 of Object A
            Point 1 of Object B
Paragraph 3:   Point 2 of Object A
            Point 2 of Object B
Paragraph 4:   Point 3 of Object A
            Point 3 of Object B
Paragraph 5:   Conclusion

Which pattern is better: *object-by-object* or *point-by-point?* Many instructors prefer the point-by-point pattern because it allows the writer to cover more details without confusing the reader, particularly with complex or involved subjects. The reader sometimes has the feeling, after reading an essay organized object-by-object, that he has read two separate essays only thinly connected. On the other hand, it is a convenient pattern for allowing the writer to deal with one item at a time. The advantage of the point-by-point pattern, with its interlocked network of ideas, is that it continuously reminds the reader of the two objects and the point being made about them.

Using transitions in the comparison and contrast paper will help your reader follow your ideas, regardless of the method of organization you use. Words like *however, too, alike, in common, moreover, on the other hand, but, similarly, instead, both,* and *so on* show relationships between ideas.

Here are outlines for two comparison and contrast papers. The first is based on the object-by-object pattern, and the second follows the point-by-point pattern.

Object-by-object

Paragraph 1:   *Introduction and thesis statement:* "Having lived in a dormitory for a semester, I believe that there are more advantages in living at home."

Paragraph 2:   *Object A:* Dormitory life

Point 1: No privacy: unpleasant roommate who smoked

Point 2: Atmosphere not conducive to study; noisy, interruptions

Point 3: Inconvenience of being responsible for laundry

Point 4: Sense of being isolated without a car

Paragraph 3:   *Object B:* Living at home

Point 1: Privacy: my own room

Point 2: Ability to regulate my own schedule: meals, study time; better able to concentrate

Point 3: Superiority of my mother's cooking

Point 4: Access to car

Conclusion: I found that living at home, to my surprise, provided more privacy, independence, and study time.

Point-by-point

Paragraph 1:   *Introduction and thesis statement:* "An examination of Japanese personnel practices reveals differences that American industry might consider adopting."

Paragraph 2:   *Point 1 of Object A (Japanese industry):* Employees and managers see themselves on the same "team"

Point 1 of Object B (American industry): Employees and managers often have adversary relationship

Paragraph 3:   *Point 2 of Object A:* Japanese workers move from one task to another, performing a variety of jobs

Point 2 of Object B: American workers specialize in one function, rarely taking another worker's position

Paragraph 4:   *Point 3 of Object A:* Japanese workers see themselves as part of a company family, using company facilities for leisure, social activities

Point 3 of Object B: American workers distinguish sharply between their place of employment and their family or social world

Paragraph 5:   *Point 4 of Object A:* Absenteeism, alcoholism, and worker discontent are virtually nonexistent in Japanese industry

Point 4 of Object B: American industry is plagued with

Paragraph 6:

problems of absenteeism, alcoholism, and worker alienation

Conclusion ("Perhaps American industry could not only increase its profits but also its employees' happiness by importing some of the Japanese customs.")

E X E R C I S E 7

Using either the object-by-object or point-by-point pattern, write an outline for a paper in which you show the differences or similarities between two objects that you are familiar with: two brands of a product, two cities that you know, two careers or life styles, two friends, two actors, or two other objects of the same class.

Guidelines for Writing an Essay Developed by Comparison and Contrast

Be certain that you are comparing items of the same general class, even though they differ in their qualities. You can compare the Baptist faith with the Methodist, because they are both Protestant denominations, and you can compare Baptist doctrine with Roman Catholic teaching because both groups are Christian. You can even compare Baptist and Jewish beliefs, because both groups are religions. But you could not compare Baptists with policemen, because there is no category that encompasses both—there is no logical basis for a comparison and contrast.

Do not try to compare more than two things in a short paper. A chapter in a book can compare and contrast three or four (or more) objects, but an essay of the usual length should keep to two.

Before writing your paper, decide what your main idea or purpose is. A comparison and contrast paper makes a point and is more than a list of likenesses and differences. It should lead to a conclusion.

Be fair; if you are trying to show the superiority of one object over another, give equal space to both objects being contrasted.

Give your reader several examples to make clear the differences and similarities between the subjects of your paper.

E X E R C I S E 8

Which of the following pairs of subjects could be developed into a comparison and contrast essay? Which could not?

1. Computers and the human brain
2. Chicago and Boston
3. Left-handed and right-handed people
4. Math majors and high school dropouts
5. The Dewey Decimal System and the Library of Congress System
6. Cable television and Burt Reynolds
7. The community college and the four-year university
8. Teen-age pregnancies and the pill
9. Lightning and the lightning bug
10. Swiss chocolate and American chocolate

Two Student-Written Essays Developed by Comparison and Contrast

The first student-written essay which follows is developed by comparison and contrast. Because there are not a great number of differences being contrasted and because neither subject is treated extensively or in depth, the writer has used the *object-by-object pattern.*

Black Comedy: Two Angles

Bill Cosby and Richard Pryor are two of the most popular black comedians today. Both are seen frequently on television and in the movies, and both have succeeded in changing the attitudes of many white Americans toward blacks. In almost every other way, however, they are different.

Bill Cosby is a polished and verbal comedian whose comedy routines reflect his educated background. He is a graduate of Temple University and continues to take an active interest in the affairs of that institution. His humor is clean and wholesome, and he appeals to the entire family. His jokes are often based on humorous accounts of his wife and children. He pokes fun at himself, as well as society and its institutions, but he is never bitter. Cosby's ethnic jokes evoke mirth and smiles, but he never attacks his white audiences. He is frequently seen on television endorsing such wholesome products as computers, soft drinks, and desserts. As a headliner at benefits for charitable organizations, he has built an image of generosity, decency, and kindness. As a result, he appeals to older, middle-class Americans of all races.

Richard Pryor, on the other hand, is a high school dropout from the tough back streets of Peoria, Illinois. His early years were spent with rough characters who introduced him to sex, crime, and drugs. As a result, his jokes are often based on his experiences with dopers, prostitutes, drunks, and criminals he met in jail. Much of his material deals with the personal scandals in his life relating to alcohol, drugs, and his divorces. He is often crude and vulgar in his language, and his routines are too obscene to be delivered in their entirety on television. When he discusses race relations, he is often harsh and bitter, displaying a biting wit. His audience is mainly young people who come to hear him in sophisticated nightclubs.

Both Cosby and Pryor have their loyal audiences, but each represents a contrasting attitude and view of the world. If you want to be soothed and gently massaged, Cosby is your man. But if you don't mind becoming agitated, angry, or even offended, then Pryor is your ticket.

E X E R C I S E 9

These questions are based on the essay above.

1. How does the opening paragraph of the essay prepare the reader for the organization of the essay?
2. Where is the thesis statement?
3. The second paragraph deals with Bill Cosby, and the third discusses Richard Pryor. Is there an abrupt shift from one to the other, or does the writer provide a transition? If so, what is it?
4. How does the concluding paragraph tie the essay together?
5. Would the essay have been more effective if it had been organized in the point-by-point pattern? Explain.

The next essay considers a complex subject. Because she wanted to illustrate many differences between men and women, the writer used the point-by-point pattern.

Sex: There Is a Difference!

Everyone agrees that men and women are different. And everyone—both men and women—believe that they understand those differences. But there are aspects of those differences that would make for better relationships and stronger marriages if they were really understood by men.

In terms of stamina, physical condition, and resistance, men are the inferiors of women. More fetuses lost in miscarriages are male. More male infants die than female. And men are less resistant to illness than women. On the average, women have more fat and less muscle tissue than men. This accounts for the fact that many women outrun men in marathon races and can remain active longer than men. It also accounts for the fact that although women cannot lift objects as heavy as those lifted by men, they do possess strength in the form of endurance and stamina.

In the ways they think, women perceive the world differently. This is partly because their brains develop somewhat differently and they use their brains differently. A girl's verbal brain develops earlier than a boy's, and a boy's visual brain develops earlier than a girl's. This is why little girls generally read and write better than little boys, and why little boys can figure out how to put things together more easily than a girl. The sides of the brain catch up with each other eventually, but it is a fact that girls get a verbal head start and boys a visual-spatial head start.

The most important difference between men's and women's brains, however, is the way they function. Women usually seem to think more intuitively, because they use both sides of their brains at the same time. Men usually use one hemisphere at a time when they approach a problem. This means that men are usually more literal in their approach.

These differences between the sexes are created, in large part, by biology. But if both sexes knew and understood the importance of these differences and how they were caused, there would be more happy couples.

E X E R C I S E. 10

These questions are based on the preceding essay.

1. Why did the author of this essay use the point-by-point method? Could she have used the object-by-object pattern just as effectively?
2. What is the purpose of the second, third, and fourth paragraphs? Why do they have a unity? On the other hand, how is each distinct?
3. Is the discussion of the differences between men and women tilted in favor of either sex? What is your evidence?

E X E R C I S E 11

Using either a point-by-point or an object-by-object pattern, select one of the following pairs of objects and develop it into an essay using comparison and contrast. If you prefer, use one of the topics suggested in Exercise 7 (page 78).

A trip by car versus a plane flight
Two cultures you are familiar with (Chicano and Anglo, black and white, etc.)
The court system as you have experienced it and as it is represented in textbooks
Living together and getting married
The qualities looked for in a mate by males and by females
Two cities you know well
Foreign and domestic luxury cars
Two authors or two novels
Two television programs of the same type

Developing an Essay by Process and Analysis

"How is it done?" "How did it happen?" These are the questions answered by essays developed by *process and analysis*. Some process papers tell the reader how to do or make something: change a tire, train a puppy, mix concrete, or plant a tree. Others explain how something happened or how it takes place: how the pyramids of Egypt were built, how the blood circulates through the body, or how the Roman Catholic Church elects a Pope. In all cases the purpose is to provide information to the reader as clearly and directly as possible.

Because all process essays essentially explain how an act is done or a process happens, their ideas are presented chronologically. Every idea follows the previous one in a *time sequence*. If the ideas are presented out of order, the results will be chaotic. Imagine trying to put together a transistor radio from a kit whose instructions began, "After receiving a radio signal, adjust the aerial to improve reception." Or imagine an essay explaining how Jonas Salk discovered the polio vaccine in which the writer first discusses the controversy over the vaccine and the tragic deaths that were caused by vaccine samples insufficiently tested, followed by an account of Salk's early experiments with polio viruses and antibodies, concluding with earlier attempts to find a cure for a virus. The reader would be justifiably bewildered in following such an account. The first requirement, then, is to make certain that all the steps are presented in a clear sequence.

When writing the process paper, you should make it more than a list of steps. Such a paper would be technically correct but would have all the excitement of a set of directions for assembling a bicycle. Give your paper direction by giving it a thesis statement. For instance, instead of just listing in order the steps in taking a blood sample, write a thesis that lets the reader see an overall pattern. "Taking a blood sample is more painful for the nurse than for the patient" is more inviting as a thesis than "There are three steps to follow in taking a blood sample." In this way your paper has a point of view; it is leading somewhere.

Organizing the Essay Developed by Process and Analysis

Because the purpose of the process and analysis paper is to explain how a procedure is done or how it occurs, the introduction should contain a thesis statement which gives the reader an overview of the process, as well as your approach to it. The process should be divided into steps, usually in a time (chronological) sequence. Each major step of the procedure normally is treated in a separate paragraph. The conclusion reviews the procedure and reinforces your thesis statement.

The outline below is for a typical process and analysis paper. Keep in mind that the outline is for illustrative purposes only. The first paragraph does not always contain the thesis statement, and the number of steps in a process and analysis paper may vary, depending on the topic.

Paragraph 1: Introduction and thesis statement: announcement of the purpose or overall view
Paragraph 2: Step 1 or Stage 1
Paragraph 3: Step 2 or Stage 2
Paragraph 4: Step 3 or Stage 3
Paragraph 5: Step 4 or Stage 4
Paragraph 6: Conclusion

The following outline is for a process essay in which the writer wants to tell the reader how to do something: how to write a term paper.

Paragraph 1: *Introduction and thesis statement:* "Writing a term paper doesn't have to be a traumatic experience if you follow six easy steps."
Paragraph 2: *Step 1:* Selecting and narrowing your topic
Paragraph 3: *Step 2:* Formulating a thesis

Paragraph 4:	*Step 3:* Finding your information
Paragraph 5:	*Step 4:* Taking notes
Paragraph 6:	*Step 5:* Writing the first draft
Paragraph 7:	*Step 6:* Revising and polishing
Paragraph 8:	*Conclusion*

The next outline is for an essay in which the writer wants to tell the reader how a process happens: the major stages in a child's intellectual development. Like the outline for an essay explaining how to do something, this outline is arranged chronologically.

Paragraph 1:	*Introduction and thesis statement:* "According to the Swiss psychologist Jean Piaget, there are four major stages in a child's intellectual development."
Paragraph 2:	*Stage 1:* The sensory-motor stage (from birth to age two)
Paragraph 3:	*Stage 2:* The preoperational stage (from the second to seventh years)
Paragraph 4:	*Stage 3:* The concrete operations stage (from the seventh to eleventh years)
Paragraph 5:	*Stage 4:* The formal operations stage (from about the twelfth to the fifteenth years)
Paragraph 6:	*Conclusion*

Guidelines for Writing an Essay Developed by Process and Analysis

Do not try to explain something you do not understand. Choose a subject that you know something about and can explain clearly.

Begin by breaking the subject into its basic steps. Make certain that you have not omitted any important ones. Then write a brief introduction telling your reader what you are going to explain or tell.

Define any technical or abstract terms early in the paper. You don't want to confuse your reader with unfamiliar terms.

Present the steps of the process or analysis chronologically. Use words like "first," "next," and "finally." These will keep you on track and let your reader follow your paper without any problems.

When you have finished your paper, check it over. Make sure you haven't omitted any steps.

Two Student-Written Essays Developed by Process and Analysis

In the first essay which follows, the student wants to tell the reader how to do something. Notice how he has stated his thesis in the first paragraph and presented the steps for making paper in a sequential or chronological order.

How to Make Your Own Stationery

When we hear the word "recycling," we usually think of beer cans and bottles or wrecked cars. But you do not have to leave your home to recycle one of the most common waste products around you: old newspapers. By following a few easy steps you can manufacture recycled paper from your old newspapers. You will have fun, save money, and get rid of those old papers that have been stacking up.

The first step is to cut a square of newspaper approximately eleven inches on a side and shred it into small pieces. Fill a large bowl one-fourth full of water, add the shredded paper, and let the mixture soak for an hour or two. Beat the mixture vigorously with an electric mixer or hand-operated egg beater until the paper breaks up into fibers and the mixture appears creamy and homogeneous.

Next, dissolve two heaping tablespoons of starch or wallpaper paste in a half-liter of warm water. Add this solution to the creamy slurry and stir. Take a piece of fine window screen and dip it into the solution. Lift the screen out horizontally. If you have done this correctly, there will be a fine layer of paper fibers on the screen. Stir up the contents of the bowl and redip the screen carefully as many times as is necessary to build up a layer about a fourth of a centimeter thick.

Now it's time to press and dry the paper. To do this, place some cloth towels on a tabletop and lay the screen over the towels so that the fiber layer is facing upward. Cover the fibers with a piece of thin plastic (a plastic bag is fine). Now squeeze down evenly on the plastic, using a block of wood for a press. Most of the water should be squeezed from between the fibers, through the screen, and on the cloth towel. Set the screen out to dry for a day or two, and then peel off the newly fabricated recycled paper.

With a little practice you will be producing paper that has a beautiful texture—and won't cost you anything. Now all you have to do is sit down and write a friend.

In the next essay, the writer wants to tell the reader how the human skeleton develops. Notice that the first paragraph concludes with the thesis statement ("The development of the human skeleton is a mysterious and exciting process"), and the second paragraph gives an overview of the process. Paragraphs three, four, and five present the growth of the skeleton in chronological order, and the last paragraph offers a concluding idea.

The Development of the Skeleton

A ballet dancer pirouetting on the stage, a pitcher throwing a baseball, and a student writing an essay all have one thing in common: they are using their musculoskeletal system to control their motions. Those motions can be graceful, powerful, rhythmic, or precise, but they depend on a collection of 206 bones that make up the human skeleton. The development of the human skeleton is a mysterious and exciting process.

In a sense, an individual has three different skeletons at different ages. The first skeleton is formed of cartilage, and it is flexible and adequate for the period when the mother's uterus protects the fetus and when its motion is limited. The second, during childhood, is composed of primitive bone. It is more rigid than cartilage and more resilient than adult bone, but adequate for the infant. The final skeleton is finer grained bone, and it provides the support and protection required for such activities as walking and running.

About twenty-eight days after conception, limb buds appear at the site of the infant's future arms and legs. By four and one-half weeks blood vessels and nerve trunks are growing into the buds. Within the limb buds a spongy network of branching cells develops, and this produces a semifluid jelly that gradually stiffens. This eventually forms primitive connective tissue and cartilage. As the cells divide and produce new cartilage, the entire mass grows both internally and externally.

About eight weeks after conception, the general shape of the limb can be seen under the microscope, and even the developing joints can be identified. As the cartilage masses continue to grow, they are gradually surrounded by fibrous cells that in turn are invaded by capillaries, or tiny blood vessels. As the capillaries advance, they lay down a type of protein known as osteoid, which is later impregnated with bone minerals like calcium and phosphorus. This forms a ring of bone. As successive layers are laid down, the bone shaft is formed. This process is repeated at the bone ends until finally there is a bony mass at each end of the bone separated from it by a thin plate of cartilage. Birth occurs at about this stage.

After birth, further growth takes place in the cartilage, known as the growth plate. This continues until about sixteen years of age in girls and eighteen in boys. When growth is completed, the growth plates disappear and no more vertical growth of the skeleton occurs.

Because they are not visible, we tend to ignore our skeletons, concentrating instead on our hair, our complexion, or our muscles. But the skeleton provides the framework and the levers for all of our organs and tissues, and allows us to control our motions. Although its development is predictable, it is a mysterious process that begins again every time a human life is conceived.

E X E R C I S E 12

1. Using the outline on page 83 as a model, write an outline for "How to Make Your Own Stationery."
2. Using the outline on page 83 as a model, write an outline for "The Development of the Skeleton."

E X E R C I S E 13

Select one of the following topics and write an essay in which you explain how to do or make something. Divide the process into steps, following the suggestions on page 84 and the outline on page 83.

How to prepare for a camping trip
How to become rich
How to rig a sailboat
How to impress your teacher
How to meditate
How to grow your own vegetables
How to tune a piano
How to get rid of an undesirable habit
How to improve your appearance
How to select the best college

E X E R C I S E 14

Select one of the following topics and write an essay in which you explain to your reader how a certain process or event occurs or has taken place. Follow the suggestions on page 84 and the outline on page 83.

How the electoral college works
How the process of aging among males or females takes place
How the federal budget is determined
How the Nobel prize winners are selected
How cable television works
How a caterpillar becomes a butterfly
How photosynthesis occurs
How the news is gathered on television
How the music for a movie is written
How food is digested

Developing an Essay by Cause and Effect

"Why did this happen?" "What will happen because of this?" Every time we ask questions like these, we are thinking in terms of *cause and effect.* The driver who wants to know why his engine keeps dying in traffic, the scientists who ponder the effects of genetic engineering, and the cook who wonders why the soufflé collapsed are all following a familiar way of thinking: leaping back and forth from effect to cause and from cause to effect.

When writing a cause and effect essay, you emphasize cause or effect depending on your purpose. Most essays follow one of these plans:

They begin with a situation (the *effect)* and then examine the probable *cause;*

or

They begin with the *cause* and then speculate on its likely *effect.*

In the first plan you are searching for causes in the past; in the second you are looking ahead, considering possible consequences. Many topics can be approached from either direction. Using the first plan you could, for instance, begin your essay by discussing today's economy in terms of unemployment figures, the prices of food and automobiles, the cost of housing, and so on. These *effects* could then be traced to their cause: high interest rates, foreign imports, wage increases, and the price of oil.

If you start with the cause you could speculate on how these effects will in turn serve as the *causes* of future *effects:* a possible depression, political unrest, an increase in welfare, a ban on foreign cars, and a decline in the housing industry, for example.

E X E R C I S E   15

Select three of the following topics. Then, following the two plans as explained above, list as many *causes* and *effects* as you can think of. Here is an example:

topic: Hunger in the United States

Causes
Low-income
Lack of information concern-
ing nutrition and well-
balanced meals
Large families
Inadequate distribution of
food surpluses
Emphasis on fatty and starchy
foods

Effects
Birth defects
High incidence of childhood
diseases
High mortality rate among
poor
Poor academic performance in
school
Undesirable social behavior
Psychological ailments
Vulnerability to debilitating
disease

Topics
1. Cheating in college
2. Working mothers
3. Minimum-wage laws
4. The Great Depression
5. Child abuse
6. Alcoholism
7. The interest in astrology
8. The turbulence of the sixties
9. Racial prejudice.
10. The exodus to the suburbs

Organizing the Essay Developed by Cause and Effect

Whether your essay moves from an effect to a cause or from a cause to an effect, its organization will be similar. Your introduction should contain a thesis statement which identifies the cause and alludes to its effect, or specifies an effect and refers to its cause. The paragraphs in the body of the essay present the causes or the effects, and the conclusion reinforces the thesis.

Here is an outline for an essay that moves from *cause to effect:*

Paragraph 1:   *Introduction, Thesis:* "The almost 100,000 foreign immigrants who arrive in Los Angeles every year are
changing the character of the city." *(Cause)*

Paragraph 2:   *First effect:* No longer a predominant Anglo-American city but a city with diverse cultures, skin, languages

Paragraph 3:   *Second effect:* Challenge to already crowded schools to educate children in English

Paragraph 4:   *Third effect:* Racial tensions among immigrants and working class as they vie for housing, jobs

Paragraph 5:   *Fourth effect:* Businesses and neighborhoods undergoing transformation as many whites move

Paragraph 6:   *Conclusion*

Here is an outline for an essay that moves from *effect to cause:*

Paragraph 1:   *Introduction, Thesis:* "Much of the eastern shore of North America has been eroding, chiefly because of four major forces." *(Effect)*

Paragraph 2:   *Cause 1:* Tectonic forces depressing the coast

Paragraph 3:   *Cause 2:* Erosion by waves

Paragraph 4:   *Cause 3:* Buildup of sediment

Paragraph 5:   *Cause 4:* World-wide changes in sea level

Paragraph 6:   *Conclusion*

Guidelines for Writing an Essay Developed by Cause and Effect

Much bad writing stems from careless cause and effect reasoning. Just saying that something is the cause of something else, or that *this* will cause *that*, will persuade no one. You can avoid the common pitfalls when writing the cause and effect essay if you follow these suggestions:

If your topic is controversial, it is important to examine and present evidence, cite statistics, and look for more than one possible cause. More often than not, there is more than one cause for a given effect.

Keep in mind that the fact that something happened before something else occurred is not proof of a cause-and-effect relationship. If you have a pain in your neck and take a pink pill, the fact that the pain disappeared is not sufficient proof that the pill was the cause of the pain's disappearance. It may be that the pain would have disappeared even if you had not taken the pill. If you failed a math test, it is probably because you did not study, rather than because you didn't take your rabbit's foot to class. See pages 142–43 for a discussion of errors in reasoning, particularly in cause-and-effect relationships.

Two Student-Written Essays Developed by Cause and Effect

Here is an essay that moves from an *effect* (stated in the first paragraph) to a series of *causes* (listed in paragraphs two through five), with a conclusion that reinforces the thesis stated in the second paragraph.

Sex, Violence, and the Media

The United States leads the world in child abuse, divorce, and violent crime. Teen pregnancies, quickie abortions, rape, and venereal disease continue to rise. Young people maim and terrorize the old in savage acts of brutality without pattern or motive. Violent crime has risen by five percent every year since 1977. These are the facts. What are the causes?

Some sociologists would claim that poverty is the cause of violence and sexual permissiveness in our society. Others claim that discrimination is the main source, or that lack of education is to blame. These claims overlook the fact that violence and illicit sexual activity occur among all economic levels and races, and that more people are being educated than ever before. The actual cause of this epidemic of violence and sexual permissiveness is closer at hand, and is all around us: the media.

The movies, song lyrics, and television are the chief causes of the social and moral attitudes that most Americans have. Adultery is flaunted on every soap opera, and explicit sex, once confined to "X" ratings, is now "R" and even "PG," so children can be exposed to it. Song lyrics are suggestive and often vulgar. The private lives and scandals of movie stars are now public knowledge as a result of magazines like People and Us. Young people in particular are impressed by articles that feature gossip about their entertainment heroes, and they assume that such behavior is acceptable.

Violence on the screen may have an even stronger effect on the lives of its viewers than does explicit sex. Beheadings, disembowelings, razor slashings, and other varieties of torture are now regarded as entertainment, and as a result our culture is increasingly dehumanized. Although filmmakers say there is no evidence for a cause-and-effect link between violence on the screen and in the streets, studies have shown just the opposite. The Eisenhower Commission's study of "Mass Media and Violence" in the 1960s linked movies and television to youth aggression, and other studies have supported those conclusions.

These studies prove that subjects exposed to violent films show a far greater tendency to aggressive reactions on stress tests than subjects who saw comedies or some other bland fare. One study revealed that a preference for violent TV shows among third graders led to aggressive behavior not only at the time, but ten years later during their adolescence. These children had been shaped emotionally by the media.

Censorship is not the answer. Self-regulation by the media is the solution. If they do not accept their responsibility, our society will continue in its downward plunge toward lawlessness, and it will not be worth saving.

Here is an essay that moves from a series of *causes* (listed in the first four paragraphs) to their *effects* (stated in the fifth paragraph).

The Betrayal of the Vietnam Veteran

The Vietnam veteran has a set of problems different from those experienced by his older brother or father who served in Korea or World War II. No war is popular, but the Vietnam war met with hostility throughout this country on all levels of society. On college campuses, in Congress, in civic organizations, and on the front pages of the newspapers, our participation in that "dirty war" was debated. The goals of the war were never established, and American soldiers did not know what they were fighting for.

When the American soldiers returned from Vietnam, they were often met with contempt and made to feel that they had taken part in a dishonorable act. Employers were often reluctant to hire the veteran, and he was sometimes called a "killer." Wherever he went, he was looked at with suspicion, as if he were a bomb ready to explode.

The government did not help make the returning veteran feel welcome. The Veterans Administration has been more concerned with politics than it has been with the problems of the veteran. Led by weak administrators and ignored by Congress, it has failed to supply the necessary psychological and medical support that many Vietnam veterans need to re-enter civilian life successfully.

The U.S. Congress has refused to pass legislation comparable to the G.I. Bill of World War II, which enabled veterans to attend college. The current educational benefits program is laughable; it pays a small monthly stipend to veterans who attend college, but it is scarcely enough to live on.

What have been the consequences of this public and governmental indifference? More than a fourth of the Vietnam veterans suffer from stress. Many admit to guilt feelings and self-punishment. Others suffer from an unusually high rate of alcoholism; divorce figures are higher than average. Of those who saw heavy combat, one-fourth have been arrested for criminal offenses. They report feelings of alienation about themselves, and mistrust and doubts of love toward others.

The returning veterans of all previous wars have suffered some of these effects. But Vietnam veterans seem particularly vulnerable to them. It is up to the public and the government to realize the consequences of their indifference.

E X E R C I S E 16

1. Using the outline on page 89 as a model, write an outline for "Sex, Violence, and the Media."
2. Using the outline on page 90 as a model, write an outline for "The Betrayal of the Vietnam Veteran."

E X E R C I S E 17

Select one of the following topics and develop it into an essay moving from causes to effects or effects to causes.

The increase in small families
The growth of private education
Demand for the death penalty
Cheating on income-tax returns
Religious conversions
The failure of many people to vote
The conservative movement
The decline in SAT scores
Increasing attempts to censor books

Developing an Essay by Definition

"What is it?" "What does it mean?" Whether asked on an examination or in a conversation, these questions call for a definition, one of the most common kinds of writing assignments. Disagreements between couples, companies, and countries often occur because of confusion over the exact meaning of words. A husband and wife might differ over what constitutes "punishment" for their child, an employee and a manager would probably disagree over "generous salary," and the Russians and the Americans disagree over "detente."

When we define, we are trying to clear up confusion. Surprisingly, it isn't always the esoteric or difficult word that needs to be clarified; often it is the familiar word or phrase whose meaning defies agreement.

E X E R C I S E 18

Familiar words can often prove to be the most difficult to define. Select five of the following items and write a precise definition of each. Compare your definitions with those of others in your class. How similar were your definitions? What do the differences suggest?

good music	a good movie
"soul"	romance
success	happiness
sin	macho
religious	beauty

Words can be defined in three ways: by a *synonym* (substituting a familiar word for the word to be defined), by a *formal definition* (the kind often used in the dictionary), and by an *extended definition*, which develops the meaning of the word in a paragraph or essay.

Definition by synonym is the most concise way to define: a *melee* is defined as "a fight," a *maxillary* as "a jawbone," and *jejune* as "immature." The advantage of a definition by synonym is that it is brief. The danger occurs when the synonym is as confusing as the word being defined. To define "redundancy" as a "tautology," for example, is not very helpful.

The *formal definition* can often be expressed in one sentence. It consists of three parts: the term to be defined, the general class it belongs to, and the way it differs from all other members of that class. Here, in chart form, are some formal definitions:

term	general class	differentiation
The *human eye*	is a *bodily organ*	of *sight*.
A *capella*	is a type of *choir*	which does not use *instrumental accompaniment*.
A *binomial*	is an *algebraic expression*	with *two variables in it*.

The formal definition can be very helpful because of its exactness, and for that reason is often used by dictionarymakers.

E X E R C I S E 19

Write formal definitions of the following items:

eyeglasses	father
desk	garage
pencil	lipstick
shirt	paper clip

As helpful as synonyms and logical definitions are, it is sometimes necessary to extend a definition if the term being defined is complex, or if we want to say something interesting or significant about it. In these instances we write *extended definitions*, often as long as an entire essay.

Organizing the Essay Developed by an Extended Definition

Unlike essays developed by the previous patterns in this chapter, the essay based on an extended definition follows no customary pattern. Its organization depends, in great part, on what is being defined and what the writer intends to say about it.

Here are some of the questions you might ask before writing your definition essay:

What are some examples of it? *(example)*
How many kinds are there? *(classification)*
What are its parts? *(division)*
What is it similar to or different from? *(comparison and contrast)*
How is it done? How does it work? *(process)*
What causes it? What are its results or effects? *(cause and effect)*

In addition to applying these questions, you can sometimes make a definition clear to your reader by describing it physically: for example, its size, color, weight, and height. If the object or term evokes personal memories or associations that are helpful in explaining the term to your reader, include those as well.

To see how this technique for defining a term works, let us examine the possible ways to develop an essay defining "socialization." This concept is used by sociologists and psychologists to describe the process by which children develop behavior patterns that fit in with the standards of their culture.

What are some examples of socialization in our culture? *(example)*

What are some examples of behavior that is *not* acquired by socialization? *(example)*

What are the parts or divisions of the socialization process? *(division)*

How many kinds of socialization processes are there? *(classification)*

How is the socialization process similar to other human behavior or processes? *(comparison)*

How is the socialization process different from other human behavior or processes? *(contrast)*

How does the socialization process start? *(process)*

How does it work? What are its stages? *(process)*

What causes it? What are its effects? *(cause and effect)*

As you can see, merely answering those questions would provide an abundance of material for an essay defining the term. And as this list of questions also demonstrates, it is usually possible (and advisable) to use more than one method of development when defining a term. By doing so, you present the term in all its aspects, and you help your reader to understand it more readily.

E X E R C I S E 20

By using the approach outlined above, show how one of the following terms could be defined by a variety of developmental patterns. Do not write an essay; just list the kinds of questions that would suggest the development of the definition.

Initiation
Nuptials
Bar mitzvah
Homecoming
Recognition
Rejection
Punishment
Falling in (or out of) love

Guidelines for Writing an Essay Developed by Definition

Begin your essay with a formal definition. This tells your reader the boundaries or limits of your definition.

Tell the reader why you are defining the term. Perhaps you want to show

how it is confused with another term, or maybe you want to present some interesting examples and facts associated with the concept.

Use several examples to make certain that your reader knows what you mean when you use the term.

Avoid using the old cliché, "According to Webster . . ."

A Student-Written Essay Developed by Definition

Here is a student-written essay defining the term "phobia." Notice how the writer uses a variety of developmental patterns to make the meaning clear: cause and effect, examples, classification and division, process, and comparison and contrast.

Who's Afraid of the Dark?

Are you afraid of high places or water? If so, you suffer from one of the more common phobias, which are strong, persistent, but unreasonable fears. The fear of high places (acrophobia) and water (hydrophobia) are only two of the more than seven hundred phobias classified by psychologists.

Most of us either have or know someone who has a phobia of some kind: a fear of snakes, enclosed spaces, open places, dogs, crowds, and so on. Some phobias, however, are exotic and unusual. There is, for example, anthophobia (fear of flowers), gephydrophobia (fear of crossing bridges), ombrophobia (fear of rain), and trichophobia (fear of hair). All of these phobias have one thing in common: they represent a persistent fear of some object or situation that often presents no danger to the person who has the phobia.

Phobias have several causes, according to psychologists. One of the more easily understood causes is the one that can be traced back to childhood. A child who was bitten by a dog or who was almost drowned will understandably grow up with a fear of dogs or water. Some phobias, however, are based on more complicated causes. According to one theory, some people are genetically predisposed toward certain neurotic symptoms and therefore are suggestible toward phobias. Another theory's hypothesis is that phobias are learned. This theory suggests that a phobia is the result of habits learned by the individual; in a typical case he or she associates "bad luck" or misfortune with a particular object or situation, and as time passes, the phobia expands. As a result, the fear often generalizes to more and more objects.

The effects of phobias can vary from behavior that is barely noticeable to behavior that is very bizarre. The patient may go to great lengths to avoid entering a small room or passageway, even when it is essential. Phobia victims often report a wide range of physical ailments: headaches, back pains, stomach upsets, dizzy spells, and sweating. They often complain of feeling generally unhappy, and speak of feelings of unreality, strangeness, and depression.

The cures for phobias range from psychotherapy to avoidance therapy. In some cases patients are urged to probe their past for the origins of the phobia. Some therapists believe, however, that it is best to ignore such probings and to emphasize the future. Their technique is to encourage the patient to confront the phobia. One such practitioner who treats people who have a fear of flying has been so successful that his patients celebrate by flying to Miami.

A surefire cure for phobias has not yet been discovered, nor has the cause. In the meantime, you should take comfort that if you hate to get back to your homework, you merely suffer from ergophobia, a phobia shared by millions of students: the fear of work.

E X E R C I S E 21

1. What is the main developmental pattern used in the first two paragraphs of this essay?
2. The third and fourth paragraphs combine cause and effect with definition. Point to specific examples of each pattern.
3. What pattern is used chiefly in the fifth paragraph?
4. Comment on the concluding paragraph: is it effective? Does it bring the essay to a close, or does it leave you anticipating more?
5. How many developmental patterns were used in this selection? What does that tell you about the strategies or patterns used to develop an essay that defines a term?

E X E R C I S E 22

Select one of the following terms and write an extended definition. Keep in mind that you will probably use more than one developmental pattern in writing your definition.

Censorship   Patriotism
Male chauvinism   A bargain

Nature	Home
Radical	Sexy
Work	Up tight
Funky	A white lie
A flirt	Sportsmanship
The Third World	Women's liberation

6

Revising
the Essay

Some people are willing to settle for the second-best in life. Refusing to expend the effort and concentration necessary to complete any worthwhile job, they prefer to take the easy way out. They are content to go through life giving it their half-best. As a consequence, they rarely produce anything that is distinguished, and they let opportunities for excellence slip through their fingers.

People with this attitude usually take the same approach to their writing. They write in a hurry, rarely looking back to revise or edit their material. If they are students, they often turn in the first draft of an essay full of rambling, undeveloped ideas and careless mistakes. They ignore the fact that every piece of writing can be improved by careful revision and editing, and that all writers—even professionals—find it necessary to revise their work.

The kinds of writers described here fail to give their work the final polishing it deserves because they think that revision means at most only the search for mistakes in spelling, grammar, and punctuation. While it is true that editing includes the correction of such errors, revision involves much more. It includes (but is not restricted to) the rearranging and reorganizing of ideas, the rewording of sentences, the addition of new material, and the deletion of unnecessary material. It is, in other words, an examination of the draft from the ground up.

7. Revising and Editing Your Essay

Revision (which comes from two Latin words meaning "to see again") also requires the development of a self-critical attitude. This is often the most difficult part—to be objective about your own writing. Writing is effective only insofar as it communicates ideas to the reader. If you can stand back and look at your essay as if you were an outsider reading it for the first time, you will save yourself disappointment later.

The revising and editing process in this chapter takes you through your essay several times as you look (and listen) for ways to improve your paper. The first step is to *hear* your essay so that you can get an overall impression of its impact. The second step is to *read* it carefully—first, for its content and organization and the development of its ideas, and next, for its style, especially its sentence structure and word choice. The third examination of your paper is to *edit* it for mistakes in grammar, punctuation, and spelling. The last step is to *proofread* the final copy for typographical errors, previously undetected spelling and punctuation mistakes, and other blemishes that would weaken the paper's overall impression.

Hearing Your Essay

One of the best ways to begin the revision of a piece of writing is to hear it. Seeing your writing is usually not enough; as you read it silently, you unconsciously fill in missing punctuation marks, letters, and even words, and you often do not catch rough sentences or awkward transitions. When you *hear* the essay, however, you use different cognitive and critical skills that will expose the errors that might escape a silent reading.

Begin by asking a friend to read your essay aloud to you. If you prefer, read it on a cassette recorder and play it back. In either case, follow along with a copy of the essay and a pen. As you listen, mark anything that bothers you. Do not try to make corrections as you listen; instead, concentrate on the following questions:

Does this essay sound like *me?*

Does it have an overall design and flow?

Is the paper smooth? Are there any words or sentences that stick out or jar?

Is it interesting? Or dull? What about the beginning: Would the reader want to know and read more?

What is my purpose? What point am I trying to make to my audience?

Do I talk down to my reader? Do I say the obvious? Do I sound too formal?

Is the essay clear? Is there enough information? Are there any sudden jumps?

Does the paper end abruptly?

You will probably notice that your reactions range from the less important ("Should I use a different word here?") to the more fundamental ("I wonder whether I ought to cut out this section"). You will also discover that revision is not just a cleaning-up operation but a process that usually triggers new ideas as you examine the structure and organization of your paper. Keep in mind that as you revise, you are *rethinking;* as a result, you are likely to change anything in your paper.

An analogy might be helpful here. When you buy a house you often need to do some remodeling. Sometimes you have only to apply a fresh coat of paint or replace some broken window panes. After living in the house a while you may find that you want to move a door or a window. You may decide to add on a room or tear down a wall. If the foundation is cracked or if the supporting beams are weak, you may have to replace the joists or shore up the footing. Only rarely can you assume that you will not have to make any repairs or modifications.

So, too, in the case of writing an essay. You may discover that your first draft needs only minor remodeling: a few words changed here, a sentence or two there, and perhaps some additional bracing and support in sections that sag. A closer examination, however, may reveal some shaky premises, windy passages, or an entire section that needs to be renovated. Rarely will you find that your first draft cannot be improved.

After you have listened to your essay and satisfied yourself on the points you have noted, you are now ready to read it. As stated above, you will read your first draft twice: the first reading to consider its content and organization, and the second to examine its style, focusing on the sentence and word level.

Revising for Content and Organization

The content and organization of an essay—its ideas and its design—are as related as the two sides of a coin. It is virtually impossible to isolate one from the other. As you revise your first draft, you will move back and forth from its content to its organization. To help you see how the revision process works, a first draft by Tom Guarnotta, a freshman, is included in this section. Read his first draft carefully. Later, you will reread it to check for content and organization. The revision checklist which follows his first draft can be your guide. You should use this checklist to go over all your own writing.

Revision Case Study: A Student Essay

Athletics Should Be Abolished

Tom Guarnotta

1. American education is coming under attack and everyone seems to have a cure for its problems. Some people push for more math, others computers, still others say we should do more writing. They have their solutions, but they have all missed the boat. The problem is that there is too much emphasis on competitive athletics.

2. In the typical high school the facilities for the football teams are very good. They boast of their record and the number of the athletic scholarships that are won. Their coaches make huge salaries. But the facilities for the rest of the students are limited and crowded. This keeps every student from devoting a period per day to physical exercise.

3.   Our country needs to change its attitude toward its schools. It should insist on the right of every student to develop to the utmost his or her athletic ability. In addition, each student should be physically fit.

4.   In high schools they play football, even at night. The parents demand interscholastic competition. They say that if the schools don't arrange games, the kids will play in leagues that are more dangerous. They have marching bands, majorettes, cheerleaders. People should compare the amount of money spent on athletics, bands, and so on with what is spent on education.

5.   The colleges don't help the situation in their recruiting practices. They have created a commercial aspect to athletics. But this is what the public, especially the parents, want. The community wants winning teams and entertainment. They think that a public spectacle is taking care of the well-being of all the kids. They are ignoring the physical fitness of all youth, boys and girls. There are a number of things the citizens could do if they wanted to.

6.   There is a need for developing all talent. There is also a need for a change in attitude of each person and community toward its secondary schools. The school should be restored to its real purpose. Only then will our nation be prepared for the challenges that lay ahead.

REVISION CHECKLIST

First Reading

1. *Is your thesis statement focused sharply so that the reader knows exactly what your controlling idea is? (See pages 41–45.)*
2. *Does the introduction catch the reader's interest and lead naturally into the thesis statement? (See pages 180–82.)*
3. *Do you have enough information to support your thesis statement? (See pages 32–33.)*
4. *Can the reader sense a direction or movement of the ideas through the essay? (See pages 47–57.)*
5. *Are all of the ideas on one subject and in the right order? Do they advance the thesis without wandering off? (See pages 154–56.)*
6. *Does each middle (body) paragraph deal with one point or aspect of the topic? Does every sentence in each body paragraph deal with that point? (See pages 159–62.)*
7. *Does each paragraph have enough development so that its topic sentence is supported? (See pages 173–75.)*
8. *Does the conclusion express a sense of finality without seeming abrupt? (See pages 182–84.)*

As you go through the following discussion, you will notice that some of the questions have been combined. This reflects the way you will revise your paper as you look for several things at the same time.

---

1. *Is your thesis statement focused sharply so that the reader knows exactly what your controlling idea is?*

The place to begin a revision is with its backbone: the thesis statement. On a separate sheet of paper write down the main idea of your essay. If you can't, your paper lacks a focus and you need to step back and reconsider what it is that you want to tell your reader. Ask a friend to read your paper and identify the main idea. If you don't agree, you need to work on making the thesis statement more specific.

Tom Guarnotta's thesis statement is reasonably clear, but it needs to be focused more sharply. He states, "The problem is that there is too much emphasis on competitive athletics." The confusion stems from the sentences that precede the statement. They refer to American education and its problems, but do not define what branch of education he refers to, nor does he define the problems. Further, his thesis, which advocates a de-emphasis on athletics, seems to conflict with his title, which implies that all athletics should be abolished. Before we can suggest a revision of the thesis statement, therefore, we need to read more of the essay so that our confusion can be dispelled.

---

2. *Does the introduction catch the reader's interest and lead into the thesis statement? Does the concluding paragraph express a sense of finality without sounding abrupt?*

Look over your opening paragraph. Did you begin with a "hook" that would catch your reader's interest and make him want to read on? Does your introduction suggest the tone and organization of your essay? Did you avoid beginning with a cliché or platitude?

Tom's opening paragraph needs rewriting because it is vague and lacks focus. His first sentence raises more problems than it solves. As noted above, he speaks ambiguously of American education; he does not tell us who is attacking education; various "people" have answers for these unspecified problems, but they too are not identified. Despite these problems, Tom's paragraph does have a semblance of organization. He begins by announcing that American education (whatever that is) has a problem (which he fails to specify) and that various solutions have been proposed (though he mentions them somewhat tersely and incompletely), and then dismisses them. He has cleared the stage, however clumsily, for his own solution, which is implied in his thesis statement: there should be less emphasis on competitive athletics.

Tom's concluding paragraph does not seem to reinforce his introduction and thesis statement; they seem to be from different essays. The conclusion consists of a series of platitudes and vague pleas for a change in attitude toward the secondary schools. The reader is left without a clear notion of what is expected of him. As with the introduction (and the title), we will be able to offer a revision after we have read the entire essay.

---

3. *Does the body of your essay support your thesis? Do you have enough ideas, facts, and information?*

After you have sharpened your thesis statement and are satisfied with it, look at your middle paragraphs to see if they contain enough support. On a separate sheet of paper jot down the ideas in each paragraph that support your thesis statement. Are you satisfied that you have developed enough material, or should you add additional supporting information? Have you supplied convincing examples, facts, and reasons that make your thesis clear to the reader?

Paragraph two of Tom's essay cites the facilities for the football team at the typical high school and contrasts them with those available for the rest of the student body. This paragraph provides support for his thesis, but is somewhat thin.

His third paragraph helps to clarify his thesis, but it does not provide additional support. He states that our country should insist on the right of every student to develop his or her athletic ability, an idea implied in his main idea but not developed here.

The fourth paragraph offers additional support for his thesis that there is too much emphasis on competitive athletics. He cites the pressure of parents and the money spent on athletics.

The last paragraph in the body of Tom's essay—paragraph five—again refers to the public, particularly parents, implying that they are the culprits responsible for the emphasis on competitive athletics and for ignoring the physical fitness of all students.

The overall impression you have after reading Tom's middle paragraphs is that he has stuck fairly consistently with his thesis statement, supporting it with a mixture of generalizations and few specific details. He needs to give more examples and to make his generalizations clear to the reader.

Before trying to revise Tom's middle paragraphs, however, we should note whether his ideas are in the right order and whether all of them should be retained in a revision.

4. *Does each paragraph deal with one point or aspect of the thesis statement, and is that point expressed in a topic sentence? Are there ideas that need to be expanded? Are there any ideas that are irrelevant and unrelated to the thesis statement? Are the paragraphs in the right order?*

This is one of the most important phases of your revision. You are looking at each paragraph as a mini-essay, testing it for its unity and development, as well as for its support of the thesis statement.

As we look again at the body paragraphs in Tom Guarnotta's essay, we can note ideas that need to be expanded, moved, or eliminated. We can also make recommendations for improving the relationship of the paragraphs in the essay to strengthen the movement of the ideas.

Tom would make a better case for his thesis if he would expand his reference in the second paragraph to the contrasting facilities available to the football team and those available to the rest of the students. Such a contrast would drive home his point that there is too much emphasis on competitive athletics at the expense of facilities and activities for nonathletes. He should revise the topic sentence of this paragraph because it does not convey this contrast, limiting itself to the facilities for the football team. At the same time, he should delete the reference to the coaches' salaries and the number of athletic scholarships won because those details do not support the topic sentence. A suggested revision for paragraph two might look like this:

Facilities for the football team in a typical high school are often luxurious, particularly when compared to those offered to the rest of the students. The football stadium holds more than ten thousand fans; the playing field is sodded and manicured; the field house provides private showers, dressing rooms, spacious lockers, and a medical dispensary. Several tackling machines, universal gyms, and sundry equipment designed to make the aspiring All-Americans faster, heavier, and stronger are supplied. The facilities for the gym classes, by contrast, are spare and ascetic. The playing area is usually too small for the hordes that fill it. There is usually a shortage of basketballs and other equipment because the budget has been tilted in favor of the athletic program. The community showers are inadequate to take care of the vast number of students, and the tiny lockers assigned to their belongings are often pilfered. Because of the shortage of facilities and equipment, the student is assigned to gym class only two or three hours a week. As a result, he and his tax-paying parents get short-changed.

Notice that the revision sharpens the focus of the thesis and gives it support by emphasizing through additional details the contrast between the amenities enjoyed by the teams and the limited opportunities available to the rest of the students.

The third paragraph in Tom's essay begins with a shift in the focus of the paper—a call for our country to change its attitude toward its schools. It concludes by asserting that each student should be physically fit, an idea implied by the thesis. Aside from its opening sentence, this paragraph does little more than restate the thesis. If Tom intends to offer a solution to the problem of overemphasis on competitive athletics, he would do better to wait until he has finished his presentation of the problem. This paragraph violates the overall unity of the paper and should be deleted.

The fourth paragraph contains, in jumbled fashion, support for Tom's thesis. His topic sentence states that high school football is played at night. He neglects to explain the significance of this fact, choosing instead to mention the pressure applied by parents on the schools. Then he alludes to marching bands, majorettes, and cheerleaders, and concludes with a reference to the amount of money spent respectively on athletics and education. The paragraph suffers from two weaknesses: it offers a chaotic series of details that need to be rearranged, and it offers several vague terms that need to be defined or clarified. Nevertheless, the paragraph contains the seeds of support for the thesis statement. A revision of this paragraph might be:

> By demanding interscholastic competition, the parents deserve much of the blame. They claim that if the schools don't arrange school-sponsored games, the students will play in leagues which allow more dangerous play. They claim that athletic competition is beneficial, but they ignore the injuries as well as the rejection that young bodies and minds are particularly sensitive to. They tacitly approve the time spent on practice instead of homework, and they gladly pay their tax dollars for marching bands, majorettes, and cheerleaders.

Notice that this revision strengthens the thesis in two ways: it cites examples of abuses in the athletic program, and it assigns much of the blame. Each sentence in the paragraph supports the two key words in the topic sentence: "parents" and "blame."

The fifth paragraph repeats some of the ideas in the preceding paragraph. It begins with an irrelevant statement about the colleges. Tom should either expand on this or abandon it. His best move would probably be to abandon it because to develop it might divert his essay away from a path he has set. The paragraph contains a charge that the schools are ignoring the physical fitness of all their students, an idea that supports his thesis. The paragraph concludes with a statement that needs clarification: "There are a number of things the citizens could do if they wanted to." This sentence is actually the turning point of the essay; it signals the introduction of Tom's solution to the problem that he has set forth. Yet he walks away from the sentence and we are left to wonder what his solution is. A revision of this paragraph, therefore, would have to start with its last sentence and clarify it with a series of examples. Here is a suggested revision:

It is within the power of the citizens of this country to make their schools once more a place to develop their children's intellectual and physical talents rather than a stage for the performance of athletic heroes. First, they can compare the amount of money spent on teams, bands, uniforms, transportation, and maintenance of facilities with the amount of money spent on books and laboratory equipment. Second, they should compare the amount of time spent practicing during the week for a forthcoming athletic spectacle with the amount of time spent on homework and time in class. Third, they should ease the pressure on the coaches for winning. Finally, they should demand to know what the schools' athletic departments are doing for those students who are not athletically inclined, and they should insist that all boys and girls are included.

Now we can return to the introduction and conclusion of Tom's essay. If we had tried to revise them earlier, the proposed paragraphs might not have accurately introduced or concluded the revised body of the essay. Now, however, we see the movement of the thesis statement and the middle paragraphs, and we can revise the introduction and conclusion. Here is a suggested revised introductory paragraph:

Everyone seems to be taking pot shots at the American high school. Critics point to declining S.A.T. scores, shortened school days, soft courses, and unprepared teachers. As a solution they offer longer days, harder courses, higher pay for the best teachers, and computers. While all of these proposals have some merit, they fail to remedy an ailment that pervades the American high school: the overemphasis on competitive athletics.

The concluding paragraph, as we already noted, is too vague to offer the reader much to think about. It consists of several platitudes that seem to have little to do with the thesis. This suggested revision asks the reader to pursue a course of action:

This generation of students will be confronted by challenges unknown by their parents or previous generations. The schools must adapt to those challenges, and they can do it only by a change in the attitude of each parent and citizen in the community. The schools should be restored to their real purpose: the physical and intellectual preparation of their students. Only then will our schools produce graduates prepared for the demands of the future.

The Title of Your Essay

A good title, like a good introduction, suggests the contents of the essay. Tom's title is unexciting in its starkness. It is too abrasive for most readers; further, it does not really reflect his thesis. A better title might be "Athletics: The Worm in the Educational Apple." Such a title takes advantage of a pun and lightens the heavy-handed approach implied by his original title.

Your title does not have to specify the exact scope of the contents of your essay; on the other hand, it should give at least a hint of what the reader will find. Do not use a general title that promises more than you intend to deliver. "New Orleans Jazz," for example, is hardly an accurate title for an essay that is restricted to a discussion of Louis Armstrong. Nor should you use a title that is too vague or ordinary: "The Importance of Education," "An Interesting Day," or "A Surprise Party."

The best titles are relatively brief, direct, and exact—and they catch the interest of the reader. Note these titles:

"American Fat" (an article about wordiness)
Custer Died for Your Sins (a study of the American Indian)
"Who's Afraid of Math, and Why?" (an analysis of the fear that math induces)
Zen and the Art of Motorcycle Maintenance (a study of Eastern philosophy)
"Four-Letter Words Can Hurt You" (an article about obscenities)
"Clothes Make the Man—Uneasy" (an article about changing styles)

E X E R C I S E 1

Improve the following titles:

My Hobby	My Vacation
Applying for a Job	My Favorite Relative
A Fishing Trip	Why I Want to Be a Nurse
Teachers	Shyness

Revising for Style

In our health-conscious society with its emphasis on fitness, it would appear that few people are satisfied with their bodies. Everyone seems to be either too heavy or too skinny. So it is with writers. They seem either to overwrite or to underwrite—either to be wordy, drowning their ideas in excess verbiage, or too lean and spare or vague, starving their ideas by failing to supply enough information. As you revise your essay for style, ask yourself whether you are an overwriter or an underwriter: whether you have written too much and therefore need to trim your verbal fat, or whether you have starved your sentences and readers and need to nourish them with more ideas.

When we discuss the style of an essay, we are usually referring to its sentences and word choice. If you read your paper aloud (or listened to it as someone else read it), perhaps you noted on your paper those sentences that were difficult to read or that caused the reader to stumble. Examine those sentences to locate the source of the problem. Similarly, look at the words that the reader stumbled over or that were incorrectly emphasized. Try to analyze what went wrong.

The revision of Tom Guarnotta's essay emphasized its content and organization. During that revision many sentences and individual words were changed. Listed below are some of them; see if you can detect others. In each case, why were the words or sentences changed?

Paragraph 1: This paragraph contains a comma splice; can you find it? Is the term "missed the boat" appropriate?

Paragraph 2: What is "very good"? Is the idea clear? Notice the sentence structure; are the sentences smooth? Are they connected with transitions? Can you improve the expression "per day"?

Paragraph 3: Does the last sentence follow logically? What does "In addition" imply?

Paragraph 4: Who is "they" in the first sentence? Is this an important detail? Is "kids" appropriate? Who is "They" in the third sentence? Who are the "People" in the last sentence? Is "and so on" acceptable? Are the sentences smooth and connected? Do the ideas seem related?

Paragraph 5: Does the first sentence serve adequately as a topic sentence? What is the "well-being" of the students (fifth sentence)? What are "the number of things" the citizens could do? Are the sentences smooth? Do the ideas flow from one sentence to another?

Paragraph 6: What kind of talent is referred to in the first sentence? What kind of attitude (second sentence)? What is the "real purpose" (third sentence)? What exactly is the writer saying?

REVISION CHECKLIST

Second Reading

1. *Are your sentences tight and concise rather than padded and lumpy? Look carefully at each sentence for redundancies, repetition, and fillers. Make sure that every sentence says as much as possible in as few words as possible without sacrificing your meaning. (See pages 186–89.)*

2. *Do your sentences vary in their length? Count the words in ten sentences and determine their average length. If you average only ten to fifteen words, your sentences are probably too short. On the other hand, if they average more than about 25 or 30, they are probably too long. (See pages 189–92.)*

3. *Are your sentences varied in structure? If most of your sentences follow the subject-verb pattern, rearrange some of them. Use a variety of strategies, including loose and periodic sentences and parallel structure. Examine every verb in the passive voice; try to replace it with a verb in the active voice. (See pages 193–203.)*

4. *Are the tone and level of your word choice appropriate to your topic? Do you move back and forth from slang to Standard English? Select the level of language and the tone that is best for your audience and subject and stick to it. (See pages 223–25.)*

5. *Do you use words that are concise and exact, avoiding triteness and clichés? Make certain that every word in your essay means exactly what you mean. Be sure that you have avoided tired language, pretentious words, and other language that masks your meaning. (See pages 215–22.)*

Editing Your Essay: Grammar, Punctuation, and Spelling

The purpose of the editing phase of the revising process is to get rid of the warts and blemishes in your paper: to correct any mistakes in grammar, punctuation, and spelling. The process is more like repairing a roadbed than building a new freeway. You are trying to make the journey smoother for the reader, not blast out a new route or head in a new direction.

This stage is important because it can ruin your image. If the kinds of errors you look for in the editing process remain in your paper, they can create the impression that you are careless and sloppy in your approach not only to writing, but to logic and thinking as well.

Mistakes like these can create the impression in your reader's mind that you should not be trusted or believed.

As you read your paper, look for the kinds of mistakes that are mentioned on page 101 and discussed in pages 297–314.

Sentence fragments
Comma splices and run-on sentences
Mistakes in subject-verb agreement
Misplaced and dangling modifiers
Problems in pronoun usage
Shifts in tense, voice, and person

The best way to catch errors like these is to read your essay aloud. Your voice will usually catch errors in usage; if you stumble over a sentence, mark it and go on. After you have read the entire essay, return to the marked passages and work on them until they sound right. Refer to the handbook section in this book (pages 333–37 if you are not certain about the kind of mistake involved.

As you look over your paper, examine carefully all punctuation marks, especially the comma. It gives writers more problems than any other punctuation mark. Be sure that you put end punctuation after every sentence, that you always use parentheses and quotation marks in pairs, and that you can substitute a period for every semicolon. Review pages 315–26 for any punctuation rules you'd like to check.

Your mind can play tricks on you when you look for spelling errors. You think you see letters that are not there, and you ignore those that are there. Reading each line of your essay backwards will help you because it forces you to read each word singly, in isolation, instead of in a phrase. Look for words that have given you trouble in past papers. Circle any words that do not look correct; use your dictionary to verify their correctness. Do not trust your intuition— use the dictionary for all words you're not sure of. Misspelled words irritate readers and makes them wonder about the accuracy of your ideas.

After you have edited your paper and are positive that you have made all of the necessary corrections, you are ready to prepare the final copy of your essay.

E X E R C I S E 2

This passage, from Charles Dickens' *Pickwick Papers*, contains a sentence fragment and three misspelled words. Find and correct the errors.

While his three companions were busily engaged in proffering their thanks to their new acquaintance, Mr. Pickwick had liesure to examine his costume and appearance. He was about the middle height, but the thinness of his body and the length of his legs gave him the appearance of being much taller. His green coat was buttoned closely up to his chin, at the imminent hazard of splitting the back. His scanty black trousers displayed here and there those shiney patches which bespeak long service, and were strapped very tightly over a pair of patched and mended shoes. As if to conceal the dirty white stockings, which were nevertheless distinctly visible. His face was thin and haggard, but an indescribable air of jaunty impudence and perfect self-possesion pervaded the whole man.

Manuscript Form and Proofreading

You would not think of wrapping an expensive gift in torn or soiled paper. Nor would you show up for a job interview in a soup-stained shirt or tattered trousers. The same principle applies when you turn in written work to your instructors—you do not want your effort and ideas to be overshadowed by a sloppy or careless manuscript. Check your paper carefully, therefore, to be sure that it represents your best work. If your instructor has not given you directions for preparing your manuscript, you should follow these suggestions as a guide.

If you type, use white unlined paper of standard size (8½ by 11 inches). Type with a clean black ribbon, double-spacing, on one side of the paper. If you write, use standard size lined white paper (*not* the kind ripped out of a spiral notebook) and black ink. Whether typing or writing, leave margins on all four sides. The first line of each paragraph should be indented about an inch.

If you use a title page, type or write the title of your essay, your name, the name of the class, and the date. Center the title about four inches from the top of the page; capitalize the first word and all other important words. Do not use a period after the title. Drop down about four or five spaces and type or write your name; about two spaces below your name, type or write the name of your class. If you do not use a title page, place the title on the first line of your essay and place your name and the name of the class in the upper right-hand corner of the first page. Number your pages, beginning with page two, in the upper right corner.

Your last job before submitting your paper is to proofread the manuscript carefully. During this stage you are looking for any errors in your essay: misspelled words, punctuation and typographical errors, and other mistakes that would distract your reader. Proofreading requires that you change the focus of your attention. No longer are you looking beneath the surface of your paper for such weaknesses as lapses in logic, undeveloped paragraphs, or irrelevant details. Now you are examining the surface structure of your essay—you are, in effect, examining the wrapping and the ribbon.

The first requirement in proofreading is to give yourself enough time. You can't spot all of your mistakes if you have to rush through the paper. As you read your final copy, look first for misspelled words. Be sure that you have correctly hyphenated words; use the dictionary if you are not certain. Draw a line neatly through all words that you wish to omit. If you want to add material, use a caret ($\wedge$).

If you have several erasures, changes, and corrections on a page, recopy it. Messiness can detract from the effectiveness and impact of your writing. When you are satisfied that you have made all necessary corrections, staple or clip the pages together.

The Progress of an Essay: A Case History

In this section you will follow the development of an essay written by Nancy Avery, a freshman. As she wrote her essay, Nancy went through the seven steps in the writing process as they are presented in this book. You will see that she continued to tinker with the wording and organization of her essay right up to the final revision.

Her English instructor had given the class the following assignment: Write an essay of 500 to 750 words discussing some of the problems faced by American college students.

1. Choosing and Limiting a Topic

Here are Nancy's notes as she tried to develop a topic for her essay:

> *Getting a part-time job*
> most employers want experience
> hard to find anything in this city now
> unemployment high
> students shouldn't work part-time if they want good grades
> tuition to be raised next year
> necessary for many students to work
> books, tuition, room and board
> most students don't have marketable skills

   Broken homes
      divorce common
      students confused; stress
      they can't given enough time to their mates because of studies
      economic hardship
  Social relationships
      sororities and fraternities
      making friends
      getting along with opposite sex
      exchange student from Spain: differences in relationships, customs
      dating; being shy
      sex: what is allowed?
      cliques
      my friends—their complaints
  College
      can't decide on major
      problems of registration; crowded
      classes filled
      too much homework

Nancy has the nucleus of some possibilities in these lists, but there are a few problems as well.

Her ideas on "getting a part-time job" are predictable, and she does not have much that is interesting or different to say. Furthermore, she does not seem to have a focus or angle in mind; her comment, "students shouldn't work part-time if they want good grades" suggests an ambivalence toward her topic. She may be able to focus this after thinking more about it and by discussing it with her friends.

"Broken homes" suffers from the same problems. She says the obvious ("divorce common") and her comment, "they can't give enough time to their mates because of studies" suggests that she has shifted from students who come from broken homes to students who get a divorce. She seems to be short on ideas, but maybe she can develop some more promising material.

"Social relationships" suffers from a lack of focus: is she thinking of boy-girl relationships, or friends in general? Her references to dating and the opposite sex, on the one hand, and sororities and fraternities, on the other hand, suggest that she hasn't yet sharpened her topic. The reference to the exchange student from Spain hints of a paper comparing American and Spanish dating customs, which is not the assigned topic. Nevertheless, this list does have some possibilities.

"College" does not sound promising as a topic for Nancy's paper. Her notes sound more like personal gripes; at any rate, it is doubtful that the problems she cites are those faced by most American college students. Furthermore, she seems to run out of gas, as evidenced by the brevity and predictability of her list. If she wants to write on this topic, she will have to develop more content and some fresh ideas.

After thinking about her lists and discussing them with her friends, Nancy realizes that not all college students have a problem getting a part-time job or come from broken homes. As for the fourth topic, she realizes that she cannot think of an approach that would present "college" as a problem faced by American students. She decides, therefore, that the third group of ideas—"social relationships"—offers the most promising possibilities.

Because she has been dating a classmate for the past year and has encountered problems in dating that most of her friends share, she believes that she will have enough information. In addition, her sociology professor has recently lectured on the stresses and problems that college students encounter with the opposite sex.

Now she is ready for the next step in the process of writing an essay.

2. Determining Your Purpose and Audience

By writing a statement of purpose and considering her audience, Nancy will give her essay direction and define its content and tone. Therefore, she writes the following statement:

> The purpose of my essay is to help my reader understand the problems that college students experience in dating.

Now she has to consider her audience: Who will read her essay? Because this is an assignment, she realizes that her instructor and classmates will read her essay. She can assume that they will be a sympathetic audience who have shared, in varying degrees and ways, the problems that she will discuss. She can also assume that they are literate; she does not have to "talk down" to them. Finally, she decides that slang and colloquialism would be out of place for a serious discussion of this topic or for her audience. She will use, instead, conventional, informal English.

3. Gathering Material

Nancy's next job is to gather material for her essay: ideas, facts, opinions, examples, and information.

She talks to her classmates and to her boyfriend, Dan, about the problems of dating. She looks over her lecture notes and textbook from her sociology class, where the topic had been raised. And to get the viewpoint of the older generation, she discusses the subject with her parents. Finally, she does some freewriting in order to get her own impressions and opinions down on paper and to compare those ideas with the ideas of others.

As a result of this search for material, two things happen. First, she discovers that her fear of not having enough ideas is groundless. As she thinks about her topic, listens to her friends and parents, and begins to take notes, she realizes that she is accumulating many more ideas than she will be able to use. Second, she finds that the uncertainties and difficulties in dating cited by almost everyone she talks to seem to fall into certain categories. As a result, her ideas are beginning to focus more sharply and precisely on the topic, and she is soon in a position to write her controlling idea, or thesis statement.

4. Writing a Thesis Statement

As Nancy tried to formulate her thesis statement, she asked herself, "What am I trying to say? What is my point?" Her English instructor had reminded the class that a good thesis statement expresses the central idea of an essay. After looking over her notes and thinking about her topic, she wrote this thesis statement:

> Many people report that they have problems in their social relationships.

This is a start, but she feels uncomfortable about it. There is a vagueness that concerns her: Who are "Many people," and what are the "problems" in their "social relationships"? She needs to be more specific, both for her reader and for herself. She looks at her statement of purpose and finds that it comes close to expressing her thesis statement. After some more fine tuning, she settles for the following:

> Many couples experience problems in dating.

This is much better: "couples" is more specific than "many people," and "dating" is narrower than "social relationships." She had tried to explain in her thesis statement what she meant by "problems," but gave up, deciding that she could not cover everything in one sentence. Besides, her thesis statement can be modified as she writes, and she will continue to look at it carefully, modifying it later to reflect any changes as she develops her material.

5. *Organizing and Outlining Your Material*

Now Nancy is ready to organize her ideas. Her first step is to list them. Here is her first list:

1. Parents interfere, but want to help
2. Dating person of different religion or race
3. Exchange student: Spanish attitudes on dating
4. Dan—very good student; wants to get married
5. Shyness; attempts to cover it
6. Sororities and fraternities: competition in popularity
7. Every generation faces same problems: parents
8. Our country: young people independent
9. College freshmen: uneasy, no experiences
10. Cliques on campus
11. Young people try to cover awkwardness with opposite sex
12. Sex: shame, guilt; fear of pregnancy; frustration
13. Young people get older, become conservative
14. Young people need someone to turn to; different opinions

As she looks over her list, she sees ideas that belong together, and others that seem to be unrelated to her thesis statement. Items three, four, six, and ten, while potentially interesting topics in themselves, have little to do with "the problems that many couples experience in dating." Her next step in organizing her material, therefore, is to group similar ideas together, placing the supporting details under important ideas.

Here is her first attempt to group her ideas:

Interference of parents
    want to express their feelings
    opinions of son's or daughter's date, mate
Dating person of different religion or race
    parents' and peers' reactions
    young people: not prejudiced
Sex—biggest problem
    shame, guilt
    frustration
    fear of pregnancy
    no one to give advice
Shyness—awkward with opposite sex
    don't know how to act with opposite sex
    no experience; can't make easy conversation
    try to cover awkwardness

Nancy prepares a scratch outline from her reorganized list, making a few additional changes as they occur to her. Before she can do that, however, she has to determine the order in which her ideas should be presented and the method of development. Because her ideas cannot be arranged chronologically or spatially, she has to arrange them in some other order. She decides to present them in their order of importance, beginning with social awkwardness and building up to what she regards as the biggest problem facing couples who date: sex.

To keep herself on track, she writes her thesis statement at the top of her outline. Notice that she has slightly modified her original thesis. She has changed the original "Many couples" to "Many college students," because it is the people of her age in college that she has in mind as she explains the problems encountered in dating.

> *Thesis:* "Many college students report that they experience problems in dating."
>   1. *Shyness*
>   —awkwardness: not at ease with opposite sex
>   —don't know what to talk about
>   —no experiences
>   —can't make conversation
>   2. *Parents*
>   —interference
>   —opinions of son's or daughter's date, mate
>   3. *Different religion, race*
>   —influence of society
>   —criticism from others
>   4. *Sex*
>   —guilt and shame
>   —frustration
>   —possibility of pregnancy
>   —conflicting opinions of others
> *Conclusion:* Problems eventually work out

Nancy's outline is rough, but detailed enough for a short essay. If she were writing a term paper, she would write a formal outline (see page 262). This one, however, is adequately detailed for her purpose. Her major headings indicate that the essay will be developed by *examples* of the problems that couples experience, and that the examples will be organized *in their order of importance.*

---

6. Writing the First Draft

Here is Nancy's first draft. It is far from polished, but her purpose at this stage was just to get her ideas on paper. After she had written this

draft, she read it aloud, and asked herself the questions listed on pages
104 and 112. As she read, she made notes in the margin and between
the lines of her draft. These notations are questions and reminders for
her revision.

DATING

Many of my friends are shy. They don't know what to talk about

Do I mean only girls have problems?

slang?

when they are with (guys) because they have had few experiences and

what kind?

This sentence is too long

they can't make (conversation.) *Do I mean interesting conversation?*

what matters?

Parents don't help matters any. I know they want to give me advice.

confusing

well, which am I? *whatever that means!* *what kind?*

They want their son or daughter to be happy and well-adjusted.

what minorities? *what kind?* *who's doing the dating?*

Dating minorities can create problems with some parents. A dif-

ferent religion can also create a (problem.) My parents are getting more

who? *my parents?*

conservative like other parents as (they) get older. I'm sure they were

check this!

critisized when they were (kids.) *best word?*

I what way? *Hmmm!* *who?*

The big problem is sex. It is a problem in (all) relationships. (They)

when? *what kind?* *who?*

don't know what to do. They get (ideas) from different people. They don't

ck this

know who to (beleive.) *about what?*

obviously *so?*

Regardless, it is my opinion that everybody has had these problems

and that history repeats itself. *what ever that means!*

*weak ending. I ran out of ideas. Smoother
sentences! It sounds choppy and rough. Use
words like "therefore" to hook my ideas together.*

7. Revising and Editing Your Essay

Nancy put her rough draft aside for a few days while she thought about her ideas on the topic. When she read it over, she realized that she needed more supporting material—more examples and facts—because the body of her paper was too thin. She also realized that she would have to work on her sentence structure. As she read her paper aloud, she could hear the choppy sentences and the abrupt shifts from one idea to another.

One weakness that seemed to run throughout the paper, she realized, was its vagueness. She needed to substitute specific words and phrases for the general statements that filled the essay. Notice her comments reminding herself of this deficiency. Nancy also realized that she needed to focus the thesis of the paper more sharply. In its present form it drifts aimlessly, touching or hinting at a number of ideas, but failing to give the reader a clear picture of its main idea. Her main challenge, she decided, was to make the paper more specific by adding and substituting clear, precise ideas instead of relying on the fuzzy statements in the first draft.

Nancy expanded each paragraph and tested her ideas for their logic and organization as well as for their style. She tightened up a few of the longer sentences, inserted some transitions to show the relationship among the ideas, and checked her spelling. When she decided that she had revised her draft sufficiently, she wrote the following essay and submitted it to her instructor.

Read it carefully, particularly her instructor's comments. Can you see how much she improved her rough draft? Do you see the sections of the paper and individual sentences or words that can be improved even further?

The Problems of Dating

Many college students report that they experience problems in dating. One of the most common problems is that they are awkward socially. Everybody is uncomfortable at times in social situations, but young people in particular are ill at ease with the opposite sex. They try [*How?*] to cover their awkwardness. They also have a difficult time thinking of things to talk about. This is because of their inexperience. [*at what?*] Most college freshmen don't have this advantage. [*what advantage?*]

Another problem is the interference of parents. It is only natural that parents would want to express their wishes with respect to their children's dates, and it is only logical that their children regard this advice as interference. Most children would probably admit that their parents are trying to be helpful, and no doubt the parents' advice is, in the long run, helpful. Nevertheless, the opinions of parents on their children's dates and choice of mate are the result of our dating system in which the young man or woman operates independently. *How?*   *totally?*

Dating persons of different religion or race can also create a prob- *How?* lem. Differences would probably *disapear* if the couple involved did not *sp* live in a larger group such as the family and society. They have to endure the comments and criticism of others if they insist on crossing such lines. Couples get older, they often get more *consearvative* on *sp* these issues. Sometimes they are just as critical of their own *kids* as *two sentences?* *diction* their parents were of them.

Last but not least the biggest problem facing couples is sex. It is an area that makes itself known in most relationships. If the couple *or just in dating?* indulges in *it* they may experience guilt and shame. If they abstain, *?* they will be frustrated and become angry or irritable with each other. If they have intercourse, there is the possibility of pregnancy. Then when they turn to others, they get conflicting opinions. *for what?* *sex?*

Students work these problems out eventually, and their children start out all over again facing the same problems. *abrupt ending*

- Some excellent ideas! Your paper is well organized and your examples are good.

- Your thesis statement is presented somewhat abruptly; your introduction needs to be developed more slowly.

- You have a few unclear or ambiguous sentences; note my queries.

- A few cloudy references; some specific details would help so that we'd know what (or whom) you had in mind.

- Read your paper aloud to catch a few sentences that are rough; using transitions, combining sentences, and varying your sentence structure would make your style smoother and add clarity

- You need to slow down your conclusion; it's somewhat terse.

Here is the revised version of Nancy's essay. Before writing it, she read carefully the revision and editing checklists on pages 104 and 112, testing her paper for its content, organization, style, and correctness. Although she is not completely satisfied with her essay, she knows that her final version is much better than her earlier drafts. Nancy has also learned that revision is a process that can go on indefinitely.

The Problems of Dating (Revised Version)

Nancy Avery

Most American college students have had their first date by their fourteenth birthday. This means that the average freshman has dated for at least four years and has dated a wide variety of people of the opposite sex. Despite this experience, many college students report that they experience several problems in dating.

One of the most common problems that young people face is social awkwardness. Even adults are often uncomfortable in a social situation, but young people in particular are often ill at ease with the opposite sex. They try to convey the appearance of being "cool" or at ease, but their loudness, giggles, and excessive laughter give them away. They also have a difficult time thinking of things to talk about. One reason is their inexperience. A good talker has a background of experiences to draw upon and has had the opportunity to practice the art of conversation. Most college freshmen do not have this advantage.

Another problem that affects the dating and courting activities of young people is the interference of their parents. It is only logical that parents would want to express their feelings and wishes with respect to their children's dates. And it is only logical that their children regard such advice as interference. Most children would probably admit that their parents are trying to be helpful, and there is no doubt that the parents' advice is, in the long run, helpful. Nevertheless, the opinions of parents concerning their children's dates and choice of mate are the natural result of the dating system in this country in which the young man or woman operates somewhat independently.

Dating people of a different religion or race can also create problems, from one's parents as well as from one's peers and society in general. Differences in religion and race would probably disappear if the couple involved did not live in a larger group such as the family and society. However, they have to endure the comments and criticism of others if they insist on crossing such lines. As couples get older, they often get more conservative on these issues and sometimes are just as critical of their own children as their parents were of them.

Perhaps the biggest problem facing couples is that of sex. It is an area that makes itself known in most dating relationships. If the couple indulges in any kind of sexual activity, they may experience guilt or shame. If they abstain, they may be frustrated and become angry or irritable with each other. If they have intercourse, there is the possibility of pregnancy. When they turn to others for advice, they encounter conflicting opinions.

One way or another, American college students overcome these problems and work out compromises and solutions that allow them to survive our dating system. They marry, have children, and the entire process starts all over again.

Comment

Nancy's final version is much better than her earlier draft, although it still has some weaknesses. Her revised introduction leads more naturally to her thesis statement, catches the reader's eye with statistics, and creates the expectation that the essay will be developed by example. As in the case of her first draft, her four examples of the kinds of problems that young people experience in dating are arranged in their order of importance. She gives her paper an overall unity and coherence by beginning every paragraph with a reference to "problem" or "problems," thereby reminding the reader of her thesis. Every paragraph has a topic sentence supported by details and examples. Notice, too, that she has improved some of her sentences; for the most part, they are smoother and tighter. Her conclusion conveys a sense of finality while looking forward.

7

Writing
the Persuasive Essay

We have already discussed expository essays, in which the writer's purpose is to inform the reader. Much college writing, however, requires you to *persuade* your reader to take a specific course of action or to accept a particular point of view. This chapter will consider the problems that are unique to persuasive writing and address its intention, its relationship to its audience, and its organization.

In a sense, every essay is persuasive because you are trying to convince your reader that you are trustworthy. But what we call persuasive essays are often based on controversial topics: Should the theory of evolution and the Biblical account of creation both be taught in the public schools? Should the death penalty be abolished? Should the military draft be reinstated? Topics like these often face hostile audiences, and the writer of a persuasive essay has to work hard to win their agreement.

There are two ways to approach a controversial topic. The first is to set out to win at any cost by proving that you are right and your opponent is wrong. Those who write essays this way are not trying to change their readers' minds. All they want to do is score points, and they will usually use any technique to do it: personal attacks and sarcasm, purely emotional appeals, quoting out of context, or evading the issue. This approach succeeds only in antagonizing the critical reader.

The other way to approach a controversial topic is to try to change the reader's mind by playing fair: by looking at the same issue from the reader's point of view, using logical arguments, citing evidence, and being rational. This does not mean that you will not appeal to your reader's emotions. It does mean, however, that you will adopt a reasonable tone and be tactful and honest.

The Assertion and the Persuasive Essay

As with the expository essay, the first step in writing a persuasive essay is to formulate your assertion in a thesis statement. If the thesis has been supplied by your instructor, your position in the paper has been decided for you. But if you have been given a topic on which to base your assertion, you should first list your ideas on the topic. This stage is similar to prewriting when writing an expository essay. You can explore your own thoughts by freewriting and brainstorming. You can talk to friends about the topic, test your ideas and get their views. After surveying the ideas you have developed, you can then write your thesis statement or assertion.

You may find that your thesis statement will be softened or

modified in the finished essay. A working thesis might be bold, as in the following:

> The best way to solve the problem of illegal migrants taking jobs away from Americans is to ship them back to where they came from.

The problem with this assertion is that while it may express the writer's feelings, it is far too aggressive to be accepted by an open-minded reader.

By revising and giving more thought to the topic, the writer might end up with a more convincing assertion as the thesis statement:

> Because of the rise in unemployment in this country, illegal migrants should not be hired in preference to U.S. citizens.

This revised assertion is calmer and more likely to encourage the reader to accept it.

The thesis statement in a persuasive essay must not be a statement of fact; it must be an assertion over which people of good will can differ. You could not, for example, write a persuasive essay based on the following thesis: "Crime in our city rose ten percent last year." Assuming this is a statement of fact, there is nothing to dispute. But you *can* argue the following assertion: "Crime in our city rose ten percent last year because of the lack of educational and recreational opportunities for youth and the reduction of welfare benefits for the poor." Such a statement is subject to challenge and could provide the basis of a lively persuasive essay.

After you have written your thesis statement, apply three tests to find out whether you can use it. First, is it a question? If so, reword it, because a question does not contain an assertion. Do not write, "Should rent control be enacted in our city?" Instead, write "A rent control law should be enacted by our city council."

The second test of your thesis statement: Is it one that everybody would agree with? If so, rule it out. A thesis statement like "Poverty is a problem in our society" is so bland that no one would disagree. As a result, your paper would never get off the ground. But if you said something like, "Poverty is a necessary condition in a democracy," you will strike a response in your readers, and you will create controversy.

The third test of your thesis statement is the one first mentioned: Does it merely state a fact? If so, it offers nothing to debate, and therefore it is unsuitable as the assertion for a persuasive essay. But if your thesis statement takes sides in a genuine controversy about which people of good will can differ, you are ready for the next step.

E X E R C I S E 1

Which of the following statements could serve as the thesis for a persuasive essay? Reword the unsuitable statements so that they can serve as acceptable assertions.

1. The difference in men's and women's earnings today is actually greater than it was twenty years ago.
2. Because of the dangers of radiation, the construction of nuclear power plants in this country should be halted.
3. The "proof" for the existence of extrasensory perception is unconvincing.
4. Isn't it true that blonds have more fun?
5. The emphasis on grades obscures the real purpose of education.
6. I prefer the beaches of Florida to those in California.
7. Growing up in the country offers many more advantages than city living.
8. Statistics show that women live longer than men.
9. Is the emphasis on the "basics" just a motto, or is there truly an emphasis on the "essentials"?
10. The expenses connected with a serious illness can be ruinous for many American families.

E X E R C I S E 2

Below are some topics that generate controversy. For each, write an arguable assertion that could be developed into a persuasive essay.

1. The Selective Service
2. The Moral Majority
3. Teenage drivers
4. Test-tube babies
5. Dress codes for high school students
6. Fraternities and sororities in college
7. Smog devices on cars
8. Capital punishment
9. Offshore drilling for oil
10. A national health insurance plan

The Audience for the Persuasive Essay

In Chapter 3 you learned the importance of keeping your audience in mind as you write an expository paper. The audience in that case wanted to learn or be informed. The audience for a persuasive paper, on the other hand, is more difficult to please: Either they are undecided, or they disagree with your thesis statement. In other words, they are either hesitant or hostile. You can assume that they are interested in the subject. You can also assume that they know some of the arguments on both sides of the issue. If they are neutral, they are waiting for you to convince them that you are right. If they are hostile, they will be looking for weaknesses in your argument. In both cases it is important that you know something about their interests, background, and knowledge of the issues.

Your readers have a right to demand proof and valid reasons for agreeing with you. Your job, therefore, is to convince them by the soundness of your arguments. It is equally important to create an impression that suggests that you understand their point of view, having examined it carefully, and that you respect their beliefs. You will not be able to do this if you adopt a tone that offends them. Above all, you should avoid personally attacking them or sounding condescending in your attitude. By taking a conciliatory and fair stance, you will invite their respect and encourage them to consider your arguments.

After you identify your audience, you can determine the best approach, the appropriate level of diction, and the most effective kinds of arguments for your paper.

E X E R C I S E 3

Your audience will affect the kinds of arguments you offer. Consider each of the following situations.

1. Imagine that you have to deliver a speech before the Society for the Prevention of Cruelty to Animals in which you defend experimentation on animals. Write a list of arguments for such a position.
2. Imagine that you are giving a speech before a convention of the American Medical Association in which you attack experimentation on animals. Write a list of arguments for such a position.
3. What arguments would you give in a speech to a building contractors' meeting urging the preservation of a downtown block of old buildings for their historical value?
4. What arguments would you present in favor of legalized gambling in a speech to a group of ministers who are against such a position?
5. What arguments would you present against legalized gambling in a speech to the city council as they prepare to vote on the issue?

Supporting Your Assertion

Having settled on your thesis statement (which contains your assertion and identifies your audience) you should now make a list of your supporting arguments as well as those that oppose your assertion. By anticipating the arguments of your opponents, you will convince your readers that you are knowledgeable and fair. More important, you will strengthen your own position by refuting those arguments as you begin to present your own view.

Most effective persuasive essays rely on three kinds of appeals to support their assertions: *rational appeals, ethical appeals,* and *emotional appeals.* The rational appeal is the most important, but the others, when used with discretion, can be very effective.

Rational Appeals

Mere opinion will not be enough to support an argument or persuade your readers—they demand and deserve *evidence.* Therefore, you will have to offer them proof.

Facts and statistics are among the most impressive kinds of rational proof and should therefore be used in abundance to support your assertion. They suggest objectivity and finality, and they can often convince a skeptical reader. For example, in a letter to your college paper arguing for the construction of additional handball courts, you could strengthen your case by furnishing such facts and statistics as the number of students who use the courts each day, the number who can't get on the crowded courts, the percentage of students by comparison who have no other opportunity to participate in organized physical activity, or the benefits of playing handball. Such evidence would be much more convincing than mere pleading or irate demands.

Or suppose that you believe in a "get tough" policy for our criminal justice system. In your opinion, stiff prison sentences rather than social reform will serve as a deterrent to crime. Such a view is controversial and would collapse if it were not supported with evidence. But suppose you happened to read an article in a recent monthly magazine that contained the following facts:

1. A 1978 report by a panel of the National Academy of Sciences concluded that the probability of a stiff punishment supported the notion of deterrence.
2. A 1977 study by Alfred Blumstein and Daniel Nagin found that the higher the probability of conviction for draft evasion, the lower the evasion rates.
3. A study in the late 1970s by investigators at Stanford University found that when antitrust laws are enforced, price fixing diminishes.

4. A study by Kenneth Wolpin of Yale demonstrated that for the period 1894 to 1967 in England, the changes in the probability of being punished varied with changes in the crime rate.*

Such a parade of facts and statistics, when added to other evidence, would strengthen a controversial thesis statement and help to sway the undecided reader. Keep in mind, however, that although facts are indisputable, they can be subjected to contradictory interpretation. When the United States Marines landed on the Caribbean island of Grenada, they found huge warehouses of munitions and a nearly finished landing strip which the American government cited as evidence that Cuba planned to use the island as a military outpost. Cuba, while not disputing the facts, argued that the munitions belonged to the Grenadan army and that the landing strip was to encourage tourism.

Statistics, like facts, can also be manipulated. Suppose that a wealthy industrialist with an annual income of $1,000,000 a year lives on a street with only one other occupant, an impoverished widow with an annual income of $2,000. The average income on that street is $500,000—at least, mathematically. But such an interpretation of the statistics would create a distorted impression of the facts and the neighborhood. If used fairly, however, facts and statistics can form the sturdy underpinning of your argument.

Examples are another effective kind of rational proof. Although by themselves they do not prove the truth of an assertion, their impact and the attention they attract can be convincing. In arguing for government aid to public television broadcasting, for instance, you might give examples of programs like "Romper Room," "Sesame Street," concerts, documentaries, and plays that are available to viewers who might not otherwise see them. Such examples would be far more effective than lofty appeals to the citizens' right to the airwaves and the need for an enlightened public.

Examples make the abstract and general more specific, and your argument will be strengthened by them. Be certain, however, that your examples are typical, and not exceptions to the rule. Careful readers will detect those that are not representative of your assertion.

Personal experience that supports your argument can be convincing because it has the qualities of urgency and relevance. Your own experience brings a controversy to the level of the concrete, the specific, and the personal. If you are arguing for bilingual education, for example, your own experience learning English in a bilingual program would be of interest to your reader. Or suppose that you are arguing

*Information is from James Q. Wilson, *Atlantic Monthly*, September 1983, pp. 72–82.

for mandatory safety inspections for automobiles and buses in your state. And suppose, too, that you describe an accident in your neighborhood in which a school bus careened down a hill out of control because of faulty brakes, resulting in injuries to several students. Evidence based on such firsthand knowledge often has more impact on a reader than any other kind of support.

When offering personal experiences as support for your thesis, be careful to select those that are not merely emotional anecdotes. Personal tales of woe usually offend readers who are looking for solid proof.

The *testimony of experts* is another effective way to support your argument. By quoting respected authorities you lend credibility to your assertion. Be sure that your authority is recognized as knowledgeable on your topic. The testimony of your Aunt Clare on the advisability of spraying the lakes and ponds in your county with a controversial new chemical to get rid of mosquitoes would not be as impressive as that of a chemist or botanist—unless Aunt Clare were the county director of public health.

Ethical Appeals

Logic, as powerful as it is, often needs to be supplemented by other kinds of appeals. The *ethical appeal* is based on *you*, the writer. It is the appeal that gets its impact from the impression you create of yourself, the writer of the essay.

You want to be respected and trusted by the audience; you want your readers to feel that you are honest and reliable. There are three ways to accomplish this. The first is to write in a rational and informed style, and avoid name-calling, personal attacks, and wild exaggerations. The second is to write straightforward, clear prose that shows you have nothing to conceal. The third way is to be in command of your evidence. By quoting authorities, presenting facts, and arguing logically, you will create the impression of a fair and informed writer.

The ultimate effect of the ethical appeal is to say to your reader, "You can believe me. I am a fair, objective, and informed person who has thoroughly investigated this controversy. The assertion that I offer you, therefore, is reliable because I am trustworthy."

Emotional Appeals

Emotions are never a substitute for logic and solid evidence. But when the facts are not in question, and action is desired, then an emotional appeal is appropriate, perhaps indispensable. An emotional appeal can help stir your audience's feelings and predispose them to take a particular course of action. It can take advantage of their sense of dignity or their sense of justice.

Advertisers are well aware of the powerful tug of the emotions on our purse strings. The American flag, laughing children, puppies, vibrant young people, and saintly, elderly faces are commonly used to sell everything from cars to corn flakes. When used to "sell" an idea, however, they should be used with caution. Readers are usually quick to detect appeals that are offering emotions rather than evidence.

In the critical days during the "Battle of Britain" in World War II, Prime Minister Winston Churchill made his great "blood, toil, tears and sweat" speech. He inspired the British people, spurring them to heroic efforts. In more recent years the late Martin Luther King, Jr., used emotional appeals to great effect in many of his speeches and essays in order to persuade Americans to support the civil rights movement.

Not only speeches but individual words or terms can carry emotional appeal. By calling industrialists "rapers of the earth" or environmentalists "barriers to progress," a writer appeals to readers' emotions. You should use such terms with caution; if not chosen carefully, they can make an audience hostile toward your argument. But when used with discretion, the emotional appeal can be an effective method for persuading your reader.

How much support in the form of rational, ethical, and emotional appeals is needed in a persuasive essay? It depends on your topic and your audience. An essay arguing against the increased use of nuclear energy in the United States would require a great deal of complex evidence, including statistics, examples, facts, and testimonials. If such an essay were addressed to an audience of executives of power companies, it would require special tact and delicacy to present the evidence. On the other hand, if the audience were a group of homeowners who live near a nuclear plant and have petitioned for the closing of the plant, the evidence could be presented more forcefully, since the audience would not be hostile.

By presenting rational, accurate proof and by convincing your readers that you are fair and objective, you will encourage them to examine the evidence from your point of view. Then, and only then, can you count on them to support your assertion.

Moving from Evidence to Conclusion: Inductive and Deductive Reasoning

Having offered your evidence, you have laid the groundwork for your conclusions. There are two ways to move from your evidence to your conclusions: *induction* and *deduction*. In *inductive reasoning*, a large number of individual cases or experiences are listed and on the basis of these cases, a probable generalization or *conclusion* is drawn. *Deductive reasoning* works from the opposite direction. It moves from a general premise or generalization (called a *major premise)* and a particular fact or instance (the *minor premise)* to a *conclusion.*

Let's assume you want to buy a personal computer. As you ponder the decision, you follow a series of steps in reasoning. You talk to your friends who have personal computers. One complains that her Alpha breaks down often and is usually in the shop for repair. Another says that the programs for other computers are not compatible with his Beta computer. Still another friend says that his Gamma is difficult to operate and does not have an adequate storage capacity. Then you talk to the instructor of the computer class at your college who tells you that her students have used Delta computers in both day and evening college classes for the past two years without any problems, and that she and the students are pleased with them. Your conclusion is that Delta is the most reliable computer. Up to this point your reasoning has been *inductive:* you have made a series of observations about the reliability of different computers and you have arrived at the generalization that Delta is the most reliable computer. You then make an *inductive leap:* you assume that the generalization arrived at on the basis of your friends' and instructor's experiences applies in your case. Having arrived at your generalization by inductive reasoning, you now use *deductive reasoning:* you move from the generalization to individual cases. You apply a premise (you want to buy a reliable computer) to a generalization (Delta is the most reliable computer) and you arrive at a conclusion (you want to buy a Delta.)

The following steps illustrate how inductive and deductive reasoning were combined in the example above:

INDUCTIVE REASONING

You made *a series of observations* about individual computers:

> Alpha
> Beta
> Gamma
> Delta

On the basis of those observations you reached *a conclusion or generalization:*

> "Delta is the most reliable computer."

DEDUCTIVE REASONING

You began with *a major premise* based on your generalization:
> *Major premise:* "Delta is the most reliable computer."

Then you applied a particular case as your *minor premise:*
> *Minor premise:* "I want to buy a reliable computer."

You then reached a *conclusion:*
    Conclusion: "I should buy a Delta computer."

You move constantly from induction to deduction in your daily life. In fact, these reasoning processes are natural ways of thinking as you evaluate evidence and apply generalizations to even the most insignificant situations. But when reasoning about complex issues and when trying to persuade others to accept your views, you use inductive and deductive reasoning more carefully and consciously. In the following pages we will examine both kinds of reasoning and their relationship to persuasive writing.

Inductive Reasoning

Most of what we know has been learned through inductive reasoning. As we saw in the computer example, induction moves from individual instances and observations to a generalization or conclusion. Observing sumo wrestlers offers another example. All of the sumo wrestlers that I have seen on television are huge and must weigh at least 300 pounds. All of the sumo wrestlers that my friends have seen in Japan were huge men. And all of the pictures of sumo wrestlers in sports magazines and newspapers that I read are of large men. I therefore conclude that all sumo wrestlers are large men. Of course, I have not seen *all* of the sumo wrestlers in the world, but I base my generalization on a fair sampling. To reach my generalization I have taken an *inductive leap,* a jump from the evidence (sumo wrestlers that my friends and I have seen or heard about) to a generalization (all sumo wrestlers are large men).

The safest inductive leap—and therefore the most reliable generalization—is based on the largest number of typical examples. If the only wrestling match I ever witnessed features midget wrestlers, and if I concluded that all wrestlers are midgets, I would be guilty of a *hasty generalization* (see pages 142–43 for an explanation of this and other errors in logic).

Most inductive arguments are more complicated than the example above about sumo wrestlers. But regardless of their complexity, they require you to make connections between particulars or samples in order to come to a generalization about the entire class of particulars or samples.

All inductive arguments must be based on two principles: the generalization must be based on a sufficient number of samples, and the samples must be typical and reliable. In discussions of certain racial groups, religions, or nationalities, we often encounter generalizations that ignore these principles: "Jaycees are corrupt. The treasurer of our chapter was indicted for bribery." "Don't tell me about Episcopalians.

We lived next door to an Episcopalian family for two months." "Professor Mobley is a terrible instructor. My friend worked very hard in his chemistry class and received a D." "Teenagers are terrible drivers."

When hearing or reading such generalizations, ask yourself whether there is sufficient evidence to justify such sweeping statements. In your own writing (as well as your reading), be wary of words such as *none, all, never,* or *every* when they are applied to generalizations. It is safer (and more likely correct) to substitute such terms as *some, many, often,* or *probably.*

Because the process of inductive reasoning begins with numerous facts, examples, instances, and observations and then leads to a conclusion or generalization, it is often an effective way to organize a persuasive essay. Many readers can be convinced or persuaded if they are first provided the evidence. For instance, if you are arguing against student evaluation of the faculty at your college, you might get the support of your readers if you show them that students are inconsistent when they evaluate their instructors. Some students want to "get even" because they received an F; others rate a teacher highly because he or she gave them an A or told jokes; still others judge the instructors on the basis of their dress or accent or ethnic background. After presenting the information you have compiled, you can then lead your readers to your concluding generalization: student evaluation is inconsistent and should be abolished. Of course, the more evidence that you can present, the more likely it is that your generalization will be sound and will be accepted by your reader. If you were to cite only one student who had evaluated an instructor unfairly, your argument would not be convincing. But it is not only the number of examples or the amount of evidence that is important; the particulars that you offer to support your generalization must be representative so that your inductive leap is justified.

Deductive Reasoning

The opposite of inductive reasoning is *deductive reasoning.* It is the process of arriving at a conclusion by starting with a generalization or assumption instead of with a specific instance. For example, if you know that all of the geography majors at your college are in the honor society and that Jo Ann is a geography major at your college, then you conclude that Jo Ann is in the honor society. These three statements comprise a *syllogism,* a three-part argument consisting of a generalization which has been arrived at by deduction (the *major premise*), a specific case of the generalization (the *minor premise*), and a *conclusion*.

> All of the geography majors at your college are in the honor society.
>
> Jo Ann is a geography major at your college.
>
> Jo Ann is in the honor society.

If both premises in a syllogism are true and if the reasoning process from one part of the syllogism to the other is valid, the conclusion is true. An inductive leap is not necessary, as it is with inductive reasoning, because the conclusion is inescapable. In this syllogism, only one conclusion can be reached. You can't say that Jo Ann is failing her courses, because that contradicts the premises; nor can you say that Jo Ann is talkative, because that goes beyond the premises.

If one of the premises is not true, the conclusion will be false, even though the syllogism follows the correct form. Consider the following:

Major premise: All cars are Japanese made.

Minor premise: My convertible is a car.

Conclusion: Therefore, my convertible is Japanese made.

But my convertible happens to be a Volkswagen. The conclusion is false because the major premise is false: All cars are *not* Japanese made. If my convertible were actually a Toyota, the conclusion would have been correct by chance, not by logic. To repeat, then: a deductive argument can be considered reliable only if the premises are true and if its form is valid.

Most of us do not employ the full-fledged syllogism when we speak. Instead, we usually present our propositions as *enthymemes*, which are compressed syllogisms. Notice the following:

> Of course my Volkswagen is well built; it's made by Germans.

If this enthymeme were expanded into a complete syllogism, it would look like this:

Major premise: German cars are well built.

Minor premise: Volkswagens are German cars.

Conclusion: My Volkswagen is well built.

By using an enthymeme, the speaker assumes that his listener or reader accepts the implied premise (in this case, that Germans build good cars).

Using enthymemes can be risky business because they ask the listener or reader to follow an argument without seeing all of the premises laid out. For premises that are not controversial ("Honesty is the best policy," "An education is important today"), this is not a problem. But if the premises are controversial, the writer or speaker will have to show their validity before proceeding further. The following sentences illustrate the problem.

> His word can't be trusted; he's a politician. [The first statement is the conclusion and the second statement is the minor premise of a syllogism whose major, unstated premise is something like "All politicians are untrustworthy."]

> I doubt that Sharon's marriage will last; her parents were divorced. [Like the preceding example, the first statement is the conclusion and the second statement is the minor premise of a syllogism; in this case, the major premise is something like "All children of divorced parents will have marriage problems."]

In both examples the unstated but implied premise is too shaky and controversial to be accepted without evidence. Any paragraph or essay based on such a premise would have to be supported to be convincing.

Deductive Reasoning and the Persuasive Essay

Using the principles of deduction to organize a persuasive essay can be very effective. The conclusion of the syllogism (which is the thesis of the essay) usually appears in the opening paragraph. The subsequent paragraphs support the truth of the conclusion. If the premises are reliable and if the conclusion follows logically from them, such a pattern is convincing.

In actual practice most writers do not base deductive essays on pure syllogisms, particularly when writing on controversial topics. It is difficult to state a meaningful or significant major premise that encompasses "all" or "none" in social sciences, politics, and related fields, areas where controversy often arises. A generalization or major premise that is true for "all" members of a group is usually self-evident and therefore likely to be bland or noncontroversial. Most writers settle for a generalization based on convincing evidence. Writers usually employ enthymemes—incompletely stated syllogisms which contain an implied premise the writer assumes readers will accept—rather than formal syllogisms.

Essays based on deduction often use a series of informally stated syllogisms. In such an essay the initial thesis statement is derived from the conclusion of the first syllogism; the essay can then move to a defense of each premise in separate paragraphs and return to an expanded explanation of the conclusion. Because the major premise of a syllogism is probably acceptable to most readers, you may not have to develop it in detail. The minor premise, however, will need extended development and explanation, and require one or two paragraphs or even an entire section. Your conclusion, in turn, may become the premise of another syllogism after being combined with another compatible premise. This syllogism, in turn, may produce another conclusion that will clarify or expand an earlier point in the essay. Each premise and conclusion can be clarified in separate paragraphs. If all of this sounds too theoretical and even confusing, applying it to a writing assignment should make it clear.

Suppose that you want to write an essay urging your readers to protest an increase in the tuition at your college. Your thesis statement might read, "If the proposed increase in tuition is approved, many able students will have to drop out of college." This thesis is a reworded version of the conclusion of the syllogism:

Major premise: The poor students at our college cannot pay higher tuition.
Minor premise: Many of our able students are poor.
Conclusion: Many of our able students cannot pay higher tuition.

This syllogism has to be adapted to serve as the basis of a persuasive essay. The major premise implies but does not state flatly that *all* poor students cannot pay higher tuition. Such a sweeping generalization would probably be inaccurate (presumably some poor students would borrow from relatives or get loans in order to pay the higher tuition), and such a sweeping statement would be offensive to some readers (they would object to the categorical statement that *no* poor students could afford higher tuition). As already mentioned, the best you can usually hope for in such premises is strong probability or likelihood. In this case it is probable that most (if not all) poor students cannot pay higher tuition.

The minor premise is the key to the argument; if you cannot prove it, the syllogism collapses. What kind of proof would be sufficient to convince skeptical readers that many of the able students are poor? An interview with the financial aid officer at your college could provide statistics and data showing that many of the low-income students are receiving top grades. Students on the dean's list or honor roll could be interviewed and asked about their income. By examining a number of particular cases and arriving at the conclusion that many able students are poor, you would be using inductive reasoning. Persuasive writing incorporates both inductive reasoning and deductive reasoning (your conclusion becomes the minor premise in your syllogism).

The conclusion (the thesis of your essay) grows naturally out of the preceding premises: if poor students at your college can't pay higher tuition (major premise), and if many students with ability at your college are poor (minor premise), then many able students cannot pay higher tuition (conclusion). To make the conclusion more dramatic and effective as a thesis statement, you can rewrite it for greater impact: "If the Board of Trustees raises the tuition, many of our best students will have to drop out of college." This conclusion can, in turn, serve as the major premise for another premise and syllogism which will expand on the consequences of the proposed tuition increase ("Many able students can't pay higher tuition; many able students will have to drop out of college; our nation will lose the potential contributions of many of its brightest citizens.") This syllogism can be expanded and can become part of your essay.

An essay organized along the lines sketched here is easy to follow and, if supported with enough evidence and proof, can be very persuasive.

Strengthening Your Argument by Avoiding Logical Fallacies

Your readers will not be persuaded if they detect mistakes in your logic or reasoning. Such flaws are called *logical fallacies;* conclusions reached using them are invalid. Avoid these common logical fallacies and keep your arguments persuasive.

Hasty Generalization. A hasty generalization is one based on an inadequate number of examples or on examples not typical or representative. "The Toyota dealer in my city reported that his sales were down twenty-five percent last month. American drivers are beginning to buy American cars instead of foreign imports." But the sales of one dealer in one city for one month are hardly the basis of an inductive leap to a conclusion applying to the entire nation.

Post Hoc, Ergo Propter Hoc. This is a Latin expression meaning, "After this, therefore because of this." This fallacy occurs when we assume that what comes *after* an event is necessarily the *result* of that event. "Our baseball team changed the color of their uniforms last month, so now they have lost five games in a row." Just because one event follows or precedes another does not necessarily mean there is a causal relationship. In fact, there are usually several causes or effects in a relationship.

False Analogy.   An analogy is a comparison used to explain or illustrate an idea. Analogies are useful because they make things clear. When you make comparisons that are not relevant to the issue or make misleading comparisons between logically unconnected ideas, you employ a false analogy: "He'll make a wonderful president. Just look at the control he exerts over his own children." The skills in running a nation are obviously not the same as those in being a parent.

False Dilemmas (Either-Or Fallacies).   This is presenting an issue as having only two sides, and ignoring the possibility of a middle ground between the two extremes. "The instructors on this campus are all too easy or too difficult." "If you take that first drink, you'll become an alcoholic." Such statements fail to acknowledge that other choices exist.

Non Sequitur.   This is a Latin expression for "It does not follow." This fallacy occurs when a conclusion does not follow from the premises that are supplied. "Why should we spend money on new buildings on this campus? Abe Lincoln attended a one-room school." The fact that Lincoln attended a one-room school does not have anything to do with the need for new buildings on campus.

Begging the Question.   Using one of your premises as the point that you are actually trying to prove is termed "begging the question." In other words, you assume the truth of something that you actually need to prove. "People should be required to vote; therefore, we should work out an effective system to make certain that they vote in every election." "When are these irrelevant math courses going to be dropped from the curriculum?" But should people be required to vote? And are the math courses really irrelevant?

Ignoring the Question.   This fallacy occurs in several forms; two of the most common are:

1. *Argumentum ad hominem* ("Argument to the man"), which is an attack not on the issue itself, but on the person who supports the view; and
2. *Glittering generalities,* using "fancy" words instead of evidence.

An example of (1): "The bond issue should be defeated. Its supporters include Letitia Winsome, who wears loud clothes and swears in public." An example of (2): "The bond issue should be passed. Its supporters are for the American way of life." In both instances the argument ignores the issue and tries to divert attention to irrelevant issues.

Strengthening Your Argument by Confronting the Opposition

In addition to arguing logically, you can strengthen your position by examining the arguments of your opposition. Your object is to convey the impression that you have listened to your opponents, considered their views, examined their evidence, and then concluded that your arguments are more persuasive. By confronting the opposition, you will gain the respect of your readers who will be impressed by your honesty and fairness.

As pointed out in the "Concession and Rebuttal" section later in this chapter, the best place to dispose of your opponent's arguments is usually before you present your main argument. If the topic is relatively simple and the opposing arguments are few, you can summarize them in one paragraph before demolishing them. If the opposing arguments are more complex and detailed, you can introduce them point by point and answer each in its turn. In both cases, the use of expressions like "nevertheless," "but," "however," and "after all" will help you structure your argument into a series of assertions and refutations that your reader can easily follow.

Assume that you are arguing against the abolition of the death penalty. If you present your thesis statement (assertion) and then launch immediately into your proof and evidence without considering the arguments of those who oppose capital punishment, your essay will be one-sided and unconvincing. But if you state, calmly and fairly, the arguments most often advanced by opponents of the death penalty, you will demonstrate your honesty and make the presentation of your own case more effective.

Most opponents of the death penalty advance four arguments, and you would do well to acknowledge and refute each before moving into the body of your essay. Notes for such a strategy might look like this:

Thesis: The death penalty should not be abolished.

*First opposing
  argument:* The death penalty is based on revenge.
Refutation: The death penalty is not rooted in revenge any more than a jail sentence for a drunk driver; it is based on the desire to protect others. Anger and vindication are not involved.

*Second opposing
  argument:* The death penalty does not deter.
Refutation: This is not the point; capital punishment deters the killer from killing again.

*Third opposing
  argument:* Innocent men are sometimes executed.

Refutation:	This criticism is misdirected; the weakness lies with the judicial system, not with capital punishment. We need to improve our jury system, the rules of evidence, the machinery of appeal, etc.
Fourth opposing argument:	The death penalty goes against the sanctity of life.
Refutation:	The sanctity of *whose* life? The murderer's or the victim's? If there is true merit to this argument, then armies and abortions should be outlawed. Furthermore, is a life term respectful of the sanctity of life?

After acknowledging the opposing arguments, you are ready to move into the body of your paper and present your evidence: the statistics, facts, examples, and other proof that support your thesis. You have shown your reader that you considered the views of your opponents, and that you found them unconvincing.

E X E R C I S E 4

Identify the logical fallacy in each of the following arguments. Explain how each assertion goes astray, and whether or not it can be corrected or rewritten.

1. I don't think that soccer should be played in this country. Soccer matches in South America are often followed by riots and even death.
2. I don't know why she received an Oscar for her film; she contributes to left-wing causes.
3. Television programming in this country is all junk. Did you see "The Vultures" last night?
4. Art majors are not very practical, because people who study modern art can't be very bright.
5. America—love it or leave it.
6. So what if the police did have to break a few skulls at the demonstration? You have to break eggs to make an omelet, don't you?
7. Everyone who lives in Utah must be a Mormon; the governor and senators are all Mormons.
8. Greg always gets better grades than I do; after all, both of his parents are college graduates.
9. Of course I believe in premarital sex! You try on a pair of shoes before you buy them, don't you?
10. Chevrolets are the best cars ever made. I know—I have owned two of them.
11. I have not had a cold since moving to Miami.
12. Either offshore drilling must be encouraged or we will have to build more nuclear energy plants.

13. A friend of mine had a nervous breakdown after taking Ms. Ross's geography class last year.
14. Students should not be allowed to evaluate their instructors. Prisoners don't evaluate their warden, do they?
15. Drunken drivers are a disease in our society. And, like germs, they should be eradicated.
16. Congressman Bradley's bill should be defeated; he was arrested for nonsupport of his wife and children.
17. Television programs like "Aegean Ecstasy," which destroy the moral fiber of our country, should be banned.
18. Mayor Wilson should be reelected. We shouldn't change horses in the middle of a stream.
19. Women are basically more intelligent than men, and therefore they should have to score higher on the S.A.T. tests.
20. He is an eloquent speaker; he must know what he's talking about.

Organizing the Persuasive Essay

After you have sharpened your assertion, assembled your strongest arguments, and tested your logic, you are ready to organize your persuasive essay. Most experienced writers arrange their ideas in the following pattern:

Introduction
Assertion
Concession and rebuttal
Proof
Conclusion

The third section, "Concession and rebuttal," is sometimes introduced before the assertion or after the proof. Your own experience will be your best guide to deciding where to place this section.

Introduction

Your persuasive essay should open with a clear explanation of the controversy. Your reader may not be familiar enough with the subject to have an opinion, or may not have recent information on which to make a decision. Your introduction brings the reader up to date and "sets the stage." This is also the section of your paper where you define the key or controversial terms which will be important to your argument.

If your paper argues, for instance, for a change in zoning regulations to allow homeowners to rent rooms to students, you should briefly summarize the debate: who opposes the proposed regulations and who is for them; the actions the city council or zoning commission has taken; and the timetable or agenda when a vote will be taken. If you will be using controversial terms, this is the place to define them.

By clearly and succinctly stating the problem or controversy, you have prepared the reader for your assertion.

Assertion

After stating the controversy, you should clearly present your assertion, which will be expressed in your thesis statement. Your reader should know what you propose without any doubt. Be careful, however, to avoid a pugnacious or belligerent tone; that will only offend uncommitted readers.

This early section is not the place to offer your proof. Before doing that, you must acknowledge opposing points of view in the concession and rebuttal section.

Concession and Rebuttal

You have to acknowledge that there are other views that differ from yours. As noted previously (page 144), if you fail to include them your readers will assume that you are either ignorant of opposing arguments or that you are dishonest and pretending that they do not exist.

It is important that you do not exaggerate or distort your opponents' arguments or resort to name-calling or scare tactics. If, for example, you are arguing for the legalization of laetrile as a possible cure for cancer, it would be unwise to begin your concession with a statement like "My opponents claim that laetrile is too expensive to produce, but they don't know what they are talking about." A more effective statement might begin with something like "Opponents of laetrile claim that the drug is prohibitively expensive to manufacture. This argument, however, is not supported by the evidence that I have gathered." Words like "admittedly," "although," "I realize," and "even though" suggest a moderate and reasonable stance and imply an open mind.

Proof

This will be the longest section of your paper. It is similar to the body of the expository essay, which presents the thesis statement's support. In a persuasive essay it presents the evidence for your assertion. As you saw in the discussion of inductive and deductive reasoning, your proof and arguments can be arranged in either of two ways. You can support your opening generalization or assertion with a series of facts, examples, instances, and observations. If you use this method, the best arrangement is in order of increasing importance, saving your best or most dramatic arguments for last. Or you can arrange your proof in the form of a syllogism, with the body of your paper developing the major and minor premises. If you use this method, you will probably use more than one syllogism, with separate paragraphs or sections for each premise and conclusion.

If you use ethical and emotional appeals, be sure that they are supported by sound reasoning. If used judiciously, they can strengthen the impact of your logic.

Conclusion

The conclusion of your persuasive essay should contain a brief but compelling restatement of your assertion. Try to avoid merely stating it in the same words. Present it in a fresh and pointed way so that your readers will remember it and reflect on it. As in the conclusion to the expository essay, do not introduce new arguments or facts in your ending. Its purpose is simply to draw together what you have said so that the reader has a clear idea of your intentions.

The Traits of a Good Persuasive Essay

A good persuasive essay encourages its reader to accept its thesis or assertion. It accomplishes this by clearly stating the issue and showing how it is related to the reader's interest. It offers a solution, avoids a "know-it-all" or offensive tone, yet conveys the impression of certainty. To be convincing, it presents the opponents' views fairly and demonstrates that the writer has examined their claims and found them weak. It provides the reader with convincing evidence: sound logic, examples, facts, testimony of authority, statistics, and reasons. The good persuasive essay avoids logical fallacies and does not call names, exaggerate, or distort evidence. Finally, the good persuasive essay concludes with a forceful restatement of the essay's assertion so that the reader knows exactly what the writer believes and why the assertion should be accepted.

Student Essay

The following persuasive essay was written by a freshman supporting the assertion, "The minimum wage law for everyone under twenty should be abolished."

The outline which precedes the essay points out the organization of its major sections, including the statement of the problem, the assertion, concession, proof, and conclusion. The comments in the right margin point out some of the rhetorical techniques used by the writer. Read the outline, essay, and the marginal comments carefully before going on to Exercise 5.

The Minimum Wage Law and Youth

Paragraph 1.
      Statement of the problem
      Evidence that problem exists
      Cause and effect established: Inductive reasoning
      Statement of assertion

Paragraph 2.
      Concession:
      Opposing Arguments #1
                       #2
                       #3
      Dismissal of opposing arguments

Paragraph 3.
      Rebuttal of opposing argument #1
      Consequences of opposing argument #1
      Examples

Paragraph 4.
      Rebuttal of opposing argument #2
      Rebuttal of opposing argument #3
      Consequences of opposing arguments #2 and #3

Paragraph 5.
      Proof for assertion: Reasons
      Shift from financial to other benefits

Paragraph 6.
      Additional proof
      Specific example

Paragraph 7.
      Emotional appeal

Paragraph 8.
      Conclusion: Consequences of opposing argument
      Restatement of assertion with benefits
      Leads up to most important benefit

The Minimum Wage Law and Youth

1.   Youth unemployment is a major problem in our country. While the unemployment rate for the general population is about ten percent, approximately twenty percent of all young people and forty-five percent of minority youth can't find jobs. Unfortunately, every time the minimun wage has gone up, joblessness among the young has spread because jobs have diminished. The solution is obvious: abolish the minimum wage law for everyone under the age of twenty.

First paragraph leads naturally to statement of assertion

2.   Those who defend the minimum wage law claim that if it were abolished for young people, small businesses would replace their adult workers with youngsters. They also argue that a subminimum wage won't help minority youth and will fail to create a single job. Although at first glance these arguments sound attractive, an examination of their claims reveals their weaknesses.

Calm, rational presentation of opposing views

Air of reasonableness

3.   In the first place, small businesses, which account for half the gross national product, are particularly harmed financially by such regulations. As a result, they are cutting out marginal jobs and moving toward automation. That is why you don't see as many movie theater ushers, car washers, and fast-food employees as you used to. If employers were allowed to pay teenagers less, small businesses would have the incentive to make more jobs available.

Use of transition ("In the first place," "As a result")

4.   Further, before the minimum wage law went into effect, the number of black adolescents working for pay was actually higher than that of whites. By abolishing the minimum law for those under twenty, Congress would encourage businesses to hire more young people, and minorities would gain employment. As the law stands now, it is actually discriminatory toward minorities.

Transition Post hoc ergo propter hoc? Statistic

5.   Those who emphasize the financial rewards of working forget an important fact: jobs reward young people with more than money. They reward teenagers with valuable experience and give them responsibility. They also provide young workers with a chance to develop skills as well as to earn money.

Reasonable tone

Lofty benefits

6.   Another neglected aspect of the minimum wage law is that it is inflationary. When the minimum is increased, adult workers use it as evidence that they are due fatter paychecks. Their raises hurt the economy and freeze kids out of the job market. If you had to pay $3.35 plus social security for a teenage baby-sitter, you'd probably hire an adult instead.

Transition: "Another"

7. Finally, most youngsters really want to work. But when jobs are not available, too many young people turn to crime. Work furnishes dignity and a sense of worth that welfare benefits fail to supply.

    Most important, dramatic reason: emotional appeal

8. By forcing employers to pay the minimum wage to everyone regardless of age, the government is discriminating against an entire class of citizens: the young. By exempting those workers under twenty from the minimum wage law, the government would provide additional jobs, increase minority employment, hold down the spiral of inflation, and restore a sense of worth to its most valuable asset, its young people.

    Emotional language: "discriminating"; "the young"; "sense of worth"; "valuable asset" Conclusion ends on lofty tone

E X E R C I S E 5

Select one of the topics in Exercise 2 for which you wrote an assertion or select one of the topics below, write an assertion, and develop it into a persuasive essay. Use the suggestions in this chapter, including the student example. After you write your first draft, read the checklist on the next page.

1. Student evaluation of instructors
2. Motorcycle regulations
3. Affirmative action programs
4. Bilingual education
5. Pollution standards
6. Social Security
7. Alternative living arrangements
8. Cult deprogramming
9. Violence on television
10. Radioactive waste
11. Noise control
12. The terminally ill
13. Terrorists' demands
14. Busing
15. Political action committees
16. Ecumenism
17. Foreign aid
18. Unions
19. Sexism
20. Sociobiology

REVISION CHECKLIST

The Persuasive Essay

After you have written the first draft of your persuasive essay, read this checklist carefully. Also consult Chapter 6, "Revising the Essay."

1. *What is the argumentative position or assertion taken in your essay? Does it discuss an issue that can be debated, or is it merely a fact that cannot be disputed?*
2. *Is your assertion clearly stated? Could it be improved? Is it too combative in tone?*
3. *Does your introduction summarize the controversy clearly so that an uninformed reader would immediately be familiar with the problem?*
4. *Is your acknowledgement of the opposing viewpoint stated calmly? Do you state opposing arguments fairly, or do you distort or misstate those views?*
5. *Is your evidence and proof clear and convincing? Is it presented in the most convincing order? Could it be arranged more effectively?*
6. *Can you think of any other examples, statistics, or evidence that would strengthen your argument?*
7. *Have you been careful to avoid the logical fallacies explained on pages 142-3?*
8. *Have you avoided name-calling, exaggeration, personal attacks, or other unfair techniques of argument?*
9. *Does your conclusion emphasize the assertion, leaving your reader with a clear idea of your assertion and why it should be accepted?*

8

Writing

Paragraphs

Paragraphs have to accomplish several important functions for your essay. The opening paragraph should catch your reader's attention; the middle paragraphs provide support and development for your main idea; and the concluding paragraph brings your essay to a close with a sense of completeness.

In this chapter we are going to show how paragraphs can perform each of those functions, beginning with *middle paragraphs*, the paragraphs in the body of the essay that support and develop the thesis statement. The most important sentence in the middle paragraph is the *topic sentence*, so we will start with it. Then we will study the important qualities that every effective middle paragraph must have: *unity*, *coherence*, and *development*.

Finally, we will look at the paragraphs that play other important roles in the essay: *introductory* and *concluding* paragraphs.

Middle Paragraphs

The job of the paragraphs in the body of the essay—the *middle* paragraphs—is to support and develop the thesis statement. Each paragraph presents one aspect of the topic, usually announced in its *topic sentence*. Because the paragraph includes a series of related sentences on one topic, it has *unity*, *coherence*, and *development*.

The Topic Sentence

Every good paragraph deals with a single topic or aspect of a topic. The sentence that states the paragraph's subject is the *topic sentence*. The topic sentence is usually the most general sentence in the paragraph; it is developed and supported by the specifics in the sentences that follow it. In a sense, the topic sentence has the same relationship to the paragraph as the thesis statement has to the essay.

Experienced writers do not include a topic sentence in every paragraph. But until you become an adept writer and are certain that your paragraphs stick to one idea, you should provide every paragraph with a topic sentence. Most topic sentences are placed at the beginning of a paragraph, although they can appear in other parts of the paragraph.

The first sentence in the following paragraph is the topic sentence, and it announces the main idea of the paragraph in a general way: there are reasons for the growing popularity of fast-food chains. The remaining sentences present several specific reasons that illustrate and support the topic sentence's idea. Like most well-written paragraphs, this one begins with a general point and then supports it with several specific details.

Reasons for the growing popularity of fast-food chains appear obvious enough. For one thing, the food is generally cheap as restaurant food goes. A hamburger, French fries, and a shake at McDonald's, for example, cost about one-half as much as a similar meal at a regular "sit down" restaurant. Another advantage of the chains is their convenience. For busy working couples who don't want to spend the time or effort cooking, fast-food restaurants offer an attractive alternative. And, judging by the fact that customers return in increasing numbers, many Americans like the taste of the food.

The advantage of the opening position for the topic sentence is clear. It tells the reader what to expect in the sentences that follow, and reminds the writer what the central idea of the paragraph is, so he or she is less likely to include sentences that wander off the topic.

A topic sentence can also be placed in the *middle* of the paragraph. This position is effective when the writer wants to begin with one or two details to lead up to the topic sentence, and then follow it with more support. In the next paragraph, notice how the topic sentence is preceded and followed by sentences that provide specific details and support. The topic sentence is italicized.

The offices of most doctors today are overloaded with people who are convinced that something dreadful is about to happen to them. At the first sign of pain they run to a doctor, failing to realize that pain is rarely an indication of poor health. *We are becoming a nation of pill-grabbers and hypochondriacs who regard the slightest ache as a searing ordeal.* Instead of attacking the most common causes of pain such as tension, worry, boredom, frustration, insufficient sleep, overeating, poor diets, smoking, or excessive drinking, too many people reach almost instinctively for the painkillers— aspirins, barbiturates, codeine, tranquilizers, sleeping pills, and dozens of other desensitizing drugs.

The topic sentence can sometimes be found at the *end* of a paragraph. This position is particularly effective in building up to a controversial or unexpected conclusion. The writer first provides a number of facts and details and then tops them off with a sentence that serves as a conclusion or summary. In the following paragraph notice that the writer offers a number of facts and then offers the topic sentence.

The dolphin's brain generally exceeds the human brain in weight and has a convoluted cortex that weighs about 1100 grams. Research indicates that, in humans, 600 to 700 grams of cortex is necessary for a vocabulary. Absolute weight of the cortex, rather than the ratio of brain weight to total body weight, is thought to be indicative of intelligence potential. The dolphin's forehead is oil filled and contains complex sound-generating devices. Tests indicate that the dolphin is sensitive to sound at frequencies up to 120 kilocycles. Whereas human vocal cords pulsate at 60 to 120 cycles per second with about 50 selective harmonics, the dolphin's pulsate at about 600 cycles per second with a choice of many more harmonics. *These facts provide convincing arguments for possible dolphin intelligence.*

One common weakness of many topic sentences is that they try to cover too much territory. If your topic sentence is vague or very broad, you will have trouble writing a paragraph that develops it fully. "Status symbols can tell us something about the people who adopt them" is not as good a topic sentence as "The person who drives a Rolls-Royce has a certain self-image." A good topic sentence must be precise so it can be developed in a paragraph and it can control the other sentences in the paragraph.

E X E R C I S E 1

Which of these sentences are narrow enough to serve as topic sentences of paragraphs?

1. There are many reasons why high school students should be required to take a course in computers.
2. Winter in San Diego is different from winter in Duluth.
3. Some psychologists claim that there are three body types, each with its own psychological characteristics and behavior.
4. Nutritionists have a ready explanation for the prevalence of taller basketball players in recent years.
5. The Soviet Union, like the United States, is populated by many ethnic groups.
6. As I approached the dentist's office, I was suddenly tempted to run away.
7. Body language as a subfield of psychology has received increased attention in recent years.
8. Cars painted in certain colors seem to attract the police more than other cars.
9. North Americans have a different concept of time from that of Latin Americans.
10. By studying Rapid Eye Movement (REM), psychologists and physiologists have come to an important conclusion about the importance of dreams.
11. When making a hook shot in basketball, keep one thing in mind.
12. The songs of the Beatles remind me of my youth.
13. The view from my dorm window is spectacular.

14. According to a recent study, education in the United States needs reform.
15. As we travelled across the country by train last summer, we were impressed by the diversity of this nation and its people.

E X E R C I S E 2

Each group of sentences below can be rearranged as a paragraph. Select the topic sentence in each group and arrange the remaining sentences in the order that seems most logical. Remember: the topic sentence is the most general sentence in the paragraph because it states the main idea of the entire paragraph and includes all the ideas in the body.

1. a. Computers speed up registration by providing up-to-date information on open classes.
   b. They assist instructors by marking multiple-choice tests.
   c. Computers now perform many tasks on my campus.
   d. Computers can supply advisors with instant and complete information on requirements, career information, and personal data while they are talking to a student.
   e. Computers keep records for the bookstore, library, cafeteria, and maintenance department.
2. a. My new Future camera has several features that I like.
   b. It advances the film after each shot and automatically rewinds it after each roll.
   c. Compared to other cameras, it is inexpensive.
   d. If I get too close to the subject, it alerts me with a buzzer.
   e. It beams out an infrared ray that focuses for me, even in the dark.
   f. It is lightweight and compact.
3. a. Sometimes rapidly, sometimes slowly, they went relentlessly upward.
   b. Last week the Labor Department reported, however, that the economy's seventeen-year inflationary spiral had, for one month at least, finally been broken.
   c. During March, inflation actually went down instead of up.
   d. This turned a trend of what economists call disinflation into outright deflation.
   e. Since 1965, prices in the U.S. economy have been heading one way.
4. a. Moving back home with his parents would save him quite a bit.

b. He was glad that he no longer had to work fulltime while going to school.

c. His income tax refund was enough to cover his expenses for the rest of the semester.

d. The dean's office approved his student loan, and he could cut his working hours.

e. He had finally paid off his car.

f. Things were beginning to look up.

5. a. Two young girls took turns throwing their Frisbee to their dog, which leaped into the air to catch it.

b. A family of tourists stood in front of the fountain, studying a map and trying to remember where they had left their car.

c. It was a typical May Sunday afternoon at the park.

d. From the freeway that circled the park the sound of a fire engine could be heard.

e. A couple sat on a blanket, their baby crawling on the nearby grass.

E X E R C I S E 3

Here are some groups of sentences that need a topic sentence to tie them together. For each set, write a sentence that would serve as a topic sentence for the paragraph.

1. *(Your topic sentence)*
Fewer male students wear long hair and more are beginning to wear ties. Women students in increasing numbers are wearing dresses and nylons. Soft music is replacing hard rock on campus juke boxes. It is no longer square to sing the National Anthem at public performances or to vote in local and national elections.

2. *(Your topic sentence)*
One of my bosses was generous and thoughtful, and answered all of my questions patiently. Another boss was rarely in the office, and when she returned from out-of-town trips, she looked at me curiously but never spoke. Another supervisor watched closely, making comments about my work, the amount of time I took for lunch or a coffee break, or letting me know that he saw everything I did.

3. *(Your topic sentence)*
There were forty of us packed on the deck, each with poles and bait boxes in hand, eager to try our luck. By the time we were through the breakers and a few miles out in the ocean, I was beginning to feel nauseated from the constant movement of

the boat. The waves pounded the boat, and it bobbed like a cork. With each dip my stomach churned. By the time the fish were spotted, it was too late. I was down below, too sick to fish.

4. *(Your topic sentence)*
   This pigment is called melanin. People who can form a little melanin are yellow-haired and blue-eyed. People who can form a fair amount of melanin have brown hair (or even black hair) and brown eyes. There is enough melanin in the skin to give them a swarthy complexion. If the amount of melanin is high enough, the skin itself is distinctly brown, sometimes quite dark brown.

5. *(Your topic sentence)*
   We are awakened by electric alarm clocks and music pouring from our radio; we operate our toaster, brush our teeth with an electric toothbrush, and shave with an electric razor. We read the day's headlines from newspapers printed on huge electric presses, and we write a letter on our electric typewriter before leaving for work to operate a computer and word processor.

E X E R C I S E   4

Develop each of the following subjects into a topic sentence. Remember that a good topic sentence is narrow enough to be covered in a paragraph.

Doctors	Prejudices
Tools	Friends
Aptitude tests	Jewelry
Trips	Columnists
Habits	Surprises

The Unified Paragraph

Every paragraph should be *unified*—that is, the topic sentence and every other sentence in the body should all relate to one main idea. The best way to be certain that your paragraphs have *unity* is to construct a specific focused topic sentence and then develop it through the entire paragraph. If the paragraph sticks to the idea promised in the topic sentence, it has unity. Any sentence that does not develop this idea violates the unity of the paragraph and should be omitted.

In the following paragraph, notice how the italicized sentence introduces another idea into the paragraph and violates the unity of the paragraph:

> Fishing for killer sharks can provide excitement for even the most experienced anglers. Mako sharks, which run over 1000 pounds and are considered to be the best fighters in the world, have jumped or "tail-walked" into the cockpit of a boat, slashed crewmen, and torn off the transom. Big white sharks have attacked boats and inflicted severe damage. *Shark meat is considered a delicacy in Australia, but it is not popular with diners in the United States.* Huge tiger sharks have shrugged off harpoons and bullets as they fought violently for hours before being landed.

The topic sentence announced the main idea of the paragraph: fishing for killer sharks can provide thrills. The fact that shark meat is a delicacy in Australia and is not popular in this country is irrelevant— the writer has introduced a sentence that does not contribute to the development of the topic sentence.

Some paragraphs lack unity because they are only a collection of unrelated ideas; they look like paragraphs because the first line is indented, but they do not develop one single topic. In the paragraph below, notice how the writer discusses a number of things, all of which are abandoned:

> I took Tammy to the concert last Friday night. It was the best concert I've ever attended. She is a good influence on me. She is majoring in biology and plans to be a physical therapist. Next week we are going to rent a two-seater bicycle and ride through the park. This is the prettiest time of year for seeing the gardens in the park.

As you can see, this paragraph is chaotic. It goes nowhere because it never started out to say anything. It is a hodgepodge of miscellaneous thoughts. The writer could salvage some of the sentences and rework them into topic sentences for separate paragraphs, but as the paragraph stands now, the impression is one of a mind bouncing from one thought to another.

One of the best ways to test the unity of a paragraph is to analyze it in terms of how the sentences support the topic sentence. This is particularly effective when the topic sentence comes at the beginning of the paragraph. This kind of paragraph will usually fall into one of two patterns. In the first pattern, all of the sentences are *coordinate;* that is, they are equal to each other, and each is a comment on the topic sentence. Using the shark fishing paragraph, here is an example of this pattern; the sentence that violated the unity of the paragraph has been deleted.

Topic sentence Fishing for killer sharks can provide excitement for even the most experienced anglers.

Supporting sentence #1 Mako sharks, which run over 1000 pounds and mare considered to be the best fighters in the world, have jumped or "tail-walked" into the cockpit of a boat, slashed crewmen, and torn off the transom.

Supporting sentence #2 Big white sharks have attacked boats and inflicted severe damage.

Supporting sentence #3 Huge tiger sharks have shrugged off harpoons and bullets as they fought violently for hours before being landed.

In this pattern, all of the supporting sentences are equal, and each is a comment on the topic sentence. As a result, the paragraph has unity.

In the second pattern, the first sentence of the paragraph is a topic sentence and the second is a development of it. The third sentence is either another comment on the topic sentence, or a comment on the sentence immediately before it, and so on. In other words, paragraphs that follow this pattern will consist of two kinds of sentences: coordinate sentences that are equal to each other and make a comment on the topic sentence, and subordinate sentences that make comments on the sentences they follow. Any sentence that fails to comment on the topic sentence or on the sentence it follows destroys the unity of the paragraph and should be deleted.

Here is an example of a unified paragraph written in this pattern. The topic sentence and supporting sentences are arranged below it so that you can see their relationship.

Country music is far more diverse than most casual listeners might think. The "original" country music continues to be played by such well-known artists as Bill Monroe and the Bluegrass Boys, Eric Weissberg, and Earl Scruggs. Their blend of quick tempos, enthusiastic fiddle playing, and high, hard tenors continues a tradition that stems from the Blue Ridge Mountains. Today's established country stars continue to stick to the themes and musical idioms that their audiences have come to expect from them. Roy Acuff, Chet Atkins, Johnny Cash, Dolly Parton, and Loretta Lynn sing of broken hearts, whiskey, family, and God, to the accompaniment of electric, slide, and pedal steel guitars. A new wave of "progressive" country music has swept the country in recent years and appeals to listeners who might not otherwise admit they listen to "country." Emmylou Harris, Willie Nelson, and Waylon Jennings, for example, are to be found regularly at the top of the pop charts. Their music, which is louder, harder, and rockishly electric, reflects the tastes of their younger, hipper listeners.

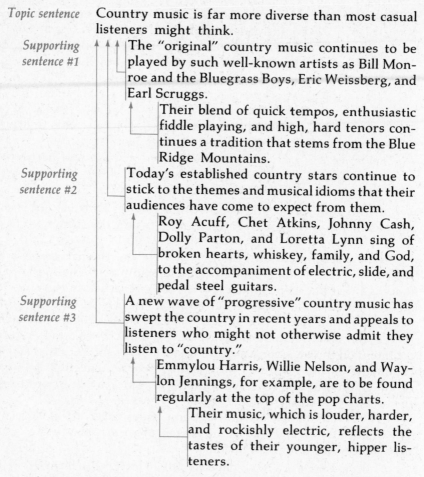

Topic sentence Country music is far more diverse than most casual listeners might think.

Supporting sentence #1 The "original" country music continues to be played by such well-known artists as Bill Monroe and the Bluegrass Boys, Eric Weissberg, and Earl Scruggs.

Their blend of quick tempos, enthusiastic fiddle playing, and high, hard tenors continues a tradition that stems from the Blue Ridge Mountains.

Supporting sentence #2 Today's established country stars continue to stick to the themes and musical idioms that their audiences have come to expect from them.

Roy Acuff, Chet Atkins, Johnny Cash, Dolly Parton, and Loretta Lynn sing of broken hearts, whiskey, family, and God, to the accompaniment of electric, slide, and pedal steel guitars.

Supporting sentence #3 A new wave of "progressive" country music has swept the country in recent years and appeals to listeners who might not otherwise admit they listen to "country."

Emmylou Harris, Willie Nelson, and Waylon Jennings, for example, are to be found regularly at the top of the pop charts.

Their music, which is louder, harder, and rockishly electric, reflects the tastes of their younger, hipper listeners.

In this paragraph the topic sentence is supported directly by three sentences ("Supporting sentences 1, 2, 3") illustrating the major "country" groups. Each of these sentences, in turn, is followed by a sentence that makes a comment on it.

By studying the pattern of support—by noticing whether or not every sentence is a paragraph makes a comment about either the topic sentence or the sentence it follows—you can easily tell whether a paragraph is unified.

E X E R C I S E 5

Each of the paragraphs below contains a sentence that destroys the unity of the paragraph. Underline that sentence. Then, for each paragraph, prepare a diagram similar to those constructed for the country music paragraph.

1. California is earthquake country. More than 1,000 miles of its coastline follow the Great Pacific Basin where 80 percent of the world's earthquakes originate. The state is laced with hundreds of faults that produce a thousand or more tremors annually. Fortunately, half of them go unnoticed except by animals and the seismograph, and only thirty are capable of minor damage. The San Francisco earthquake of 1906 left 600 dead and 300,000 homeless. A major earthquake occurs about once every 100 years and takes an awesome toll of lives and property.

2. The controversy over the death of Bessie Smith, the great blues singer, has never ended. On September 26, 1937, Bessie was killed in an automobile accident on a Mississippi road. One account has it that she bled to death on the road while waiting for medical attention. Supposedly an ambulance arrived, but its driver picked up a less seriously injured white woman first, then came back for Bessie. Other sources claim that Bessie Smith died in the back of an ambulance on the way to a black hospital after she had been refused admittance to a white hospital. Columbia Records has released over 150 of her recordings in recent years.

3. The atmosphere of the planet Venus is mostly carbon dioxide with traces of water vapor, oxygen, poisonous hydrogen chloride, and carbon monoxide. It took *Mariner 2* 109 days to come close to Venus. The atmosphere bears down on the planet's surface with a pressure 15 to 22 times what it is on earth. The hidden surface of Venus is not smooth, but rugged, mountainous, and arid. All of this makes Venus a hostile world.

4. As our plane broke through the clouds, we got our first glimpse of the ground. Immediately below us were isolated cabins nestled among the foothills of the Piedmont range. To the left, the hills dipped sharply down to the valley, which was dotted with small cabins and patches of cultivated gardens. Directly ahead of us lay the landing strip, a narrow ribbon of asphalt bordered on one side by a muddy stream and on the other by a row of trees. I knew by the fuel gauge that we were arriving just in time. To the right we could trace the outlines of Lake Bregaun.

5. If you read the headlines, listen to the radio, and watch television, you can easily get the idea that we are living in the most dangerous of all times. Problems dominate the news. The threat of nuclear warfare, poverty, discrimination, pollution, and the high unemployment rate present crises never before faced by our society. Added to these are the special problems of today's young people: competition for jobs, a bleak future for

college graduates in the marketplace, and the difficulty of buying a home. Some politicians believe these problems will bring
about the Administration's defeat in the next election. But
before you get too discouraged, you should consider the gains
that society has made in the last few years.

EXERCISE 6

Develop two topic sentences from the subjects in Exercise 4; for
one of them, write a paragraph organized like the model on page
160; for the other, write a paragraph organized like the model on
page 161.

Coherence in the Paragraph

You have seen that when a paragraph is unified, all the other sentences support or develop the topic sentence. But unity alone is not
enough to make a paragraph clear. It must also have coherence.
Coherence means "sticking together," and in a coherent paragraph, all
the ideas stick together. A coherent paragraph is one in which the
ideas are put in the right order with the right connecting words so that
the reader is never confused. This makes the writer's thought easy to
follow from sentence to sentence and paragraph to paragraph.

Good writers rely on two ways of making their paragraphs
coherent: arranging their ideas in a logical order, and using linking
words or phrases between their sentences to help the reader understand how the ideas are related.

Coherence Through Order

The best way to make the middle or supporting paragraphs of your
essay coherent is also the most obvious way: by arranging their ideas
in a pattern that makes sense to your reader. After jotting down your
ideas but before writing the paragraph, you should decide which ideas
to discuss first, which second, and so on, according to a logical order.
The purpose or content of the paragraph will usually suggest the most
appropriate arrangement.

To explain an idea or defend an opinion—the purposes of expository and persuasive writing—you would probably arrange your ideas
in one of the following patterns: *order-of-importance, general-to-specific*
(sometimes called *deductive*), and *specific-to-general* (or *inductive*). When you

wish to narrate an experience or present the steps in a process, you would normally arrange your details in *chronological order*, the sequence in which they happened. And when you wish to describe a person or a scene, you will organize the details in a *spatial order*. (For a detailed discussion of chronological and spatial order, see pages 47–54 in Chapter 4.)

Order of Importance. One of the most useful ways of arranging ideas in a paragraph is *in their order of importance.* Technically speaking, such a paragraph can be arranged in two ways: by beginning with the most important idea and proceeding to the least important, or by beginning with the least important and building up to the most important. The disadvantage of the first pattern—from most important to least—is that it is anticlimactic. There is a letdown after the opening sentence or two, and the paragraph dwindles away. The advantages of building up to the most important ideas stem from the suspense involved and the tendency for readers to remember best what they read last. The paragraph that concludes with a surprise, a clever comment, an appeal for action, or with some other strong ending is more likely to be successful.

To organize the ideas in a paragraph according to their order of importance, you should first make a list of the ideas supporting your topic sentence. The most important ideas should come first, then the next most important, and so on. In writing the paragraph, take your ideas from the list in reverse order. Not every paragraph can be constructed in this pattern, of course, but it can be an emphatic way to arrange ideas.

In the paragraph below, notice how the writer introduces his least important ideas first, then presents his most important idea in the last sentence:

> My boss's dinner party was a dismal experience for me. It began when I picked up my fiancée thirty minutes late, then lost the directions to my boss's home, arriving over an hour after everyone had been seated and was being served. I had forgotten my boss's husband's name and mistakenly called him by the wrong name. I had not realized that it was actually a birthday party and that everyone was to bring a gift. Later in the evening, imagining a certain coolness on the part of my fiancée, I began to flirt with an attractive guest at the party, only to be ignored by her and later learn she was the daughter of my boss. But worst of all, on the way home from the party, my fiancée announced that she wanted to break our engagement, and she returned the ring I had given her only a month before.

In the preceding paragraph, the writer presented a series of unfortunate or unhappy incidents during the course of an evening—some funny, others not so funny. But the most serious event of the evening is announced in the last sentence.

In the next paragraph, also written by a student, notice a similar structure: a series of facts about bulimia pave the way for the most important fact at the conclusion of the paragraph.

> Until recently, physicians and scientists have been unable to provide a reliable cure for bulimia, a syndrome of gorging on food followed by voluntary vomiting. The illness, which afflicts up to two million American women, had been treated by a variety of remedies. Some patients tried hypnosis, but without success. Others tried radical changes in diet, with limited success. Still others tried therapy or large doses of vitamins, but without notable improvement. But a scientist from Harvard Medical School announced last week that ninety percent of the women treated with an antidepressant reported that they "binged" on food half as frequently when on the medication. This finding suggests that bulimia has a chemical and hereditary basis and gives researchers hope that a complete cure will be found soon.

General-to-Specific. The *general-to-specific* (or *deductive*) pattern is the most common type of paragraph order. This arrangement begins with a topic sentence that makes a general statement followed by a series of supporting sentences which supply specifics: details, examples, and facts. Because the reader knows what the main point is, he can follow the development of the thought more easily. For this reason, it minimizes the chances for reader misunderstanding and is particularly effective for informing and clarifying.

Notice how the following paragraphs begin with a general statement (the topic sentence) and then proceed to specifics which support the generalization.

> Modern geologists agree that the earth, like an onion, is made up of layers. The crust is a thin skin, from two to twenty-five miles thick, made up of granite in continental areas and of sedimentary rock layers under much of the ocean. The mantle, which lies beneath the crust, is composed of a basalt layer nearly 1800 miles thick. The outer core is liquid, molten because of the great internal heat. The inner core, still very hot, is iron, solid because of the great pressure exerted at the depth. The inside core of the earth is probably still heating up from the radioactive decay of uranium, thorium, and potassium.

> The first day is one of activity. Students new to the campus enter the classroom late, while others discover that they are in the wrong room. The instructor is handing out reading lists and textbook assignments. Students who want to "crash" come in and interrupt the instructor to inquire whether there are spaces avail-

able in the class. Students ask questions, someone complains about the lack of ventilation in the room, and someone else reports that the bookstore is sold out of the textbook required for the class.

Specific-to-General.   In the general-to-specific pattern, the opening topic is followed by supporting sentences that are more specific. The *specific-to-general* (or *inductive*) pattern reverses this order. It presents a series of individual, specific facts, details, impressions or observations, and ends with a generalization or conclusion, usually the topic sentence.

This pattern is less common than the general-to-specific because it is more difficult for the reader to follow. On the other hand, it is useful in holding in suspense an opinion or conclusion that might be contrary to what the reader believes or expects. For this reason, it is especially appropriate for persuasive writing.

Notice the pattern of the following paragraph: the author presents a series of facts and then presents her conclusion, which serves as the topic sentence.

> Insurance for private pleasure boats has increased almost one-hundred percent in the last year. There is a severe shortage of docking slips in our city, and when one is available, the rental fee is about five dollars per foot per month. This means that for a typical twenty-five-foot sloop, it costs $125 a month just to tie the boat up. In addition, the Coast Guard has enacted new laws requiring expensive safety equipment, and the city recently passed a personal property tax on all private boats; other surcharges are in the works. Most boats have to be hauled out of the water at least once a year to be cleaned. All of these expenses are in addition to the hundreds of hours spent on painting, repairing, sanding, finishing, sail mending, and the other annoying, time-consuming tasks that take a boatowner's time. For these reasons, I have decided that it is more practical to rent a sailboat than to own one.

Below is another example of a paragraph which follows the *specific-to-general* pattern. It, too, presents a series of facts and concludes with a general statement.

> There are 23 million functionally illiterate adults in this country. Almost fourteen percent of all 17-year-olds cannot read, write, or comprehend the written language. The average teacher in America makes $17,000 a year and must moonlight to stay out of the poorhouse. There are severe shortages of instructors in math, science, and foreign languages. Half of those now teaching these subjects are not qualified to do so. There is a rising tide of mediocrity in American education that threatens our very future as a nation.

Chronological Order.   In paragraphs organized *chronologically*, events and details are arranged in the order in which they occurred, usually moving from the first or earliest to the last or latest. Not all paragraphs arranged chronologically tell stories. Some give directions or explain a process; others summarize historical events, and still others report on the steps or actions taken by an individual or an organization. Nevertheless, they all share an underlying similarity: they present their ideas in the order in which they happened.

In the following paragraph notice that all of the details are presented in the order in which they happened:

> Man's first walk on the moon began on the Morning of July 16, 1969, when American astronauts Neil Armstrong, Mike Collins, and Ed Aldrin lifted off in *Apollo II*. After thirty-four hours in flight, they began a live color broadcast of their activities. On the third day, after travelling about 250,000 miles, they went into an elliptical orbit around the moon. Gradually their landing craft approached the surface of the moon. With advice from Houston headquarters they brought the ship down toward the surface above a rocky crater. Then Armstrong changed his mind and decided to aim for another landing site. After touching down, the astronauts remained in their cabin for six hours. Then they opened the hatch and slowly went down the ladder. When he reached the second rung, Armstrong let down a television camera. Then his foot landed on the surface. He stopped to say his now famous words: "That's one small step for a man, one giant leap for mankind."

When you use chronological order, it is important that you relate the events in the order in which they occurred. The paragraph above would have been confusing to readers if the writer had started with Armstrong's decision to change the landing site, then detailed the lift-off, and so on. You can avoid such confusion by including all points or incidents as they happened.

Spatial Order.   If the purpose of your paragraph is to tell how something looks, the most effective organization pattern is usually *spatial*. If you write a description of your neighborhood, your room, or the view from the top of the Empire State Building, you will want your readers to have a mental picture of what you are describing. Like a movie photographer with a handheld camera, you may choose to focus the scene from your vantage point and then move outward, from left to right, from right to left, or from near to far. In describing a house or a building, you would probably first describe the exterior and then the interior. By moving systematically rather than haphazardly over the scene, you convey to the viewer the overall plan or arrangement of the scene.

A description of a person also makes use of the spatial pattern. If you were writing a description of your father, for instance, you would bewilder your reader if you were to describe his shoes, then his hair, then his eyes, and so on. But following closely the order in which eyes see (or movie cameras move), spatial order gives the reader a clear picture of the object being described.

Below is a paragraph based on spatial organization. Notice that the details are not presented in a hit-or-miss fashion; instead, they follow a pattern that lets us visualize the subject.

> Although I was only ten years old when my grandmother died, I can still remember her as clearly as if she were before me now. Although she was in her early eighties when I was a child, her hair had remained shiny black and, like the other natives of her tiny village in Guatemala, she tied it in a kind of ponytail secured with a bright ribbon. Her tanned face was wrinkled, yet the creases of her face would rearrange themselves into a smile when she was happy. Her eyes were the darkest brown I have ever seen, and they sparkled and glistened as she laughed. As a widow she always dressed in black, and over her tiny shoulders she usually wore a heavy *jorongo*, the shawl worn by the women in her native country. Her tiny feet were encased in slippers made of black leather that made a slapping sound as she walked.

In the next paragraph notice how the details are arranged in a spatial pattern: from the left, ahead of us, and to the right of us, like the movement of a movie camera being swung in an arc.

> As I entered Professor Walta's office, I could see that it is a reflection of his brisk, efficient personality. On the left wall, bookcases from floor to ceiling contain neat rows of books arranged in order by their subject. Directly ahead, two windows look out over the quad, their shades drawn precisely level, their curtains tied neatly back on either side. Centered on the wall on both sides of the windows are prints of Greek statues. In front of the windows are two modernistic chairs of chrome and vinyl, looking as though they have never been occupied, their backs reflecting the glare from the windows. On the right is Professor Walta's desk, on which are neatly placed a pipe-holder, a black vase with a single red rose, and, in the center of the desk, a square notebook that lies open as if waiting to record every breath taken in that room.

Spatial order presents a visual effect. In order for your reader to see your subject, you have to select details that make the subject clear, and you have to present those details in a pattern that your reader can follow. This lends order to your descriptive paragraphs.

There are other ways of arranging your ideas in a logical order so that your paragraphs will be coherent. The patterns described here, however, are used most often. The material itself will usually determine the best order to follow. The point is to put your ideas in an order so that the thought follows naturally from sentence to sentence.

E X E R C I S E 7

Following the directions given, write paragraphs arranged in each of the specified patterns.

1. Arranging your ideas *in the order of importance,* write a paragraph of at least 100 words on one of the following topics:
   A day full of disappointments
   The pleasures of . . .
   Reasons for majoring in . . .
   Effects of alcoholism
   Arguments for or against disarmament
   Effects of budget cuts on the college
   The advantages of being single
   The advantages of being married
   Study techniques
2. Arranging your ideas in either *general-to-specific* or *specific-to-general order,* write a paragraph of at least 100 words on one of the following topics:
   Advantages of a degree in the liberal arts
   Hazards of being a referee
   Women and job discrimination
   Coin collecting (or some other hobby) can be expensive
   Job opportunities for young people
   Benefits of a large family
   Invasion of privacy
   Swap meets as a recent American phenomenon
   Responsibilities of being a pet owner
   Problems in being from a non-English speaking family
3. Arranging your ideas in *chronological* order, write a paragraph of at least 100 words on one of the following topics:
   Ending a relationship
   Using a personal computer
   Making a fool of yourself
   Moving to a new home or apartment
   Celebrating a big occasion
   A close call
   A familiar street from dawn to noon
   A wedding
4. Arranging your ideas in *spatial* order, write a paragraph of at least 100 words on one of the following topics:
   The ugliest building or place in town
   I wish I looked like . . .
   An unusually neat person

An unusually sloppy person
My roommate's desk
The view of my campus from the air
The layout of a record store
The campus "hangout"

Coherence Through Linking Devices

In addition to arranging ideas in a logical order, the writer can make paragraphs coherent by linking one sentence to the next by using *transitional words and phrases and other linking devices.* They signal the curve and direction of the thought as you read through the paragraph. With them, the reader is prepared for each new idea and can relate each new statement to the last. Without them, a paragraph can sound like a list of unrelated ideas.

Notice how each sentence stands isolated from the next in this paragraph, making it sound wooden and stiff:

> Speaking and writing are different in many ways. Speech depends on sounds. Writing uses written symbols. Speech developed about 500,000 year ago. Written language is a recent development. It was invented only about six thousand years ago. Speech is usually informal. The word choice of writing is often relatively formal. Pronunciation and accent often tell where the speaker is from. Pronunciation and accent are ignored in writing. A standard diction and spelling system prevails in the written language of most countries. Speech relies on gesture, loudness, and the rise and fall of the voice. Writing lacks gesture, loudness, and the rise and fall of the voice. Careful speakers and writers are aware of the differences.

Now notice how much smoother this paragraph becomes when transitional words, phrases, and other linking devices are used; they make the paragraph more coherent.

> Speaking and writing are different in many ways. Speech depends on sounds; writing, *on the other hand,* uses written symbols. Speech was developed about 500,000 years ago, *but* written language is a recent development, invented only about six thousand years ago. Speech is usually informal, while the word choice of writing, *by contrast,* is often relatively formal. *Although* pronunciation and accent often tell where the speaker is from, *they* are ignored in writing because a standard diction and spelling system prevails in most countries. Speech relies on gesture, loudness, and the rise and fall of the voice, *but* writing lacks *these* features. Careful speakers and writers are aware of the differences.

Transition words and phrases show the relationship between sentences. In some ways they are like traffic signs. They tell the reader what is ahead, warning of a turn or curve, advising when to slow up, and so on.

Examine the following sentences for their use of transitions:

The shortstop took an extra hour of batting practice. *As a result,* he hit two home runs in the game. *("As a result" shows how the second sentence is the effect or consequence of the first.)*

Many older people look forward to retirement. *However,* some want to continue to work beyond the maximum age limit. *("However" alerts the reader to a contrasting idea ahead.)*

Here is a list of some of the most common transition words that connect sentences, making them more coherent:

also	however	next
although	in addition	on the contrary
and	that is	on the other hand
as a result	in conclusion	second
besides	in fact	similarly
but	later	still
consequently	likewise	therefore
finally	meanwhile	though
for example	moreover	whereas
furthermore	nevertheless	yet

E X E R C I S E 8

Here are ten sentences. Supply the missing transition that seems most fitting for each. Try to avoid using the same transition more than once.

1. Bruce was the most popular student on the campus; _____, his defeat in the Homecoming King election was a surprise.
2. Most employers want their job applicants to have experience; a few, _____, are willing to provide on-the-job training.
3. He vowed never to call her again; _____, he would try to forget her.
4. Venezuela produces more oil than it needs; Japan, _____, imports all of its oil.
5. Carol ignored her sister's advice; _____, she paid too much for her car.
6. Many so-called American cars are made in other countries; the Behemoth, _____, is made in Japan.
7. Don put the steaks on the grill and then went out to the backyard to talk to his guests; _____, the steaks were burning.

8. Henry's doctor advised him to lose weight; _____, he ate several large potatoes and ice cream.
9. Some college graduates have a choice of jobs awaiting them; electrical engineers, _____, usually receive handsome offers.
10. _____ she had promised to return in an hour, she never came back; _____, her friend began to look for her.

Another device to link sentences in the paragraph is the *pronoun*, particularly when it refers to the subject of a previous sentence.

> *Jogging* has been popular with people of all ages. *Its* benefits include cures for problems ranging from insomnia to depression.

The use of *Its* makes it clear that the benefits of jogging are being discussed.

By *repeating key words,* you can also connect your sentences more smoothly:

> The *Israeli* army is considered to be one of the most efficient in the world. *Israeli* citizens regard it as an honor to serve in their country's armed forces.

If *Israeli* were not repeated, the relationship between the two sentences would not be clear.

The *repetition of sentence structure* is another way of establishing a connection between two sentences:

> In the United States, most men and women marry before the age of twenty-five. In Ireland, most men and women marry after the age of thirty.

By repeating the structure of the first sentence, the writer has smoothly connected the second sentence.

Developing Paragraphs

One of the most common weaknesses in college writing is thin and underdeveloped paragraphs. While there is no exact rule about the minimum number of sentences required in a paragraph, a short paragraph is often a sign that the writer did not follow through in his or her thinking about the topic. As a result, many weak paragraphs consist of little more than a topic sentence and one or two generalities, as if the writer hoped that the reader would complete the thought for the writer.

You will often encounter brief paragraphs in newspaper writing, where the narrow column of the page requires shorter paragraphs for the readers' convenience. Brief paragraphs are also used to show a division or shift in the section of an essay or to draw attention to a startling fact or an important statement. In general, however, it is a good rule to examine carefully any paragraphs that you have written which contain only one, two, or three sentences. The chances are good that they are too thin and skimpy.

The length of a paragraph depends on the topic. The best measuring stick is your topic sentence: what promise did you make in it to your reader? As a result of your topic sentence, are a series of examples expected? Is a definition of a term used in the topic sentence promised? Or do you imply that you will present a comparison or contrast between two objects or people? The expectations raised by your topic sentence determine, to a great degree, the length and the kind of development of your paragraph.

Here is a student-written paragraph describing the last few minutes in a grocery store before it closes for the weekend. The paragraph is underdeveloped because the writer makes a few vague observations, but nothing that we can see or hear—nothing that makes the topic sentence come alive.

> The last few minutes before closing time are chaotic at the Safeway market where I work. There is confusion everywhere, and everyone is trying to leave on time. Customers and clerks are frantic, and there is always a problem at the last minute.

Notice how vague the paragraph is: "There is confusion everywhere," "Customers and clerks are frantic," and "there is always a problem." But what kind of confusion? Why are the customers and clerks frantic? And what kinds of problems erupt at the last minute? We do not know the answers to these questions, and as a result, the paragraph is blurred and indistinct.

Here is a revised version of the same paragraph. Notice how the writer has developed the topic sentence with details that make the scene more vivid.

> The last few minutes before closing time are chaotic at the Safeway market where I work. As the checkout clerks begin to total their registers, the store is invaded by last-minute shoppers desperate for cigarettes, milk, or bread. A few customers are still in the vegetable section squeezing each tomato or cantaloupe as the manager paces by nervously. The butcher and his assistants are removing the meat from the display case and putting it in the freezer, slamming the doors like the guards at Fort Knox. A little boy is running up and down the aisles crying and calling out for his mother who returns to the store hysterically looking for him. My

friend Vince, who restocks the shelves, waits impatiently for all of us to leave so that he can bring out his carts full of boxes of canned goods. Finally, the last customer is escorted to the door, and I sit down on an upturned soda case to rest for a few minutes before changing my clothes. In the stockroom a transistor radio begins to blare out rock lyrics. Suddenly there is a tap on the front door of the store. A customer says he didn't get his deposit back on the soda bottle he had returned.

As you can easily see, the revised paragraph is fully developed. It offers the sights and sounds of closing time, helping us to see and hear the chaos mentioned in the topic sentence. By comparing the two versions you can appreciate the difference between an undeveloped and a developed paragraph.

Strategies for Developing Paragraphs

The strategies or patterns for developing paragraphs are similar to those discussed in Chapter 5, "Developing the Essay: Six Patterns." An individual paragraph can be developed by example, comparison and contrast, and so on. Like essays, some paragraphs may combine patterns in their development; a definition paragraph, for example, may combine examples with division and classification.

You may find it helpful to refer to the six developmental patterns as you study this section, which includes illustrations of them.

⑥ EXEMPLIFICATION

Every culture has its own insult signals to show disrespect and contempt for others. Although they vary greatly from culture to culture and are often meaningless outside their home range, they can be very insulting to those who understand them. In Saudi Arabia, for example, a gesture in which the tips of the fingers and thumb of the left hand are brought together, and the straightened forefinger of the right hand is moved across to touch the ring of bunched tips announces, "You are the son of a whore." In certain Spanish-speaking countries "thumbnail applause" is offered as an act of derision. Instead of clapping loudly with the palms of the hands, the "applauder" taps the back of one thumbnail against the other. In Syria, picking one's nostrils with the right forefinger and thumb means "go to hell." In Italy, the *tirare-saliva*—throwing the saliva—gesture is a threatening insult in which the hand "pulls" saliva from the mouth and throws it at the insulted person. Among gypsies a final insult, ending a relationship, consists of shaking imaginary dirt from the clothes, followed by spitting on the floor.

E X E R C I S E 9

Write a paragraph of at least six sentences on one of the topics below, using examples to develop your paragraph. Begin by writing your topic sentence and listing at least three specific examples that make the topic sentence clear. Then write your paragraph.

The benefits of coming from a large family
Athletes who do not fit the image
Immigrants who have overcome handicaps
Corruption in public office
Outstanding local attractions to visit
A friend with many accomplishments
People to avoid at a party
Advice to a kid brother or sister
Some stereotypes that are true
Commercials that are actually enjoyable

DIVISION AND CLASSIFICATION

done

Division

The book of Leviticus describes five basic types of sacrifice among the ancient Hebrews. The first was the burnt offering, in which the entire carcass of an animal was burned as an offering by fire. The second type was the cereal offering, an offering of a product of the field and obviously not of such serious character as a burnt offering. Third was the peace offering, apparently the form of animal sacrifice for ordinary occasions. Fourth was the sin offering, made for sins committed unwittingly. Fifth was the sacrifice required when one committed a breach against God or against his neighbor through deception, perjury, or robbery.

Classification

According to William H. Sheldon, people can be classified according to their body types and personalities. Those who enjoy the company of others and seek comfort and are fat and rounded are termed "endomorphs." Those who are aggressive and fearless and whose bodies are muscular and firm are labelled "mesomorphs." Those who are socially inhibited, unlikely to enjoy physical competition, and who possess thin, flat bodies are designated "ectomorphs."

E X E R C I S E 10

Select one of the following topics and develop it into a paragraph based on division, classification, or both.

Your neighborhood
Techniques for procrastination
An athletic team
Your high school friends
Daytime television
Zoning regulations
Churches in your city
Part-time jobs

---

done — ① **COMPARISON AND CONTRAST**

Block method

The kill shot and the passing shot are the most effective offensive weapons in racquetball, but each has its specific use. The kill shot is a high-percentage shot; if executed perfectly, you are assured of a point. The target should be the near corner, approximately six to twelve inches off the floor. Always aim for the back wall, never for a side wall. Regardless of your position on the floor, it will go. The kill shot is best executed with maximum speed. The passing shot, by contrast, is risky; if it is not made with precision, your opponent can convert it into a kill shot. The target should be the side wall, rather than the corner; such balls are harder to play. The angle of the passing shot is important because the idea is to make the ball pass on the side opposite your opponent's racquet hand. A soft touch is best for this shot.

Point-by-point

Property as defined legally is either real or personal. Real property may be transferred from owner to owner by a formal instrument that is recorded in a public office. Personal property does not have to have its transfer documented publicly. Real property includes land, buildings on the land, mineral deposits, bodies of water, anything attached to the land, and the air above the land. By contrast, personal property includes such items as one's furniture, money, clothing, automobiles, and books.

E X E R C I S E 11

Select one of the following pairs and write a paragraph developed by comparison and contrast using either the block arrangement or point-by-point.

Kung fu and karate
Two pets
Two television comedians
A high school teacher and a college instructor

The influence of two friends
Two cities or neighborhoods
Intelligence and "horse sense"
Classical music and rock

---

(1) **PROCESS AND ANALYSIS**

How to do something

If you should capsize your boat, there are certain steps to follow in righting it. The first job is to remove the sails, beginning with the mainsail. Release the halyard but make the end fast. Pull the sail in toward the boat, pulling it all the way to the boom, and then secure it with a piece of line or the main sheet. Now do the same with the jib and then make all halyards and sheets fast. Now stand on the end of the centerboard and take a grip on the shrouds, a cleat, or the rail. Lean backwards and push down. One of the crew perhaps can try to push up the mast and tread water at the same time. The craft should slowly right itself.

How a process occurs

The story of the creation of coal goes back about 345 billion years to the time when vast swampy areas of the earth were covered by dense, sun-drenched plant forests. As the plants died in the marshes, crustal disturbances occurred. Shallow seas and layers of sediments inundated the forests, and later new swamps grew in their place. In some areas this alternation of swamp and sea occurred hundreds of times. Slowly, great pressures and ample time worked chemical changes, hardening and fossilizing the layers of decayed vegetation. The result was seams of coal.

E X E R C I S E 12

Select one of the subjects below and write a paragraph explaining how to do something, or how something happened or came about. Write at least 125 words.

The signs of spring or winter
How to tune a motorcycle or car
How to organize a musical group
The formation of the solar system
How a particular discovery was made
How to give a speech
How to write a term paper
How the referendum system works
How to impress the parents of your girlfriend or boyfriend
How the Spanish-American War came about
The establishment of the Republican party

How to barbecue a side of ribs
The splitting of an atom

love

① **CAUSE AND EFFECT**

Cause to effect

When the 55-mile speed limit was first passed, even its most enthusiastic supporters did not envision its consequences. Automobile owners began to notice that their cars were getting better gasoline mileage because of the reduced speed. Many drivers reported that their cars ran better and needed fewer tuneups. In many cities, smog levels decreased because of more efficient driving habits. Perhaps the most significant consequence, however, was the decline in the number of automobile-related accidents and fatalities throughout the country.

Effect to cause

Monday Night Football has become show business rather than a football game. The causes for this situation can be seen by any television viewer. It all starts with the ceremonies before kickoff. Interviews with celebrities who are only remotely connected with football are conducted, and movie starlets and television personalities are paraded before the camera. During the game, players on the sidelines mug for the cameras and timeouts are called by the network for the convenience of its advertisers. Halftime entertainment becomes the focal point of the game, followed in the second half by reminders of movies of the week, pilots for programs making their debut, and late-night specials that are to follow the game.

E X E R C I S E 13

Select one of the following topics and write a paragraph developed by cause or effect.

The effect of clothing on The effect of clothing on behavior
The decline of the American city
Registering firearms
Inflation and the problems it causes
Modern conveniences and their headaches
Television and the behavior of children
Advertising and the grocery shopper
Voter apathy
Church attendance in your community
Grades and what is learned

done

②DEFINITION

The family is a social unit, consisting minimally of a married couple with any children that the couple may have. Families are as nearly universal as marriage. The members of the family, particularly the parents and their young children, usually live in a common household and acknowledge certain mutual rights and obligations, especially with regard to economic activity. In a lifetime a person generally belongs to at least one family—the one that he or she is born into. Later, upon marrying, a person forms a new family.

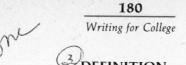

E X E R C I S E **14**

Select one of the following terms and define it in a paragraph of at least 125 words.

Success	Beauty
Maturity	Faith
Evil	A slang term you often use
Liberal	A technical term you are familiar with
Goodness	✳A term from a science textbook
Failure	A term from one of your history or political science textbooks

Introductory and Concluding Paragraphs

The introductory and concluding paragraphs are important parts of the essay. The introduction creates the first impression and therefore must be effective. The conclusion is the writer's last chance to influence or impress readers, while leaving them with a sense of completion.

Some writers write the introduction first, but others prefer to write it after the rest of the essay has been written. Similarly, some write the conclusion first, using it as a kind of final destination point to aim for as they write. Regardless of when the introduction and conclusion are written, they are vital parts of the essay.

Introductions

A good introduction to an essay performs several jobs. The most obvious is to introduce the subject that you will develop and to pave the way for the thesis statement or controlling idea of the essay. The introduction should also catch the readers' interest, making them want to read on. A good introduction informs readers of the writer's intention and suggests the tone of the essay, indicating whether it will be humorous, angry, serious, and so on.

Here are some suggestions for writing introductions with examples from student papers.

Begin with a Direct Statement of Your Topic and Thesis.   Every January, millions of American men huddle around their television sets to watch football's Super Bowl. Although the typical viewer would probably tell you he is watching the game because he admires the players' abilities or a certain team, he is actually watching the game because it fulfills several of his unconscious needs and desires.

Begin with a Personal Anecdote.   I was fifteen when my father was transferred to an American base in Japan and our entire family was moved from our home in Texas. Because there would not be an opening in the base school for a semester, and because my parents did not want me to lose any school time, I was enrolled in the nearby public school in Osaka. From that experience I have learned the importance of tolerance and understanding of others whose skin, culture, or language might be different.

Begin with a Scene or Narrative.   On Friday, November 22, 1963, President John F. Kennedy and Mrs. Kennedy were in a motorcade riding slowly through downtown Dallas in an open limousine. As the President's car moved slowly, he and his wife Jackie waved to the crowds. At 12:30 P.M. a sniper opened fire. Two rifle bullets struck the President and he died immediately. Lee Harvey Oswald, the alleged assassin, himself was shot to death by Jack Ruby, a local nightclub owner, in the basement of the Dallas police station. A presidential commission headed by the United States Supreme Court Chief Justice Earl Warren later found that neither Oswald or Ruby was part of any conspiracy to assassinate the president, but that Oswald had acted alone. Many people, however, refuse to accept the findings of the commission, and they still believe that Oswald and Ruby were part of a larger conspiracy to kill Kennedy. They think that the American people have not been told the truth about the assassination.

Begin with a Question.   What are the chances of a nuclear war in the near future? How many Americans would survive a nuclear attack? Would such an attack make living conditions impossible for the survivors? These and similar questions are being asked by citizens' groups throughout this country as they debate the issue of arms control and nuclear disarmament.

Begin with Statistics.   Almost sixty percent of the couples who married this year will get a divorce. Approximately one-third of the teenagers who marry are already pregnant. Almost half of the women who become pregnant this year will have an abortion. These and similar statistics indicate that there has been a breakdown of morality among today's young people.

Begin with a Quotation.   "To be or not to be; that is the question." Every year an increasing number of young people are answering those words of Hamlet's by taking their own lives. Suicide is becoming a major cause of death among Americans under the age of 25.

Begin with an Imaginary Scene or a "What If" Situation.   Can you imagine living your life without being able to see or hear anyone or anything? As if that were not bad enough, imagine not being able to speak. You would feel totally isolated and cut off from the world, unable to communicate your feelings and needs, and unable to share or understand those of others. That is how Helen Keller felt, before she met her teacher, Anne Mansfield Sullivan.

Begin with a Surprising Statement.   Staying up all night to study before a final exam is one of the most harmful and least productive ways to prepare for a test. Although hundreds of thousands of college students might believe otherwise, psychologists and college counselors say that a good night's rest is actually more helpful than spending the time cramming. Here are some introductions to avoid:

> *Don't begin with an apology:* "Although I don't know very much about the topic, I will try to discuss . . ."
> *Don't begin with a cliché or trite opening:* "According to Webster's dictionary, . . ."
> *Don't begin with platitudes and sweeping generalizations:* "Honesty is the best policy."
> *Don't begin with an opening that restates or defines the title of the essay:* For an essay titled "Mutations and Their Causes," the following opening: "This refers to the process that sometimes occurs during cell division" is not a strong beginning.

Conclusions

The conclusion of your essay, like its introduction, can fulfill several purposes. It can summarize your main points or restate your thesis, avoiding the same words and expressions that were used throughout the essay. It can suggest a sense of "closure" by referring to a quotation or fact used in the introduction. Some introductions ask the reader to do something—to take some action, consider another alternative, or think more deeply about an issue or problem. Other introductions speculate on the future by predicting what will happen as a result of the situation described in the essay.

Your conclusion should be in proportion to the length of the body of the essay. For a short paper, a few sentences are enough. For longer papers, one or two paragraphs would be appropriate. Regardless of length, it should convey a sense of completion to the reader.

Here are some suggestions for writing conclusions, with examples from student papers.

End with a Summary of Your Main Points. These steps should be reviewed before the actual interview. A neat, organized résumé will let your prospective employer see your qualifications at a glance. A clear idea of the salary you expect gives both you and your interviewer a starting point for a discussion of wages. A businesslike, serious approach to the interview indicates your attitude toward the position. These steps are the best way to prepare for an interview.

End with a Restatement of Your Thesis. The facts, as we have seen, do not justify a belief in the existence of life in outer space. The conditions necessary for life found on Earth cannot be duplicated anywhere else in the universe. Man is unique, and to think otherwise is to ignore the evidence.

End with a Fact or Quotation Used in the Introduction. "All men are created equal" does not mean that all men and women are identical. What the writers of our Declaration of Independence meant is that individuals should be given their rights as unique human beings and respected for their common humanity.

End by Asking Your Audience to Do Something. There will be no improvement in the schools until there is a change of attitude in the home. Insist that your children attend classes regularly. Ask them about their assignments and homework. Spend some time every day reading to your children and listening to them read. Stress the importance of punctuality, neatness, and accuracy. By your attitude and behavior you will show that you value education and believe in the importance of the schools.

End with a Prediction. If gun control legislation is not passed, the consequences will be tragic for America. As the ownership of guns increases, violence will escalate. Crimes involving handguns will multiply, and this country will become an armed camp. Vigilante groups will roam the streets. But there is still time to stop this madness. All it takes is courage on the part of our legislators. Here are some things to avoid when writing a conclusion:

Don't apologize for what you have written or for the way you have written it: "I realize much more could have been presented about this topic, but I was unable to get much information . . ."

Don't use clichés to introduce your conclusion: "Last but not least . . ."

Don't raise ideas that contradict your thesis, or ideas that belong in the body of your essay: "Some people would argue that hitchhiking should not be prohibited in our city. They point out that our public transportation system is inadequate and that many students do not own cars. Nevertheless, I believe that hitchhiking should be prohibited on the streets of this city."

Don't introduce new ideas that are unrelated to your thesis: "Taking a year off after graduating from high school, therefore, allows the young person time to plan his or her future and to choose, without the pressure of the college environment, the most satisfying and rewarding course of action. Graduates of vocational trade schools often receive excellent starting salaries . . ."

Don't make the conclusion abrupt. The following sentence would be too abrupt if it comprised the entire conclusion: "These are my reasons for allowing prayers in the public schools."

CHAPTER

9

Writing

Effective Sentences

What are effective sentences? Most experienced writers would agree that they are *concise, varied,* and *emphatic.* Effective sentences say as much as possible as economically as possible without sacrificing clarity. They use a variety of structures and are different lengths. They emphasize the important ideas so that the reader can spot the writer's intentions.

Conciseness

The best sentences contain no flab or unnecessary words. Compare the following sentences:

> *Wordy:* One of my close personal friends who lives in the city of Indianapolis at the present time has under consideration moving his residence to Buffalo for the reason that he has been offered a position in that metropolis. *(38 words)*
>
> *Concise:* One of my friends in Indianapolis is considering moving to Buffalo because he has been offered a job there. *(19 words)*

By cutting the verbiage in half, we have made the sentence clearer and stripped it of its pomposity. This does not mean that all sentences must be brief or "bare bones." When you want to emphasize certain words or ideas, then concrete, specific details to make the meaning clear and precise and repetition may be necessary. But empty phrases, padding, and unnecessary repetition add nothing to the meaning of a sentence and are barriers between you and your reader.

When you write a first draft, you will probably be wordy. As you revise, you should look out for padding and unnecessary words. In particular, watch for the following constructions.

Redundancies

A redundant phrase is one that contains unnecessary repetition; it says the same things twice. Here are some common examples: *blue in color, cooperate together, few in number, fundamental principles, smaller in size,* and so on. Notice the following sentences.

> *Redundant:* She left Chicago at three P.M. in the afternoon.
> *Concise:* She left Chicago at three P.M.
> *Redundant:* The same identical answer was given by three students on the test.
> *Concise:* The same answer was given by three students on the test.

Redundant: The tax committee, after much debate, finally reached a consensus of opinion.

Concise: The tax committee, after much debate, finally reached a consensus.

You will occasionally want to repeat an idea in different words to emphasize a particular point. Except in those instances, cut out any repetitive words or phrases that do not emphasize or clarify your point.

Unnecessary Words

Unnecessary words clutter up a sentence because they add nothing to its meaning. They make sentences flabby and, like redundancies, they are no more than padding. Compare the following sentences:

Wordy: With regard to the fact that our environment is polluted, members of Congress should draft and consequently enact laws that prohibit pollution in our nation.

Concise: Because our environment is polluted, Congress should pass laws prohibiting pollution.

The left column below contains typical wordy expressions; the right column contains concise phrases.

Wordy	Concise
Make inquiry regarding	Inquire, ask
At this point in time	Now
Have under consideration	Are considering
In view of the fact that	Because, since
For the purpose of	For, to
Of an indefinite nature	Indefinite
At the present time	Now
In order to	To
For the reason that	Because
In the final analysis	Finally
In the case that	If

This is not an exhaustive list, but it suggests how familiar and subtle wordy expressions can be. As you revise your writing, delete any unnecessary words.

All-purpose Nouns. Words like "aspect," "factor," "field," "kind," "thing," "element," and "situation" are overused. They are often resorted to by writers who cannot think of a more precise word; they can usually be deleted by rewording the sentence.

Wordy: Having entered the field of fire science as my major, I have become personally aware of the factors that contribute to various accidental fires.

Concise: Since majoring in fire science, I have learned why fires accidentally start.

Sentences that begin with "It is" and "There is" (and the plural, "There are") are usually weaker and less assertive than sentences that begin with the real subject.

Wordy: There were four strangers pounding on the door.

Concise: Four strangers were pounding on the door.

Wordy: It is a fact that people have lost confidence in their elected leaders.

Concise: People have lost confidence in their elected leaders.

Phrases like "in my opinion," "it seems," "I believe," and "I think" can usually be cut from a sentence without damaging it; the result is usually a more forceful sentence.

Wordy: In my opinion, the voting age should be raised to 21.

Concise: The voting age should be raised to 21.

Wordy: It seems to me that a course in computers should be required.

Concise: A course in computers should be required.

E X E R C I S E 1

Revise the following sentences, making them as concise as possible without changing their meaning.

1. At a public ceremony in front of the student body, Rose Diaz was presented a scholarship as a gift from the Alumni Club.

2. At approximately eight P.M. last night, I found a quiet and peaceful spot in the park and perused my academic lecture notes.

3. Insofar as learning to play a musical instrument is concerned, the harp, in my personal opinion, would be in the category of the kind that is difficult to learn to play.

4. The average worker who works in a surrounding environment that contains poisonous pollutants sometimes dies of a mortal illness connected with the pollutants.

5. The arbitrator, who is an acknowledged expert in the field of labor negotiations, recommended that each chairman of both sides meet with him tomorrow morning at ten A.M.

6. Although they were few in number, the early settlers who

came to this country brought with them strong and devout religious faith and beliefs.

7. Many kinds of factors determine the decision of an admissions committee in selecting applicants for admittance to medical school.

8. In view of the fact that the job market is constantly changing, the counselor urged each and every student to plan alternate plans for the future.

9. It is a fact that there are many individuals who do not vote in elections.

10. Various aspects of personal behavior are studied and analyzed by specialists in the field of psychology.

E X E R C I S E 2

Revise the following paragraph, making it as concise as possible without changing its meaning.

(In past years, and) until recently, Mexican food was popular among many people (chiefly) in the American Southwest and in (the state of) California. Within the period of the last year, however, (it would appear that) Mexican food has become the favorite (preferred item) on the East Coast as well. Food establishments that serve Mexican food have opened in the states of New York and Pennsylvania, states that normally are not usually thought of having a sizeable population comprised of Mexican individuals. It would appear that there are several factors giving rise to the popularity of Mexican food. First and foremost, perhaps, is the facet of cost. Mexican food is economical in price, not requiring huge expenditures of money. Second is the taste of the food. Mexican food offers to its consumers a different contrast to the kinds and types of food they have previously been accustomed to. Third and last is the convenience. Mexican food can be prepared quickly and without requiring much time. Several restaurant owners are planning ahead for the future and predicting an even greater number of customers who demonstrate a preference for this type of food product.

Sentence Variety

A good writer's essays include a variety of sentence types. He or she mixes shorter with longer sentences and employs a variety of sentence patterns. The relationship between the ideas is clear, and the reader can follow the writer's thought without any problems. A weak writer, by contrast, produces sentences that are often choppy, repetitious, and monotonous. In this section we will look at several ways to write varied sentences that are smooth and mature.

Sentence Length

Good writers use sentences of different lengths. A paragraph filled with sentences of the same length is monotonous. A series of short sentences sounds immature, as the following paragraph demonstrates.

> At least 50,000 grizzly bears ranged from Texas to Oregon. That was before the white man came. Today, no more than 1,000 survive in the lower 48 states. This is the result of hunting, poaching, and encroachment on their habitat. In the 1960s the National Park Service issued a decree. They stated that the animals could no longer be fed by the public. The bears had long foraged in old dump sites. The sites were abruptly closed. Hotelkeepers used to put food out for the bears. They were no longer allowed to do this. The bears began to look for food. They looked in campgrounds. They looked outside the parks as well. Inevitably, the grizzlies began to be shot. They would be shot just for showing up. Conservationists must devise a solution. The grizzly will eventually disappear.

This paragraph suffers from monotonous sentence structure. By combining some of the shorter sentences, you can avoid the boring style:

> Before the white man came, at least 50,000 grizzly bears ranged from Texas to Oregon. Today, as a result of hunting, poaching, and encroachment on their habitat, no more than 1,000 survive in the lower 48 states. In the 1960s the National Park Service decreed that the animals could no longer be fed by the public. Old dump sites, where the bears had long foraged, were abruptly closed. Hotelkeepers were no longer allowed to put food out for the bears. As a result, the bears began looking for food not only in campgrounds but outside the parks as well. Inevitably, the grizzlies began to be shot just for showing up. Unless conservationists can devise a solution, the grizzly will soon disappear.

Do not get the idea that short sentences should always be avoided. They can be effective for summing up a point or for making the reader stop abruptly to consider a key comment or observation.

A short sentence can often be effective at the beginning of a paragraph:

Consider this. For years now we have witnessed the agony of refugees from Asia, starving Cambodian men, women, and children, fleeing Vietnamese, struggling ashore on Malaysia from some leaky boat after a horrid passage across the South China Sea. Some of these boats make it; many do not. But all of these boats, as has been written, carry on them the same inscription: "This is what happens to friends of the United States."

A short sentence can also be effective at the end of a paragraph:

Some observers predict hard times ahead for this country: increasing unemployment, high interest rates, business failures, and inflation. They talk about the revival of racial tensions, the gap between generations, the pollution of the environment, growing cynicism on the part of the young toward political institutions, and a decline in ethics, responsibility, and tradition. But they are wrong.

In both passages, a short sentence is contrasted with a series of longer sentences. As a result, the short ones catch the reader's attention.

E X E R C I S E 3

By varying the length of the sentences, revise the following paragraph:

The first recorded Olympic games were held in Olympia, Greece. The year was 776 B.C. They were held thereafter every four years for 1,200 years. Men came from all over Greece to participate. The competition included foot races, wrestling, and chariot races. The games were held in a stadium that seated 45,000 spectators. The original inspiration of the games was religious. Another reason was to keep the soldiers in practice for war. The games lasted five days. During this time a truce was declared throughout Greece between city-states that were at war. Married women were not allowed to compete or even watch. If a woman appeared, she was thrown off a nearby cliff. Virgins were permitted to compete. If a person cheated, he was fined. The money went to build a statue of Zeus. On the base of the statue was placed the name of the offender and his offense. The games reached their height in the fifth and fourth centuries B.C. They were abolished by the Emperor Theodosius I in 393 A.D. because they were a pagan spectacle. They were not revived until modern times. The first modern Olympics was held in Athens in 1896.

Word Order

Inexperienced writers tend to begin every sentence with the subject. This is natural, because the subject-verb pattern is the most common arrangement in English sentences. A series of such sentences, however, can be boring and monotonous. By beginning some of your sentences with something other than the subject you can make them more interesting. Two methods for doing this can be employed: placing modifiers before the subject, and inverting the normal word order.

Normal order:	Canada is the world's second largest country in land size, and it stretches 3,223 miles from east to west.
Appositive first:	The world's second largest country in land size, Canada stretches 3,223 miles from east to west.
Normal order:	Coach Downing slumped on the bench, exhausted and discouraged.
Participles first:	Exhausted and discouraged, Coach Downing slumped on the bench.
Normal order:	The marshal walked through the crowd fearlessly.
Adverb first:	Fearlessly, the marshal walked through the crowd.
Normal order:	I found an important letter on my desk.
Prepositional phrase first:	On my desk I found an important letter.
Normal order:	He detested cigarette smokers.
Object first:	Cigarette smokers he detested.
Normal order:	A moan came from under the bed.
Subject-verb inversion:	From under the bed came a moan.

Additional suggestions for varying sentence patterns and for combining shorter sentences are on pages 203–10, "Sentence Combining."

E X E R C I S E 4

Each of the following sentences follows the subject-verb pattern. Rewrite the sentences, following the suggestions given above.

1. Doctor Samuel Mudd was a physician in Maryland who was falsely accused of conspiring to assassinate Abraham Lincoln.
2. Scientists have made a number of breakthroughs in recent years in their search for the cause of cancer.
3. The coaches and parents were proud of their team as the players received the trophy.
4. Some people believe that the earth is flat.

5. Sue complained that she could not get to sleep until after midnight because her neighbors were arguing and playing loud music.

6. I found a note pinned to my door when I came home this afternoon.

7. The foreman of the jury adjusted her notes hurriedly and nervously and began to speak to the judge.

8. The piercing tones of the trumpet sounded throughout the valley.

9. The Soviet Union exerts influence on Mongolia because of the vast amount of economic and technological assistance it has poured into the country.

10. The spring rains have relentlessly and tirelessly threatened the city's drainage system.

Loose and Periodic Sentences

Another technique for achieving sentence variety is to use a mixture of *loose* and *periodic* sentences. In a *loose* sentence the main idea comes first, and less important ideas follow. In the *periodic* sentence, the main idea comes at the end of the sentence.

Loose: I could tell that he was disappointed by the tone of his voice and the look on his face.

Periodic: By the tone of his voice and the look on his face, I could tell that he was disappointed.

Loose: Christopher Columbus finally reached the shores of San Salvador after months of uncertainty at sea, the threat of mutiny, and a growing shortage of food and water.

Periodic: After months of uncertainty at sea, the threat of mutiny, and a growing shortage of food and water, Christopher Columbus finally reached the shores of San Salvador.

As you can see, the loose sentence is built in stages. It completes the main statement and then explains or amplifies it. Most of our conversations and writing consist of loose sentences, as we pile details on details as we think of them. For this reason the loose sentence is sometimes called a *cumulative* sentence. The loose sentence usually lacks the suspense of the periodic sentence because the details and qualifiers that follow its main idea weaken its impact. The periodic sentence, on the other hand, holds the reader in suspense because it holds the main statement until the end. Everything that precedes it builds up the idea in the main clause at the conclusion. The periodic

sentence is more emphatic, therefore, because it creates more suspense—
the reader (or listener) has to pay attention to the very end.

A word of caution: Don't overdo periodic sentences. The suspense that they generate can be overdone, and they can become just as
monotonous as any other structure that you rely on heavily. But used
occasionally to break up the sameness of loose sentences, they will
improve your style.

E X E R C I S E 5

Change the loose sentences to periodic sentences, and the periodic
sentences to loose.

1. Built at a cost of 16 million dollars, with a mile-long center
   span and supported at either end by stone towers that were
   once the tallest buildings in the country, the Brooklyn Bridge
   celebrated its centenary in 1983.
2. She sang the National Anthem, holding the sheet music in her
   hand in case she forgot the words.
3. He chased the robber, ignoring his own safety and the likelihood that the robber was armed.
4. Directly ahead of them, standing in the middle of the road
   casually munching on a mouthful of hay, was a large cow.
5. He stood silently for a moment, wondering what to say,
   nervously rubbing his nose.
6. Because of the popularity of video cassette recorders and the
   profits to be made in copying films, video piracy is a huge and
   growing problem.
7. You should select your speakers first when you are buying a
   stereo set.
8. The Spanish invaders murdered or raped many of the Indians
   they met despite the fact that the vast majority of the Indians
   were friendly.
9. He served the stew with embarrassment, knowing that several of his guests were excellent cooks who were too polite to
   complain.
10. A master of court tactics with a flair for the dramatic who
    combined an overpowering forehand with a rifle-shot serve,
    Bill Tilden dominated world tennis during the twenties.

Sentence Imitation

Sentence imitation is an excellent way to improve your own sentence
construction. The process is simple: copy several sentences that you
like by writers you admire. Analyze the structure of the sentences,

noticing, for example, where the subject and verb are, where the main idea is placed, where the modifiers and unimportant parts are located, and so on. Then write an original sentence, following as closely as possible the same pattern. It isn't necessary to have the exact number of words as the model sentence; the object is to write a sentence that follows the same pattern.

You will notice several things happening in your own writing after you practice sentence imitation. You will discover why some sentences work and others don't, and by paying close attention to how professional writers put words together, you will be using patterns in your own writing that would never have occurred to you. A side benefit to this exercise is that you will add new words to your vocabulary.

Study these model sentences and their imitations, written by students. You will notice that most of the model sentences, as well as those in the exercise below, are loose or cumulative sentences.

Model:	To err is human, to forgive, divine. *(Alexander Pope)*
Imitation:	To work is exahusting, to loaf, refreshing. *(Student)*
ANALYSIS:	The writer of this example has tried to imitate Pope closely. Notice that Pope's sentence links pairs of words opposite in meaning: *err, forgive; human, divine.* The student's version attempts this same contrast: *work, loaf; exhausting, refreshing.*
Model:	To be, or not to be—that is the question. *(William Shakespeare)*
Imitation:	To study, or not to study—that is the dilemma. *(Student)*
Model:	The jockeys sat bowed and relaxed, moving a little at the waist with the movement of their horses. *(Katherine Anne Porter)*
Imitation:	The hunters crouched nervous and alert, peering over the blind at the flight of the ducks. *(Student)*
Model:	He dipped his hands in the bichloride solution and shook them, a quick shake, fingers down, like the fingers of a pianist above the keys. *(Sinclair Lewis)*
Imitation:	She slipped her fingers into the mixing bowl and licked them, a sneaky taste, head low, like the eyes of a dog below the table. *(Student)*
Model:	Calico-coated, small-bodied, with delicate legs and pink faces in which their mismatched eyes rolled wild and subdued, they huddled, gaudy motionless and alert, wild as deer, deadly as rattlesnakes, quiet as doves. *(William Faulkner)*

Imitation: Deeply tanned, bikini clad, with hopeful eyes and flirtatious smiles and lean bodies that swung smooth and
            practiced, they walked, giggling loudly and nervously,
            coy like a breeze, rushing like a wind, waiting like a
            storm. *(Student)*

Model: Women don't want to exchange places with men. *(Gloria Steinem)*

Imitation: Teenagers don't want to go to parties with their parents. *(Student)*

E X E R C I S E   6

Write original sentences of your own, imitating the structure of
the following sentences.

1. Rage cannot be hidden; it can only be dissembled. *(James Baldwin)*

2. There is a vague idea floating around that only dimwits can really enjoy bringing up babies because their conversation is so repetitive and they are, let's face it, little better than animals. Agreed. *(Elaine Morgan)*

3. The quality of strength lined with tenderness is an unbeatable combination, as are intelligence and necessity when unblunted by formal education. *(Maya Angelou)*

4. In the far corner the man was still asleep, snoring slightly on the intaking breath, his head back against the wall. *(Ernest Hemingway)*

5. It is not the happiness of the individual convert that concerns me; it is the happiness of mankind. *(Bertrand Russell)*

6. The only advice that one person can give another about reading is to take no advice, to follow your own instincts, to use your own reason, to come to your own conclusions. *(Virginia Woolf)*

7. Let them eat cake. *(Marie-Antoinette)*

8. Ask not what your country can do for you, but what you can do for your country. *(John F. Kennedy)*

9. Next morning when the first light came into the sky and the sparrows stirred in the trees, when the cows rattled their chains and the rooster crowed and the early automobiles went whispering along the road, Wilbur awoke and looked for Charlotte. *(E. B. White)*

10. It was the best of times, it was the worst of times, it was the age of wisdom, it was the age of foolishness, it was the epoch of belief, it was the epoch of incredulity, it was the season of light, it was the season of darkness. . . . *(Charles Dickens)*

Emphasis

Effective sentences emphasize their main ideas, keeping related but less important ideas in the background. *Coordination, subordination, parallelism,* and *the use of the active voice* are techniques that will make your sentences more emphatic and your ideas more forceful.

Coordination

To show the relative importance of two or more ideas in a sentence, you can connect them by means of *coordination* or *subordination*. You *coordinate* two or more ideas that are equally important. Ideas that deserve equal emphasis can be linked in several ways: by coordinating conjunctions (usually *and, but, or,* and *nor*) and by conjunctive adverbs such as *however* and *therefore* (see pages 203–208).

Here are two examples of coordination:

Two simple sentences:	Tim worked as a mechanic during the day. At night he took classes in business.
Coordinated with a conjunction:	Tim worked as a mechanic during the day, *but* at night he took classes in business.
Coordinated with a conjunctive adverb:	Tim worked as a mechanic during the day; *however*, at night he took classes in business.

When combining ideas, be careful that you do not end up merely stringing them together with a series of and's and but's. Excessive coordination is just as ineffective as a series of choppy simple sentences.

Excessive coordination:	The weather was mild, and the leaves were turning, and we took a trip to the mountains.
Revised:	Because the weather was mild and the leaves were turning, we took a trip to the mountains.

Faulty coordination occurs when there seems to be no logical connection between two coordinated statements. In such cases, you can show the relationship between the clauses by subordinating one of the ideas to the other one.

Faulty coordination:	Hank did not get a promotion, but he was not surprised.
Revised:	Although he did not get a promotion, Hank was not surprised.

Subordination

To subordinate is to show that one idea is less important than another in a sentence by putting it in a subordinate structure. The task in subordinating, therefore, is to identify the main idea and place it in a main clause and then place the less important material in a dependent or subordinate construction.

The writer and reader can usually agree on which idea in a sentence is more important:

> *The telephone rang as I got out of the tub.* (Most readers would agree that the *less* important idea is what the writer was doing when the phone rang. *As I got out of the tub* is a subordinate clause.)

At times, however, only the context can suggest which idea should be emphasized:

> When Mozart was five, he wrote his first composition for the piano.

> When he wrote his first composition for the piano. Mozart was five.

The first version emphasizes that it was a composition for the piano that Mozart wrote; note that this information is in the coordinate or main clause. In the second sentence, the emphasis is on the fact that Mozart was five, as stated in the main clause. These sentences illustrate the principle that the main idea should normally be placed in the main clause, with supporting information in subordinate elements.

Excessive subordination occurs when a writer crams too many loosely connected details and subordinate structures into one sentence, as in the following:

> The houses that were on the market when the recession, which has affected prices throughout the country, began have remained unsold because their builders are burdened with mortgages with high interest rates, because of inflation, which no one could predict.

The best way to revise such a sentence is to break it up into two or more sentences, putting the main ideas in main clauses:

> The houses that were on the market when the recession began have remained unsold. Because of inflation which no one could predict, their builders are burdened with mortgages with high interest rates.

Faulty subordination (or "upside-down" subordination) occurs when the logically important idea is placed in a subordinate position:

> Kevin has taken typing for only three weeks, although he can already type forty words a minute.

This sentence suggests that the main idea is that Kevin has taken typing for only three weeks; it is likely, however, that the idea to be emphasized is that he can already type forty words a minute. By putting the main idea in the main clause, we can make the sentence more emphatic:

> Although Kevin has taken typing for only three weeks, he can already type forty words a minute.

E X E R C I S E 7

Rewrite the following sentences by subordinating less important ideas to more important ones.

1. Charles Darwin wrote a book, and it contains a controversial theory.
2. It was an unbelievable performance by the understudy in the role she performed in without advance warning.
3. Sam lost his eyesight because of a childhood disease, and he can read braille.
4. Hockey is a game that often erupts into violence, and it has led to injuries.
5. Years ago students memorized hundreds of lines of poetry, and today this is no longer done.
6. Although Mary Ellen finally sold her car, she had tried to sell it for two months.
7. Carole Stunning was once the toast of Hollywood, and now she was ignored by all of the producers and directors.
8. The rocket launch, which I watched on a television set that was in my dentist's office, was on Wednesday.
9. Air Force Captain Charles Yeager flew the Bell X-1, and he exceeded the speed of sound, and therefore he became the world's first supersonic flyer.
10. At one time condors were prevalent in the western half of the United States although they are an endangered species today.

E X E R C I S E 8

Rewrite the following paragraph, subordinating less important ideas to more important ones.

Sometimes Pele, the Hawaiian goddess of fire, feels neglected. She rises up in flaming wrath from her home in Kilauea crater.

Last January, Pele indulged in one of her most spectacular outbursts. She spewed more than thirteen million cubic yards of molten lava over the southeastern corner of the island of Hawaii. Residents of the island chain are familiar with such pyrotechnics, and the whole geological history of Hawaii has been forged by fire. Layer upon layer of molten rock welled up from the ocean floor to build islands. Hawaiian volcanoes sit on molten rock which can create curtains of flame and which create a fiery caldron from which the entire archipelago continues to grow.

Parallelism

Parallelism is the use of similar grammatical forms in a sentence to express ideas of similar importance. Parallel structure can make sentences smoother and make clear the connection between the ideas in those sentences.

Compare the following sentences:

　　　　　　　　　　　　　　　　　 adj.　　 adj.　　　　　　 clause
Faulty:　 The solution was *simple, obvious,* and *it did not cost much.*
　　　　　　　　　　　　　　　　　 adj.　　 adj.　　　　　 adj.
Parallel:　 The solution was *simple, obvious,* and *inexpensive.*

Read the following pairs of sentences carefully; try to determine which sentence in each pair is smoother and more emphatic because of parallelism.

He entered the room angry; he was happy when he left.
He entered the room angry; he left happy.

Because the food was good, the rent was reasonable, and also because they thought the service was reliable, they preferred the old hotel.

Because the food was good, the rent was reasonable, and the service was reliable, they preferred the old hotel.

The second sentence in each pair uses parallelism, and therefore is smoother and more emphatic.

As you probably noticed from the preceding examples, parallel structure can employ single words, phrases, or whole clauses:

The movie was *long, boring,* and *predictable.* (adjectives)

She was confident *on the playing field, before the camera,* and *in the courtroom.* (prepositional phrases)

What he has, what he knows, and *what he believes* can be attributed to his family background. (dependent clauses)

E ·X E R C I S E 9

Improve the following sentences by using parallel structure.

1. Despite the steel fences, electronic sensors, cipher locks, and the fact that all of the checkpoints are guarded, thieves broke into the underground vaults.
2. They vowed never to return and they would always remember.
3. My job consisted of sweeping the floor, opening up in the morning, and customers had to be waited on when the others were at lunch.
4. Despite the governor's duties, he liked to hunt, to ski, and fishing.
5. The congregation complained that the new pastor's sermons were boring and contained little humor.
6. With a new typewriter and not having to work, Con decided to write a novel.
7. She played her stereo too loud, refused to clean her room, and she was careless in her appearance. *neglected*.
8. The judge decided that the witness was either telling a lie or he was confused.
9. The recipe calls for a cup of flour and you also need a cup of milk.
10. Because the weather was mild, and also we were able to take a few days off, we decided to hike in the Blue Ridge Mountains.

Active and Passive Voice

You will often be able to choose between active and passive voice when composing sentences. The active voice is usually more direct. For this reason you should use active verbs except in cases when you have good reason to use passive ones.

In a sentence built upon an *active* verb, the subject performs the action:

Active: Mark attended a concert.

The *passive* voice turns the sentence around. The doer remains the same but is placed in a less important position, and the object becomes the subject:

Passive: The concert was attended by Mark.

As you can see, active voice emphasizes the *doer* of the action, and passive emphasizes the *object* or *receiver* of the action. Therefore, the choice of active or passive voice depends on the relative importance of the doer and the recipient of the action. Compare these sentences:

The second-string quarterback called the play.
The play was called by the second-string quarterback.

In the first sentence the verb *(called)* is active and stresses the *doer* of the action *(The second-string quarterback)*. In the second sentence the verb *(was called)* is passive and stresses the *recipient* of the action *(The play)*. When the result of the action is more important than the performer, use the passive voice. Passive voice is also acceptable when the doer of the action is unknown:

> *Passive:* German children *are taught* to read and speak English in the early grades. (In this case, the *doer* is unimportant.)

In general, however, avoid the passive voice because it is wordy and less direct. Notice the difference between these sentences:

> *Passive:* It was decided by the class that a ham would be purchased and would be given to a needy family. *(20 words)*
>
> *Active:* The class decided to buy a ham and give it to a needy family. *(14 words)*

Another consequence of the passive voice is that it obscures the performer or doer of the action:

> *Passive:* A proposal to do away with final exams has been suggested. *(Suggested by whom?)*
>
> *Passive:* It is recommended that the radio be turned off. *(Who is making the recommendation? Who is to turn the radio off?)*

E X E R C I S E 10

Change the following sentences from passive to active voice to make them more emphatic.

1. Control gates were installed on the river by engineers and will be tested during the coming flood season.
2. It was decided by the judges that Tom's chocolate cake was the best in the fair.
3. The auto wreck was witnessed by Esther as she was driving to work.
4. New evidence that brain damage can be caused by boxing was cited by a panel of physicians last week.
5. Spectators were warned by the police of the danger.
6. New safeguards were approved by the hospital administrator so that the chance of a mistaken dosage given by a nurse would be eliminated.
7. The changes in the election bylaws were approved by the chairman of the election commission.

8. The silken fiber that is spun by orb spiders is twisted into an endless variety of patterns.
9. The use of body language in communications has been studied by psychologists.
10. Your letter was postmarked last Thursday, and it was received yesterday, but it has been decided by the awards committee that they are prohibited from making an exception.

E X E R C I S E 11

Rewrite the following paragraph, making the sentences more emphatic by using active voice where appropriate.

It has been agreed by members of the department that term papers will be written by students in all freshman English courses that are given transfer credit by the university. It was further decided when the last meeting was held that a grade of F could be given by an instructor to any student whose term peaper is plagiarized. Exception to these regulations may be granted by a committee to be named later by the department.

Sentence-Combining

Sentence-combining is an important and effective way to improve your writing. By learning how to combine short sentences into longer, smoother, and more interesting sentences, you can develop an arsenal of ways to develop your writing style. Because sentence-combining uses most of the techniques already discussed in this chapter, it is introduced in this concluding section. Sentence-combining employs a series of steps which we will follow, beginning with the easiest and progressing to more subtle patterns.

Using Coordination to Combine Sentences

The most obvious (though not always the best) way to combine two or more short sentences is with a *coordinating conjunction (and, but, or, for, nor, yet, so* preceded by a comma) or a *semicolon*. This will produce a compound sentence.

Simple sentences: Phil received ski boots for Christmas. His sister received a fishing rod.

Combined:	Phil received ski boots for Christmas, *and* his sister received a fishing rod.
Combined:	Phil received ski boots for Christmas; his sister received a fishing rod.
Simple sentences:	In recent years many critics have attacked the public schools. No one seems to have any answers.
Combined:	In recent years many critics have attacked the public schools, *but* no one seems to have any answers.

By using coordinating conjunctions you will often be able to combine short sentences into single sentences containing one main clause. Sentences can be combined this way when both of the original sentences have the same subject or the same verb. A comma does not precede the conjunction in sentences constructed this way.

Same subject:	Toni ran the hurdles. She threw the javelin.
Combined:	Toni ran the hurdles *and* threw the javelin.
Same verb:	Morris tried out for the hockey team. André tried out for the hockey team.
Combined:	Morris and André tried out for the hockey team.

E X E R C I S E 12

Following the preceding examples, combine the following pairs of sentences in the most appropriate way, using either a coordinating conjunction or a semicolon.

1. Many innocent prisoners have been executed. Others have been found innocent prior to execution.
2. We can stay until he gets here. We can leave now.
3. She asked him to stop whistling. He continued to do it.
4. The authorities would not let him leave the country. He did not give up hope.
5. You should check the oil dipstick every week. You should also check the tire pressure.
6. The tax bill will be approved by the budget committee. It will probably be vetoed by the governor.
7. The people who rent from you are the lessees. You are the lessor.
8. Experience always teaches us something. We can learn from it.
9. In last night's movie I loved the character of the old man. His wife irritated me.
10. Our team has superior fielders. It needs two or three power hitters.

Using Subordination to Combine Sentences

Another way to combine shorter sentences is by using *subordination*, or making a single complex sentence out of two simple sentences. A complex sentence consists of an independent clause and a dependent clause. Dependent clauses begin with *connecting words* that indicate that the clauses are incomplete or dependent thoughts. By placing a connecting word in front of a simple sentence, you change it into a dependent clause. By attaching that dependent clause to a simple sentence, you create a complex sentence. The two kinds of connecting words that you can put in front of dependent clauses are *relatives* and *subordinating conjunctions*.

When a relative *(who, which, that, whom, whose)* begins a clause, the result is a *dependent clause*. Notice what happens to the following sentences when they are combined by changing one of them to a dependent clause:

Simple sentences: Dolores Chavez speaks three languages fluently. She sits next to me in history class.

Combined: Dolores Chavez, *who sits next to me in history class*, speaks three languages fluently. (*Or:* Dolores Chavez, *who speaks three languages fluently*, sits next to me in history class.)

In general, the idea that you want to emphasize should be placed in the independent clause.

Notice how the following pairs of sentences have been effectively combined by using relatives:

Simple sentences: Melville L. Dewey was the creator of the Dewey Decimal System. He established the first library school in the United States.

Combined using who: Melville L. Dewey, who was the creator of the Dewey Decimal System, established the first library school in the United States.

Simple sentences: The dinosaur roamed the earth over 100 million years ago. It was the largest meat-eater ever to inhabit dry land.

Combined using which: The dinosaur, which roamed the earth over 100 million years ago, was the largest meat-eater ever to inhabit dry land.

Simple sentences: I bought a guitar in Mexico. I paid fifty dollars for it.

Combined using that: I paid fifty dollars for a guitar that I bought in Mexico.

Simple sentences:	Many Americans remember Ronald Reagan as a movie star. Later he became President of the United States.
Combined using whom:	Ronald Reagan, whom many Americans remember as a movie star, later became President of the United States.
Simple sentences:	Mark Twain's real name was Samuel Longhorne Clemens. He wrote *The Adventures of Huckleberry Finn.*
Combined using whose:	Mark Twain, whose real name was Samuel Longhorne Clemens, wrote *The Adventures of Huckleberry Finn.*

Notice that some dependent clauses are set off by commas. For a discussion of the use of commas with essential and nonessential clauses, see pages 317–20.

E X E R C I S E 13

Combine the shorter sentences in each section below according to the directions, supplying commas when necessary.

1. Combine the following pairs of sentences by changing one of the sentences to a *who* clause:
   a. Ted Williams is one of the great baseball hitters of all time. He is also a well-known sports fisherman.
   b. Veronica became interested in politics after retiring from her job. She has just been reelected city treasurer.
   c. Franklin Delano Roosevelt's father was a wealthy financier. He was fifty-four when Franklin was born.
2. Combine the following pairs of sentences by changing one of the sentences to a *which* clause:
   a. Honey contains an enzyme. The enzyme prevents it from molding.
   b. Hindu culture is based upon the caste system. The system divides society into a multitude of hereditary groups.
   c. The movie *The Ten Commandments* is based on the Old Testament. It is a dramatization of Moses' life.
3. Combine the following pairs of sentences by changing one of the sentences to a *that* clause:
   a. She had only one copy of her rental agreement. It was destroyed in the fire in her apartment.
   b. The physician discussed the patient's ailment. His explanation was in confusing and technical language.
   c. Claire is head cashier of a bank.

4. Combine the following pairs of sentences by changing one of the sentences to a *whom* clause:
   a. The customer did not leave a tip.
      Jackie waited on him.
   b. Ms. Maxey retired last year.
      Everyone loved her.
   c. We will meet a man at the box office.
      He will have our tickets.
5. Combine the following pairs of sentences by changing one of the sentences to a *whose* clause:
   a. An expensive limousine was left abandoned at the scene of the accident.
      Its owner is unknown.
   b. Muhammad Ali was born in Kentucky.
      His baptismal name was Cassius Clay.
   c. Sally Ride was the first American female astronaut.
      Her home is in Encino, California.

Combining with Subordinating Conjunctions. Sometimes you can improve your sentences by combining them through the use of *subordinating conjunctions*. Here are some of the most common: *after, although, as, as soon as, because, before, if, since, unless, until, while* and *when*. This is not a complete list of all the subordinating conjunctions, but it suggests the kinds of words you can put before short sentences to combine them with other sentences, thereby creating longer, smoother sentences.

Notice how each of the following pairs of sentences is combined into a smoother sentence by the use of a subordinating conjunction.

Simple sentences:	The sounds of the music faded. The audience reluctantly filed out of the theater.
Combined using as:	As the sounds of the music faded, the audience reluctantly filed out of the theater.
Simple sentences:	List your answers in a column. They will be easier to check.
Combined using if:	If you list your answers in a column, they will be easier to check.
Simple sentences:	Carl has trouble understanding algebra. His father is a math teacher.
Combined using although:	Although his father is a math teacher, Carl has trouble understanding algebra.
Simple sentences:	The music began to play. Tears started to roll down my cheeks.
Combined using when:	When the music began to play, tears started to roll down my cheeks.

Simple sentences:	His mother had thrown him into a pool when he was young. He was afraid of the water.
Combined using because:	Because his mother had thrown him into a pool when he was young, he was afraid of the water.
Simple sentences:	The United States Football League signed Herschel Walker. Cynics began to take the new league seriously.
Combined using after:	After the United States Football League signed Herschel Walker, cynics began to take the league seriously.

Each of the introductory clauses in the above sentences was followed by a comma. Introductory words, phrases, or clauses should be separated from the main (independent) clause by a comma in order to make the sentence easier to read and to prevent misreading by the reader. Consider the possible confusion in the following sentence: *After we had eaten the dog was fed.* When a comma is inserted after the introductory clause, the sentence is easier to read: *After we had eaten, the dog was fed.*

E X E R C I S E 14

Combine each of the following pairs of sentences by using one of the following subordinating conjunctions: *after, although, as, as soon as, because, before, if, since, unless, until, while,* and *when.*

1. The writer James Thurber revised his short stories many times. He was never satisfied with the first draft.
2. The water in the reservoir dam spilled over the neighboring fields. The rains continued for six days.
3. Frank took a course in television repair. He was able to repair his neighbors' television sets.
4. The referendum was not given much of a chance. It won by a big margin.
5. The first Russian sputnik orbited the earth for fifteen weeks. It fell back through the atmosphere and burned up.
6. The telephone rang. I had a feeling it was bad news.
7. The idea of Atlantis has fascinated mankind. Plato first wrote about it in 335 B.C.
8. The understudy nervously rehearsed his lines. He waited for news of the star's condition.
9. The workers carefully sifted through the rubble. Spectators strained to get a better view of the excavation.

10. The police learned of the three-car collision. They took off in their cruiser despite the blizzard.

Using Phrases to Combine Sentences. The third way to combine your sentences is to reduce or condense a simple sentence into a phrase and combine it with another simple sentence. The most commonly used phrases are *appositives, participial phrases, prepositional phrases, infinitives,* and *gerunds. An appositive* is a noun phrase that is set beside another noun and identifies or explains it. When two related sentences describe or identify the same subject, one of the sentences can usually be made into an appositive.

Simple sentences:	Chris Evert Lloyd is one of this country's best tennis players. She has often been criticized for her colorless style.
Combined using appositive:	Chris Evert Lloyd, one of this country's best tennis players, has often been criticized for her colorless style.

Two sentences can sometimes be combined by changing one of them into an adjective phrase by using an *-ing* or *-ed* word, or *participial phrase.*

Simple sentences:	Ichabod Crane sang hymns as he rode home late at night. He was trying to appear nonchalant.
Combined using -ing:	Trying to appear nonchalant, Ichabod Crane sang hymns as he rode home late at night.
Simple sentences:	Memorial Day is celebrated on May 30. It is dedicated to the memory of all who died serving their country.
Combined using -ed:	Celebrated on May 30, Memorial Day is dedicated to the memory of all who died serving their country.

You can sometimes combine choppy sentences by using a *prepositional phrase.*

Simple sentences:	During the safety inspection the highway patrol officer looked under the car. She looked inside the engine compartment. She looked behind the wheels.
Combined using a prepositional phrase:	During the safety inspection the highway patrol officer looked under the car, inside the engine compartment, and behind the wheels.

By changing one of the verbs to the *infinitive* (the "to" form of the verb), you can often combine shorter sentences.

Simple sentences:	Sheila wears very little makeup. She emphasizes her clear complexion.

To emphasize her clear complexion, Sheila wears very little makeup.

Verbs ending in -ing are called *gerunds*. By adding *-ing* to a verb so that it can function as a noun, you can often combine sentences.

Simple sentences: Elizabeth listened carefully to the lectures. She took notes on her reading. She found that these techniques helped her.

Combined using a gerund: Elizabeth found that listening carefully to the lectures and taking notes on her reading were techniques that helped her.

E X E R C I S E   15

Combine or rearrange each of the following groups of sentences into a single smoother sentence by condensing one of the sentences into a phrase.

1. The sports commentator listed the opponent's many winning matches. He wanted to emphasize her experience.
2. The advertisement featured fresh peaches and plums. The advertisement caught my eye.
3. The driver flashed his lights and leaned on the horn. He brought the car to a screeching halt.
4. Our skis hang on brackets. The brackets are on the side of the garage. The brackets are just below the rafters.
5. Doris avoided talking nonsense. She decided to memorize her campaign speech.
6. Alfred Nobel was the Swedish inventor of dynamite. He established the Nobel Prizes with a bequest of nine million dollars.
7. The children were fascinated by the magician. They pressed closer in order to study his hands.
8. The defendant testified that she had been tortured. She showed the jury her scars.
9. The winner of the decathlon was sweating and panting. He staggered to the microphone.
10. New Orleans is an exciting city. It has many beautiful neighborhoods and also has many tourist attractions.
11. The Olympic games are held every four years. They have developed political overtones.
12. The sales of record albums are decreasing. Record albums are expensive.

13. The first recipient of an "Oscar" for acting was Janet Gaynor. She was only twenty-one when she received the trophy.
14. Our mail-carrier was attacked by a neighbor's dog. She no longer delivers mail to our neighbors.
15. The spectators were stunned. They were surprised. They refused to believe the announcement.

Evaluating Your Sentence Combinations

By this time you have discovered and practiced many techniques for combining sentences. You have probably also noticed that there are several ways to combine even the simplest set of sentences. Perhaps you are wondering whether there is a "right" way to combine each particular set of sentences. And maybe you are wondering whether longer sentences are always better than shorter sentences. This is a good time to consider both questions before we move to the concluding set of exercises.

No particular method of sentence-combining is better than all of the others. In particular situations, however, some sentence combinations are, in fact, better than others. The most effective sentences are those that are the most direct in their meaning, the smoothest in rhythm, and most appropriate in their emphasis. No sentence can be said to be effective if its meaning is not clear, if more than one meaning can be construed from it, or if is difficult to understand. The first requirement, then, is clarity of meaning. But a sentence should not only clearly convey an idea. It should please the reader by its rhythm, its balanced parts, and the satisfying arrangement of its ideas. Finally, an effective sentence directs the reader's attention to the point that the writer wants to emphasize, rather than to an irrelevant or trivial detail.

Is a longer sentence always better than a short one? It depends. It depends on the purpose of the sentence, its location in the paragraph, and its relations to other sentences in the paragraph. In the section on sentence length you saw that a short sentence can be more effective than a longer one, for example, because it can abruptly interrupt the flow of a paragraph and force the reader to brake to a sudden stop and consider a particular point. On the other hand, you should remember that the sentences of professional writers are, in general, longer than those of beginning writers. Only by experimenting with the vast number of sentence-combining strategies available and by trying them out in your own writing will you become confident at selecting the most appropriate sentences to fit the situation.

E X E R C I S E 16

Read the lists of sentences which follow. For each group of sentences determine what the central idea or topic sentence of the paragraph is. Then combine the sentences in the most appropriate order, using the sentence-combining techniques you think are most effective for developing the topic.

1. You can raise or lower your blood pressure.
    Biofeedback machines monitor functions of the body.
    They give you a continuous visual or aural report.
    You can learn to change the signal.
    When you do that, you are changing some part of your body.
    You can raise or lower your heartbeat.
    You do it by concentrating.
    People can control their own autonomic functions.
    They can also relax and get to sleep.
    They can unlearn bad habits.
    Some of the bad habits include smoking and drinking.

2. The Seven Wonders of the ancient world were designated by Alexander the Great.
    He was a military strategist.
    He came to the Macedonian throne in 336 B.C.
    From age 13 to 16, he was taught by the philosopher Aristotle.
    The Seven Wonders were a way of emphasizing the extent and glory of his empire.
    His greatest military victory was storming the city of Tyre in 332 B.C.
    He subdued Egypt and occupied Babylon after his victory in Tyre.
    He invaded India in 326 B.C.
    He consolidated his empire.
    He died ten days after being taken ill, in 323 B.C.
    He became ill after a prolonged banquet and drinking bout.

3. Much of our knowledge about the way of life of the earliest humans comes from the Olduvai Gorge.
    Mary Leakey plotted and recorded several living sites.
    The sites were at the base of the gorge.
    The gorge is in Tanzania in East Africa.
    One site contained more than four thousand artifacts and bones.
    Another campsite yielded not only stone artifacts and bones.
    It also yielded a crude semicircle of stones.
    Mary Leakey interprets this as the foundation of a two-million-year-old windbreak.
    The windbreak is perhaps the oldest living structure yet discovered.

The Olduvai living sites were well established, temporary home bases.
Their occupants returned to the sites to live, eat, and sleep.

E X E R C I S E 17

Rewrite the following paragraphs so that their sentences are smoother and the relationship between their ideas is clearer. Use the sentence-combining techniques that seem most appropriate.

1. Claire looked up at the east bank of the river. She dipped her head. Her eyes were red. They were filled with tears. She felt as if the first step would take the little strength left in her. She sighed and stooped to put on her shoes. She picked up her basket. She started to walk through the reeds and shrubbery. She watched a few paces ahead for snakes. Long blades of grass whispered around her ragged skirt. The blades slashed at her bare shins. The sunlight reflected from the river. It was hot on the left side of her face. Huge dragonflies hovered and drifted away. Birds rose and shrilled. They skimmed close over the water. Claire began to think of freedom. As she thought of freedom, she began to walk faster.

2. *E.T., The Extra-Terrestrial* is a big moneymaker. It is one of the biggest moneymakers of all time. *E.T.* is a fairy tale for the preadolescent child. Many have seen the movie several times. *E.T.* appeals to audiences because of its space-age setting. The space-age setting is more relevant than a story set in a castle. The character E.T. is unattractive physically. He is unaggressive, benevolent, and charming. The film teaches something. The film teaches you to believe. You can reach out to a strange person in a strange land. The film has two heroes. One of the heroes is E.T. himself. The other hero is Elliott, the ten-year-old boy who finds and saves E.T. E.T. has been left behind by his spaceship. Elliott feels alone. His parents have separated. He finds a friend whom he can protect. The friend also provides him companionship. The film presents a conflict. The conflict is between the need to grow up and the desire to stay a child.

10

Using the Right Word

Choosing the right words to express ideas is a troublesome task for all writers and speakers. Part of the problem stems from the vast array of available words. The English language includes over a half-million words, and thousands of new ones are added every year. Of course, no one can master more than a small portion of the entire English vocabulary. But by reading widely, being curious about words, and carefully choosing the words that we use, we can communicate our ideas precisely and effectively.

What are the right words? They are the ones that keep the reader's interest; the wrong words distract or confuse. The right words are exact, fresh, vivid, and appropriate to the situation and audience. The wrong words are vague, inaccurate, stale, insincere, and inappropriate.

In this chapter we will look at some of the problems that writers face when searching for the right words and consider some of the ways to find them. In addition to this chapter, two other sources for advice on word choice that you should consult are Appendix A: A Glossary of Usage at the back of this book and a good college-level dictionary.

Vague Words Versus Specific Words

Much weak writing is caused by the overuse of vague and general words. Words and terms like *aspect, factors, kinds of things,* and *situations* have a tendency to crowd out the ideas in a paragraph just as weeds can overrun a garden.

Good writing, by contrast, uses exact and specific words and avoids those terms that are not clear to the reader. This does not mean that you should never use a general word. At times you will want to introduce a concept or topic whose exact meaning is not immediately clear. In those cases you will later have to clarify your meaning with specific and precise words that your reader understands. You should use the most specific or precise words possible when describing or discussing something that is important to your topic.

The two lists below make this principle clear. Notice the difference in meaning between the words in the left column and those in the right column.

General	*Specific*
car	Camaro
book	*The Godfather*
team	Atlanta Braves
illness	runny nose
disappointment	being jilted
food	a Big Mac with cheese

E X E R C I S E 1

Make a list of more specific words for each of the following general terms. For example, for *walk*, you could list *strut, trudge, slouch, slink, bounce, crawl, saunter, wiggle,* and so on. Use your dictionary or thesaurus if necessary.

say	look
cute	cute
beverage	smart
nice	excitement

Being Specific

Writing that is filled with too many vague or general expressions is useless. It leaves too many unanswered questions in the reader's mind. Consider the following sentence:

> Vicki's room is a real sight.

Were you able to see or imagine Vicki's room? What is "a real sight"? Here is a more concrete version:

> Vicki's room looks like the city dump.

This sentence is focused more sharply, but it can be improved by adding additional specific details:

> The floor of Vicki's room is strewn with soda bottles, dirty laundry, old magazines, and the remnants of several uneaten coffee cakes.

Now we have a better chance of imagining Vicki's room. The word choice is more exact, and we don't have to use our imagination as much.

Consider the following pairs of sentences. Notice how the first sentence in each pair has been improved by the use of specific words and details.

Vague: We had fun at the beach.
Specific: Last Sunday night we barbecued hamburgers at Sagamore Beach, played volleyball, and then sat around singing and telling ghost stories.

Vague: I have many responsibilities in my new job.
Specific: My duties in my new job as a clerk at Bond's Drug Store include opening up in the morning, sweeping out the store, delivering prescriptions in Mr. Bond's

	1955 Nash Rambler, and calling physicians to have requests for refills approved.
Vague:	She remembered many pleasant things about her home town.
Specific:	She remembered the Fourth of July parade down Washington Avenue, the Jewel Box in Forest Park, the view from the arch near the river, and the university where she had met her husband.

E X E R C I S E 2

Rewrite the following sentences, adding specific details and substituting exact words for any that are too vague.

1. My first day at college was really exciting.
2. Mr. Grissom did not like some of the duties connected with his new assignment.
3. Arlene's new residence overlooks a beautiful scene.
4. The doctor recommended a program of physical exercise and proper diet to cure Jerry's ailment.
5. The play's success was attributed to the performance of one of its actors.
6. Roberta's trip to Chicago was memorable for its many interesting events.
7. Several aspects of the president's tax program were regarded as inequitable by the opposition.
8. The critic's comments about the painting indicated his displeasure.
9. An animal was making a loud noise.
10. After doing our errands, we decided to have some fun.

Denotation and Connotation

To use the right word, you must be aware of its denotation and connotation. The *denotation* of a word is its dictionary meaning—the literal meaning that most readers would agree on. According to *The Random House Dictionary*, a "home" is "a house, apartment, or other place of residence." But "home" has other meanings, as well. Those meanings or associations are a word's *connotation:* what it suggests or implies in the reader's mind. "Home," for instance, may suggest childhood, family memories, a sense of belonging, and other comforting thoughts.

The meaning of a word is affected by its connotations and by its context—the way it is used in a particular passage. Consider, for instance, the following: *associate, buddy, confederate, confidant.* They all denote essentially the same thing, but each word has a special connotation and therefore a different meaning:

associate—The connotation is of a somewhat formal business relationship.

buddy—This word implies a pal.

confederate—This implies a co-conspirator in a plan or scheme.

confidant—This suggests a person who knows our secrets.

To speak of a businessperson and her "confederates," therefore, would be to suggest that they were engaged in illegal activities: "associates," on the other hand, would imply a more savory relationship. For the unsuspecting user of "confederates," the wrong meaning would be implied.

Words can be correct in one situation but inappropriate in another because of their connotations. A well-known sequence of sentences makes this point clear:

I am determined.

You are stubborn.

He is pig-headed.

Each means essentially the same thing, but most of us would probably prefer to be known as "determined" because of its "flavor" or connotation, particularly when contrasted with "stubborn" or pig-headed."

E X E R C I S E 3

Find the inappropriate word in each of the following sentences and replace it with a word with the right denotation.

1. Mother Teresa is notorious for her work with the poor and sick in India.
2. Because he did not know either party, the arbitrator was able to take an uninterested view of the dispute.
3. The businessperson has upheld a reputation for deception and deceit.
4. This restaurant is infamous for its tasty food, prompt service, and reasonable prices.
5. Through the use of cunning and guile, Heidi gave a successful surprise party for her husband.

The connotation of a word includes the feelings or associations that surround it or that it evokes. A "clunker" and a "hot rod" denote the same thing: automobile. But "clunker" suggests an older car badly in need of repair, while "hot rod" evokes a picture of a "souped up" or modified car that has been maintained by its youthful owner. Similarly, "children" and "offspring" have essentially the same denotation, but differ in their connotation. "Children" is more personal, and perhaps suggest more affection; "offspring" is neutral and carries a biological nuance.

E X E R C I S E 4

Each of the words below has a standard denotation as well as a common connotation. Using your dictionary when necessary, explain the denotation and connotation of each.

gay	cohort
square	tight
collaborator	child
chick	black
dogma	dog

Clichés

Good writing uses lively and original words and phrases. It avoids *clichés*, which are worn out, tired expressions that have lost their impact because they have been overused.

The first person who wrote or said "This is a tempest in a teapot" or "That's water under the bridge" was using his or her imagination. But having been repeated untold millions of times, both expressions have lost their original punch and now suggest only that their users are too lazy to think up fresh ways to express their thoughts. Users of clichés think they are saying something meaningful; in fact, they're just making noise.

Here is a list of clichés often heard on college campuses and elsewhere. See if you recognize any of your favorites.

acid test	in the nick of time
a crying shame	on the ball
after all is said and done	one in a million
all work and no play	out of sight

as luck would have it
at a loss for words
beating around the bush
better late than never
the bitter end
blushing bride
in broad daylight
bored to death
the bottom line
burn the midnight oil
busy as a bee
by leaps and bounds
cool as a cucumber
at the crack of dawn
doing your own thing
easier said than done
fit to be tied
for better or worse
green with envy
hard as a rock
high as a kite
heartfelt thanks
in all its glory
in this day and age
last but not least
light as a feather
mother nature
neat as a pin

needless to say
pave the way
picture of health
point with pride
the powers that be
pretty as a picture
pride and joy
quick as a flash
ripe old age
sadder but wiser
sharp as a tack
short and sweet
slept like a log
slow but sure
tell it like it is
tried and true
under the weather
uphill battle
view with alarm
water over the dam
water under the bridge
wend our way
where it's at
white as snow
without further ado
work like a horse
worth its weight in gold
young in spirit

As you can see, clichés are everywhere—we are all guilty of using them. You cannot purge them completely for all speech or writing, but you can reduce your reliance on them. First, be suspicious of phrases that come to your mind too quickly and patly—expressions like "straight from the shoulder," "beat a hasty retreat," and so on. Second, search for your own original phrases and words to express *your* ideas—not those that were coined years ago. By becoming aware of clichés and the ease with which you can be seduced by them, you can reduce your reliance on them.

E X E R C I S E 5

Rewrite each of the following sentences, using specific and fresh language to replace any clichés.

1. The pay that she receives is a mere drop in the bucket.
2. The batter walked to the plate, cool as a cucumber.
3. I try to save enough for a rainy day.
4. Money doesn't grow on trees, you know.
5. He will have to burn the midnight oil if he wants to finish his essay in the nick of time.
6. I'm sure there's a method to your madness, but it's over my head.
7. After his date with Helen, he avoided her like the plague.
8. Rachel caught the football and in the twinkling of an eye, she was gone.
9. Mary left the examination room, sadder but wiser.
10. He boasted that he told it like it is without beating around the bush.

Euphemisms and Pretentious Writing

One of the deadly enemies of clear writing is insincerity and phoniness. Euphemisms and pretentious word choice contribute to these vices. A *euphemism* is a word or expression used to avoid a word with unpleasant or painful associations. Some euphemisms are acceptable; just think what "to make love" or "to go to the bathroom" spares us. But euphemisms can be used to mislead or to magnify. Thus, janitors are sometimes called "sanitary engineers" and used-car salesmen become "transportation counselors."

Pretentious writing makes something trivial or plain seem very important or complicated. The result is often a series of hollow words or sentences that disguise commonplace ideas. Here is a typical example of pretentious writing; it was written by Talcott Parsons, a famous American sociologist:

> The problem of order, and thus of the nature of the integration of stable systems of social interaction, that is, of social structure, thus focuses on the integration of the motivation of actors with the normative cultural standards which integrate the action system, in our context interpersonally. These standards are, in the terms used in the preceding chapter, patterns of value-orientation, and as such are a particularly crucial part of the cultural tradition of the social system.

This passage is pretentious because it disguises a somewhat obvious idea. Parsons is attempting to say that people who share standards expect one another to stick to them; to the extent they do, their society will be orderly.

Euphemisms and pretentious writing overlap in many cases;

both should be avoided because they mislead the reader by masking the writer's real meaning and intention. Euphemisms and pretentious writing are used in advertising, bureaucratic publications, and statements by politicians when the writer or speaker wants to gloss over an unpleasant truth or magnify something unimportant. As in the case of clichés, everyone occasionally uses them because of their easy availability.

The following list contains some examples of euphemisms and pretentious phrases. The meaning of each term is in parentheses. See if you can add examples to the list.

adult entertainment (dirty movies)
orderly withdrawal (retreat)
facial blemishes (pimples)
the disadvantaged (the poor)
custodian (janitor)
viable alternative (choice)
modification (change)
dentures (false teeth)
correctional officer (prison guard)
prioritize (arrange)
reprioritize (rearrange)
sanitation engineer (garbage collector)
domestic (maid or butler)
passed on, laid to rest, met his or her Maker (died)
detention center (jail)
culturally deprived environment (slum)
members of a career offender cartel (gangsters)
counter-factual propositions (lies)
misspeak (lie)
fair trade (price-fixing)
down-sized car (small car)
bathroom tissue (toilet paper)
to suffer irregularity (to be constipated)
radiation enhancement device (neutron bomb)
pacification of the enemy infrastructure (attacking an enemy village)
a combat emplacement evacuator (shovel)
aerodynamic personnel decelerator (parachute)
antipersonnel detonating devices (bombs)
revenue enhancement (a tax increase)
engage in the decision making process (decide)
parameters (limits)
interface (meet)
at this point in time (now)

E X E R C I S E 6

Here are some sentences containing euphemisms and pretentious writing. Reword them if you can, using direct and clear language.

1. "We believe it is in the interest of international stability and the American people to avoid the tendency that we have experienced on occasions in the past to rush to summitry for summitry's sake and to bring about euphoric expectations and then to dash that euphoria against the rocks of ill-prepared summitry." *(From a statement by former Secretary of State Alexander Haig)*

2. "To draw a link from cost-effectiveness studies to realized human potential is a payoff for internal business management just as important as the impact such cost savings studies and their results have on the taxpaying clientele of the District. The single endeavor, in this case a cost-effectiveness improvement project, realizes both an internal necessity for responsible management *viz-à-viz* evaluation and an external necessity for accountability." *(From a letter written by a school administrator)*

3. "Stamps in this book have been gummed with a matte finish adhesive which permits the elimination of the separation tissues." *(From a publication of the U.S. Postal Service)*

4. "The findings of ongoing research have shown that a number of physiological effects occur under conditions of noise exposure. These studies demonstrate that noise exposure does influence bodily changes, such as the so-called vegetative functions, by inhibition of gastric juices, lowered skin resistance, modified pulse rate and increased metabolism." *(From a document published by the Federal Aviation Administration)*

5. "We were not micromanaging Grenada intelligencewise until about that time frame." *(From a statement by Admiral Wesley L. McDonald, United States Navy)*

Levels of Usage

At times you might be Jimmy Johnson; at other times, you are Jim Johnson, James Johnson, or even Mister James Johnson. The *situation*, in other words, determines how you will be presented to the world. So, too, with the kinds of words you use in writing. As noted in Chapter 2, we have different "voices," which can range from the intimate and slangy to the highly impersonal and formal. Your word choice should reflect the voice you have chosen for that particular writing situation, just as your choice of clothing suggests the way you want to be viewed in a particular social situation. The dictionary can suggest the status or level of many words, but in most cases, you will have to decide what the correct word is yourself.

Your attitude toward your audience and your subject will also determine the level of your diction or word choice. If you have ever told a traffic judge how you were driving and then retold the story to your friends, you already understand the importance of the audience, the situation, and the subject in the selection of the words you use. This principle can also be seen at work in the letters written by Chris to his friend and parents in Chapter 3 (pages 36–37).

When writing or speaking to your superiors or to public figures or in formal situations, a formal tone and diction is appropriate. However, in essays and other college writing, an informal level of diction is best. When talking to close friends in informal social situations, a mixture of informal diction and slang can be suitable. The following sequence, which ranges from the most formal to the most informal, illustrates the range of options available to you and suggests how an idea can be modified according to the audience and situation.

> The occasion was most delightful.
>
> The evening was enjoyable.
>
> We had a good time.
>
> We had a fantastic time!
>
> We had a ball!

Slang

Everybody uses slang. It adds a dash of humor and "hipness" to speech and gives its user a chance to be different. Slang is also a symbol of being a member of an "in group." But there are two problems with slang. First, it usually doesn't last long, becoming outdated within a few weeks or months. Words like *chick* and *heavy*, for example, were once popular but now seem headed for oblivion. The other problem with slang is that it quickly loses any precise meaning. Ask several friends what "bad" or "cool" means *exactly*, and you will see that slang terms are usually vague and general. For these reasons it is best to limit slang to informal conversation and to avoid it in serious writing.

When we forget or ignore the audience or situation, we can make some inappropriate word choices. Notice how jarring the conclusion of the following sentence sounds because its writer ignored this principle.

> The trustees of the National Gallery of Art announced reluctantly that electronic-monitoring devices will be installed at all exits of the museum because a painting by the Dutch artist Rembrandt was ripped off.

Informal English

Informal English is the level of language used in most college writing. It is more casual than Standard English but more precise and formal than slang. It is the language of magazine articles and newspaper and television stories, as well as most classroom lectures. It uses slang to achieve a humorous or ironic tone, but never at the risk of destroying the overall tone of the sentence or passage.

Informal English often uses contractions but avoids an excessive "slangy" or conversational tone. As you can sense, Informal English is hard to define precisely. It uses a variety of expressions and words to achieve its effect, but never in excess. It strives for a middle level of diction, the normal level for most college writing.

Standard English

At the other end of the spectrum from slang in terms of formality is Standard English. One student described the relationship between Standard English and slang as similar to that of a formal tuxedo and blue jeans. Standard English is more dignified and serious; it avoids slang and uses contractions (*it's, doesn't* and so on) sparingly. This does not mean that Standard English is stiff, wooden, or pretentious. It *does* mean that it is used on those occasions when precision and accuracy and a formal tone are required. Although it doesn't have to use long words, Standard English uses more words of Greek and Latin origin than slang or Informal English does.

As in the case of slang, Standard English can sound ridiculous when the situation or audience is not appropriate. Notice, for example, how pompous the following excerpt sounds:

> Summoning his courage and clearing his throat, Ralph said nervously, "Gee, Wanda, I'd sure like to osculate you. If that offends you, I'd settle for some interdigitation."

If you were Wanda, what would your response be?

The following pairs of words suggest the difference between Standard English and Informal English.

Standard	Informal
inebriated	drunk
disclaim	deny
initiate	start
vacillate	hesitate
cogitate	think
imbibe	drink
discard	throw away

E X E R C I S E 7

Read the following three paragraphs carefully. Which one is written in slang, which in Informal English, and which in Standard English? Notice the differences in word choice, particularly in the use of personal pronouns, contractions, passive voice, and level of diction. Which one is more specific? Which one is easier to read? What would be the proper situation for each paragraph? For example, would the first one be suitable for reading to a convention of psychiatrists?

1. So okay, you say, these loonies don't have any known disease, but I know a loose bolt when I see one. Be careful, brother, there are lots of other people that would say the same about you. There are lots of shrinks who are oddballs, but they're calling the shots on deciding who gets locked up.

2. When I raise my arm there is some corresponding change in my brain. When I see the stars on a winter's night, there's a corresponding action or reaction in my thinking equipment. If I were to strip and run down the street shouting "Eureka," having just discovered my navel, for example, there'd likewise be a corresponding condition in my head. Discovering how these physical and mental events are correlated is an interesting process, I suppose. But the fact that some mental conditions are unusual doesn't mean they're sick.

3. Every physical action may at least in principle be correlated with some set of neuro-chemical factors. This is not to say, however, that such factors initiate my behavior in the first instance, or that the correlation explains the behavior. Nor is the designation of such behavior as a manifestation of mental illness justified merely by the aberrant nature of the behavior and our social judgment of same.

E X E R C I S E 8

Using your dictionary if necessary, arrange the expressions in each of the following groups in order from the most informal to the most formal.

1. drunk; inebriated; loaded
2. improverished; poor; broke
3. shrewd; perspicacious; sharp
4. kisser; countenance; face
5. kids; children; descendants
6. guy; individual; man

 7. thrills; kicks; gratification
 8. investigate; pry; sneak
 9. pooped; exhausted; tired
10. pedagogue; prof; teacher

E X E R C I S E 9

Rewrite the following sentences, replacing any words that are not appropriate.

1. Despite the preparations and rehearsals, the master of ceremonies screwed up the winners' names.
2. We rented a summer cottage for the entire family. It was near the lake, clean, inexpensive, and roomy. My husband complained that it was inadequately fenestrated, however.
3. In recent years several excellent films have been written and produced for the idiot box.
4. Carl Sagan's popularity stems, in part, from the guy's ability to explain his abstract scientific concepts to his viewers and readers.
5. The speaker made a series of smart-aleck remarks that indicated his refusal to treat seriously the inquiries of the audience.

E X E R C I S E 10

Select one of the situations below and write it in three different versions: first, in slang; next, in Informal English; finally, in Standard English. Write about five or six sentences for each version.

1. a description of a drunk crossing the street
2. a summary of the plot of a movie you have seen recently
3. welcoming remarks to three groups of visitors to your campus: the Governor of your state and his aides; students from another college; a group of jazz musicians
4. the benefits of living in a dorm
5. what to listen for in music.

CHAPTER

11

Writing the Term Paper

Writing the term paper is an extension of the skills and techniques you have learned in the preceding chapters of *Writing for College*. In fact, it is often the "grand finale" of writing courses because it is the last major assignment in many composition classes.

If you do not understand its benefits and purposes, writing the term paper can be a frustrating and discouraging task. If you approach it in the right way, however, it will be an exciting and informative experience.

What Is the Term Paper?

Whether it is called a research paper, reference paper, library paper, or term paper, it typically presents the results of the writer's investigation on a specific topic. It can range from 1,500 to 3,000 words, or approximately six to twelve typewritten pages. As presented in this chapter, the paper follows the guidelines set forth in the Modern Language Association *MLA Handbook for Writers of Research Papers, Theses, and Dissertations* (1984), which reflects the practices required by most college instructors throughout the United States and Canada. Some instructors, particularly those in the social sciences and physical sciences, want their students to follow the guidelines in the *Publication Manual of the American Psychological Association* (1983). Although the styles of the two publications are similar, most instructors prefer the *MLA Handbook*, the model followed in this chapter.

The term paper written for most composition classes will usually be one of two kinds: a report or a thesis paper. A *report* is essentially a survey of facts and opinions; because it is primarily expository, it does not offer an argument. Rather, it relates facts to inform the reader, usually from a fresh point of view.

The *thesis* paper does considerably more. It argues a point by presenting and evaluating facts to persuade the reader to accept a particular hypothesis or to take a certain course of action.

If you are writing a report, your instructor does not want a collection of quotations and paraphrases that you have pasted together which do not represent your own conclusions. If it is a thesis paper, he or she does not expect you to present a brilliant new solution to a problem or the answer to an age-old question that has troubled scholars. In both cases what your instructor *does* expect is a studious inquiry into a subject in which you evaluate and interpret information and offer your audience evidence to support a thesis or point of view.

The Benefits of the Term Paper

Because term papers require you to locate and investigate sources of information other than your opinion or personal knowledge, you will derive several benefits from the assignment. The most obvious is that you will learn a great deal about a topic that interests you. This means that you will learn how to find information in the library (and sometimes find information that is *not* in the library). You will learn to evaluate, summarize, and synthesize a large body of material, reading it analytically and critically and presenting it in an organized and readable form, documenting your sources in acceptable style.

Writing term papers has some long-range benefits as well. After learning research techniques, you will be able to identify a problem, process information, and develop the skills of critical thinking. These are all benefits that can be used after you have finished college. And, of course, there is the sense of accomplishment that comes from doing a challenging job to the best of your ability.

Choosing and Limiting a Topic

The first step in writing the term paper is choosing and limiting your topic. Of course, if your instructor has assigned your topic, that step has been taken care of for you. But if you are given the responsibility for determining your topic, you are immediately faced with some opportunities as well as dangers. We will consider both.

The best topic for a term paper is usually one that you are interested in and want to learn more about. It could be a subject that was mentioned in a class lecture, or something that has been on your mind and has aroused your curiosity. It might be a subject that has been written about in magazines and newspapers. Or it might be related to a hobby or interest that you have. But what if you can't think of a topic? You might try the following techniques.

One of the best sources of topics for a term paper is the *Library of Congress Subject Headings*, a large, red, two-volume set usually found near the card catalog in most libraries. It is the standard guide used by most libraries to catalog books according to the Library of Congress system. It lists subjects as they appear in the card catalog, as well as related headings and subtopics. By glancing through its pages you will see hundreds of possible topics that you might want to investigate in your term paper. When you find a topic that interests you, you can look in the card catalog to see whether your library has books on it.

Here is a very small excerpt from the hundreds of topics listed under "Environment" in the *Library of Congress Subject Headings*.

Library of Congress Subject Headings.

Environment
  See Acclimatization
      Adaptation (Biology)
      Anthropo-geography
      Ecology
      Euthenics
      Human ecology
      Man—Influence of environment
      Man—Influence on nature
      Nature and nurture
      subdivision Environmental aspects
          under special subjects, e.g.
          Agricultural chemicals—
          Environmental aspects; Atomic
          power-plants—Environmental
          aspects; *and headings beginning with
          the word* Environmental
Environment, College
  See College environment
Environment, High school
  See High school environment
Environment, Human
  See Human ecology
Environment, School
  See School environment
Environment, Space
  See Space environment
Environment (Art) *(Direct)*
  xx Art, Modern—20th century
      Assemblage (Art)
Environment and mass media
  See Mass media and the environment
Environment and state
  See Environmental policy
Environment simulation (Teaching method)
  See Simulated environment (Teaching
      method)
Environment testing
  See Environmental testing
Environmental control
  See Environmental engineering
      Environmental law
      Environmental policy
Environmental education
  See Conservation of natural resources—
      Study and teaching
      Ecology—Study and teaching
      Human ecology—Study and teaching
Environmental effects
  See Environmental engineering
Environmental engineering
  sa Electric power-plants—Environmental
      aspects
      Environmental health
      Environmental policy

Environmental protection
Environmental testing
Extraterrestrial bases
Human engineering
Life support systems (Space
    environment)
Motor-trucks—Environmental aspects
Noise control
Petroleum chemicals industry—
    Environmental aspects
Pollution
Sanitary engineering
Space simulators
subdivision Influence of environment
    under subjects, e.g. United States.
    Army—Ordnance and ordnance
    stores—Influence of environment
  x Environmental control
      Environmental effects
      Environmental management
      Environmental stresses
  xx Design, Industrial
      Engineering
      Engineering meteorology
      Environmental health
      Environmental protection
      Pollution
      Testing
— Computer programs
— Information services *(Direct)*
— Research *(Direct)*
— Research grants *(Direct)*
— Vocational guidance
      See Environmental engineering as a
          profession
Environmental engineering (Buildings)
  sa Air conditioning
      Architectural acoustics
      Buildings—Vibration
      Clean rooms
      Heating
      Interior decoration
      Lighting
      Sanitation, Household
      Ventilation
  x Buildings—Environmental engineering
  xx Architecture
      Building
      Sanitation, Household
— Problems, exercises, etc.
— Tables, calculations, etc.
Environmental engineering as a profession
  x Environmental engineering—Vocational
      guidance

Another source of topics is the encyclopedia. The *Columbia Encyclopedia* and *The Random House Encyclopedia* are both single volumes and are therefore convenient for a random search for an interesting topic. By looking over the pages of either encyclopedia, you will come across many suggestions for further investigation.

Your textbooks can often yield topics for term papers. Suggestions for research are often placed at the end of chapters or units, and the table of contents will often give you some ideas.

There are certain kinds of topics to avoid as you make your choice. The first is a topic on which your library has no books or articles. This is not likely to be a problem if you have access to a major university library; smaller libraries with limited holdings, however, may lack enough material for some topics. Another topic to avoid is the "single-source" topic—one that could be exhausted by consulting only one book. An example is the biography of a famous person. The life of former President Lyndon B. Johnson, for instance, could easily be derived from a single book, but a comparison of his first hundred days in office with the first hundred days of Franklin Delano Roosevelt's first term would be based on several sources.

Be careful, too, of topics that have become clichés. Examples include the effect of television on violence, the debate over capital punishment, and the history of jazz. These are painfully familiar to most experienced instructors and will possibly evoke little more than a yawn. On the other hand, don't select a topic that is so new that no books have been written on it yet. It is doubtful, for example, that you could find many books on the foreign policy of Konstantin Chernenko, the Premier of the U.S.S.R.

You must be careful that your topic is specific enough to be covered in a paper of the length assigned. The suggestions for narrowing a topic given in Chapter 3 apply to term-paper topics as well. Some of the steps you took to select your topic will also be helpful in further narrowing it. For example, the *Library of Congress Subject Headings*, because it divides and subdivides topics, can help you narrow your topic to manageable proportions. The index of an encyclopedia will often list subtopics of a larger subject that are suitable for a paper.

Other ways to narrow the topic include studying the subheadings of the topic in the card catalog of your library, the *Reader's Guide to Periodical Literature*, and *The New York Times Index*. All of these break topics up into additional subtopics that are often narrow enough for a term paper.

Determining Your Purpose and Audience

If your term paper is a report, your purpose will be to inform your audience by presenting information on a topic. Knowing something about your audience will determine the kind of information you include and the way you present it. What can you expect your readers to know already about your topic? What terms or concepts will you have to define or explain? By keeping your audience in mind as you write, you will make your paper clearer and more informative.

If your paper argues a point—if your purpose is to persuade the reader—you will have to investigate and present the claims and arguments of your opposition. By confronting the opposition, you will impress skeptical readers and convince your audience that you are fair and informed. (See pages 144–45 in Chapter 7, "Writing the Persuasive Essay.")

Writing a Thesis Statement

When you have narrowed your topic, you will be ready to determine your preliminary thesis, the main point you hope to make in your paper. Notice that it is *preliminary;* you will probably change it as you read further, enlarging or restricting its scope as you develop new information and ideas.

The value of knowing your thesis now—even if it is only preliminary—is that it will steer you away from books and articles that will not be useful and toward those that will be helpful in writing your paper. You will be able to select only those items that contribute to your central idea, and ignore those that are off the subject. Most of the ideas in Chapter 3 for developing the thesis statement apply to the term paper, with one exception: because of its length and complexity, the thesis of the term paper may be several sentences long. Its purpose, however, is the same: to give your paper a focus.

Your thesis statement will reflect the purpose of your term paper. If you are writing a *report*, you may wish to relate facts and clear up any superficial or erroneous notions about a subject that is unfamiliar or unknown to most of your readers. The following thesis statement would be appropriate for this kind of paper: "The feminist movement has it roots in the nineteenth-century suffragettes." The purpose implied in this statement is to inform the reader of the existence and activities of those predecessors of today's feminist leaders and to show the link between them.

If you are writing a *thesis* paper, you will probably attempt to argue a point or defend a particular hypothesis in order to persuade your reader. The following thesis reflects this kind of paper: "The Social Security system must be revised drastically to prevent it from going bankrupt." Such a statement is designed to encourage the reader to accept the writer's argument.

You don't have to worry about the precise wording of your thesis statement at this stage. The main thing is to have a reasonably clear idea of where you are heading. By knowing what the point of your paper is, you will be better able to determine the worth of the books and articles you find in the next step: the search strategy.

The Search Strategy: Gathering Material

Too many students lose time "spinning their wheels" in confusion in the library as they try to find books and articles dealing with the topic of their term paper. They do not realize that by following a "search strategy"—a step-by-step process of collecting and evaluating information—they can not only save time, but also find the most useful and relevant information on their topic. In that sense the search strategy preceding the writing of the term paper is comparable to the prewriting stage when one writes an essay. In both cases the time spent searching for material and ideas is one of the most essential steps in the writing process. The search strategy explained here is an organized and systematic plan in which you move from general to more specific information. If you follow this sequence you will find the material you need with a minimum of difficulty and make the best use of your time.

You will notice that the search strategy takes you first to the reference section or room of your library. This—and *not* the card catalog, as many students think—is the best place to look for information for your term paper. By beginning with encyclopedias and the other general reference works listed below, you will have an overview of your subject and see its relationship to other topics. Then you can consult the card catalog, periodical and newspaper indexes, and more specialized sources.

Here are the basic steps in the search strategy, followed by an explanation of each step.

1. Consult a general or special encyclopedia for an overview of your topic. Look for bibliographies at the end of the encyclopedia article or for recommended readings.

2. If appropriate, consult biographical reference works, atlases, gazetteers, yearbooks, and subject dictionaries associated with your topic.
3. Use the bibliographies from the above sources to begin your search for books by author or title in the card catalog. Use the *Library of Congress Subject Headings* to find the subject headings for your topic in the card catalog.
4. Use relevant terms found in the encyclopedias, dictionaries, and other reference works in periodical and newspaper indexes for journal article citations.

Encyclopedias

The best place to start your background reading is the encyclopedia. Although your instructor will not want you to quote from it in your term paper, the encyclopedia will give you an overview of your topic and provide plenty of leads for further reading.

When looking for information in the encyclopedia, always consult the index first. The index will list two kinds of entries: those subjects that have a separate article, and those subjects covered in the encyclopedia but as part of another entry.

At the end of most encyclopedia articles you will find a list of books and articles on the topic. These are very helpful because they guide you to other reliable sources of information. Look over the bibliographies and make a note of those titles that sound interesting and promising. On a separate card for each, write *the author's name, the title of the article or book*, and *the facts of publication*. These cards (called *bibliography cards*) will form the basis of the list of books and articles that you must turn in with your term paper. (See pages 247–8 for examples of bibliography cards for magazines and books.)

General Encyclopedias

These give a summary of what is known on a subject, as well as bibliographies. They are the best place to start. Always use the most recent edition.

The Encyclopedia Americana. 30 vols. New York: Grolier, 1982. It is particularly useful for its articles on science and mathematics, as well as for its biographies. Volume 30 is the index.

Encyclopaedia Britannica. 30 vols. Chicago: Encyclopaedia Britannica, 1980. The most scholarly of the general encyclopedias, it is divided into three sections: (1) the *Propaedia,* a one-volume index;

(2) the *Micropaedia,* a ten-volume set of short articles; and (3) the *Macropaedia,* a nineteen-volume set of longer, detailed articles.

Collier's Encyclopedia. 24 vols. New York: Crowell-Collier, 1981. The articles are less detailed and usually briefer than those in the above encyclopedias, but easier to read. Volume 24 is the index.

New Columbia Encyclopedia. 1 vol. New York: Columbia University Press, 1975. This is a reliable one-volume reference work that will give you condensed information on a topic.

Random House Encyclopedia. 1 vol. New York: Random House, 1977. Like the encyclopedia above, this is a reliable desk encyclopedia designed for quick reference.

Specialized Encyclopedias and Dictionaries

These are reference works that cover just one area of knowledge. The following list below is merely a sampler; special encyclopedias are available for almost every important subject. To find the encyclopedia you need, check the latest edition of Eugene P. Sheehy's *Guide to Reference Books,* available in most libraries. Like the general encyclopedias listed above, special encyclopedias and dictionaries have bibliographies and lists of recommended readings. As you look at them, make a bibliography card for each title that looks helpful. Be sure to include the name of the author and publisher on the card so that you can locate them easily.

THE ARTS

Encyclopedia of World Art. 15 vols. New York: McGraw-Hill, 1968.

Lucas, Edna Louise. *Art Books: A Basic Bibliography on the Fine Arts.* Greenwich, Conn.: New York Graphic Society, 1968.

Maillard, Robert, ed. *New Dictionary of Modern Sculpture.* Trans. Bettina Wadia. New York: Tudor, 1971.

Myers, Bernard S. *Encyclopedia of Painting.* New York: Crown, 1955.

New Grove Dictionary of Music and Musicians. 20 vols. Washington, D.C.: Grove's Dictionaries of Music, 1980.

BUSINESS

Buell, Victor P., ed. *Handbook of Modern Marketing.* New York: McGraw-Hill, 1970.

Graham, Irwin. *Encyclopedia of Advertising.* 2nd ed. New York: Fairchild, 1969.

Lazarus, Harold. *American Business Directory.* New York: Philosophical Library, 1957.

Munn, Glenn G. *Encyclopedia of Banking and Finance.* 7th ed. Ed. Ferdinand L. Garcia. Boston: Bankers, 1973.

Sloan, Harold S., and Arnold Zurcher. *A Dictionary of Economics.* 5th ed. New York: Barnes & Noble, 1970.

HISTORY

Adams, James T. *Dictionary of American History.* 6 vols. New York: Charles Scribner's Sons, 1963.

American Historical Association: Guide to Historical Literature. New York: Macmillan, 1961.

Commager, Henry Steele. *Documents of American History.* 9th ed. 2 vols. New York: Appleton-Century-Crofts, 1973.

Friedl, Frank, ed. *Harvard Guide to American History.* Cambridge: Belknap Press of Harvard University Press, 1974.

Hodge, Frederick W. *Handbook of American Indians North of Mexico.* 2 vols. Washington, D.C.: Government Printing Office, 1910.

Martin, Michael R., *et al. An Encyclopedia of Latin-American History.* Indianapolis: Bobbs-Merrill, 1968.

Miller, Elizabeth. *The Negro in America: A Bibliography.* Cambridge: Harvard University Press, 1970.

LITERATURE

Baugh, Albert C., *et al.*, eds. *Literary History of England.* 2nd ed. 4 vols. New York: Appleton-Century-Crofts, 1967.

Blanck, Jacob N. *Bibliography of American Literature.* 6 vols. New Haven: Yale University Press, 1973.

Hart, James D. *The Oxford Companion to American Literature.* New York: Oxford University Press, 1965.

Harvey, Paul. *The Oxford Companion to English Literature.* New York: Oxford University Press, 1967.

Spiller, Robert, *et al. Literary History of the United States.* 4th ed. 2 vols. New York: Macmillan, 1974.

Watson, George, ed. *Cambridge Bibliography of English Literature.* 5 vols. Cambridge University Press, 1965.

MUSIC AND DANCE

Apel, Willi. *The Harvard Dictionary of Music.* 2nd rev. ed. Cambridge: Harvard University Press, 1969.

Blom, Eric. *Everyman's Dictionary of Music.* New York: New American Library, 1973.

Chujoy, Anatole, and P. W. Manchester. *The Dance Encyclopedia.* New York: Simon and Schuster, 1967.

Stambler, Irwin. *Encyclopedia of Pop, Rock, and Soul.* New York: St. Martin's, 1977.

Thompson, Oscar. *International Cyclopedia of Music and Musicians.* 10th ed. New York: Dodd, Mead, 1975.

RELIGION AND PHILOSOPHY

Buttrick, George A., ed. *The Interpreter's Dictionary of the Bible.* 5 vols. New York: Abingdon, 1976.

The Catholic Encyclopedia. 18 vols. New York: Thomas Nelson, 1976.

Edwards, Paul, ed. *The Encyclopedia of Philosophy.* 4 vols. New York: Macmillan, 1973.

Fern, Vergilius, ed. *An Encyclopedia of Religion.* Westport, Conn.: Greenwood Press, 1976.

Roth, Cecil, ed. *The New Standard Jewish Encyclopedia.* 5th ed. New rev. ed. edited by Geoffrey Wigoder. Garden City, N.Y.: Doubleday, 1977.

SOCIAL SCIENCES

Beigel, Hugo G. *A Dictionary of Psychology and Related Fields.* New York: Frederick Ungar, 1974.

Kreslins, Janis A., ed. *Foreign Affairs Bibliography.* New York: R. R. Bowker, 1976.

McGraw-Hill Dictionary of Modern Economics. New York: McGraw-Hill, 1973.

Mitchell, G. Duncan, ed. *A Dictionary of Sociology.* Chicago: Aldine, 1967.

Sills, David L., ed. *International Encyclopedia of the Social Sciences.* 8 vols. New York: Free Press, 1977.

White, Carl M., *et al. Sources of Information in the Social Sciences: A Guide to the Literature.* 2nd ed. Chicago: American Library Association, 1973.

SCIENCES

Fairbridge, Rhodes W., ed. *The Encyclopedia of Oceanography.* New York: Van Nostrand Reinhold, 1966.

Gray, Peter. *The Encyclopedia of Biological Sciences.* 2nd ed. New York: Van Nostrand Reinhold, 1970.

Hampel, Clifford A., and Gessner G. Hawley, eds. *The Encyclopedia of Chemistry,* 3rd ed. New York: Van Nostrand Reinhold, 1973.

The International Dictionary of Physics and Electronics. 2nd ed. Princeton, N.J.: Van Nostrand Reinhold, 1961.

Lapedes, Daniel N., ed. *The McGraw-Hill Encyclopedia of Science and Technology.* New York: McGraw-Hill, 1977.

Thewlis, J., ed. *Encyclopaedic Dictionary of Physics.* 9 vols. Elmsford, N.Y.: Pergamon, 1971.

ENGLISH LANGUAGE

The Oxford English Dictionary. 13 vols. plus supplements. New York: Oxford University Press, 1933–76.

Webster's Third New International Dictionary of the English Language. Springfield, Mass.: G. & C. Merriam, 1981.

Biographical Works, Atlases, Gazetteers, and Other Reference Works

Biographical Reference Works

Although your instructor may not allow you to write a term paper based on the life of a person, you may find it necessary to consult biographical reference works.

FOR LIVING PEOPLE

American Men and Women of Science. 12th ed. 8 vols. New York: R. R. Bowker, 1971.

Contemporary Authors. 44 vols. Detroit: Gale, 1965–73.

Current Biography. New York: H. W. Wilson, published annually since 1940.

Who's Who in America. 2 vols. Chicago: Marquis Who's Who, published biennially since 1899.

Who's Who of American Women. Chicago: Marquis Who's Who, published biennially since 1958.

FOR PEOPLE NO LONGER LIVING

Dictionary of American Biography. 20 vols. plus supplements. New York: Charles Scribner's Sons, 1928–50.

Dictionary of National Biography (British). 22 vols. plus supplements. London: Smith, Elder, published annually since 1908.

Atlases and Gazetteers

An atlas is a bound collection of maps; a gazetteer is a geographical dictionary.

Atlas of American History. Ed. Edward W. Fox. New York: Scribner's, 1978.

Encyclopaedia Britannica World Atlas International. Chicago: Encyclopaedia Britannica, 1974.

Goode's World Atlas. 16th ed. Chicago: Rand McNally, 1983.

National Geographic Atlas of the World. 4th ed. Washington, D.C.: National Geographic Society, 1981.

The New York Times Atlas of the World. New York: Times Books, 1981.

Rand-McNally Cosmopolitan World Atlas. Rev. ed. Chicago: Rand McNally, 1971.

The Times Atlas of the World. New York: Times Books, 1980.

Almanacs and Yearbooks

These are published annually and record information about the previous year: charts, lists, facts, statistics, and dates on a variety of subjects.

Britannica Book of the Year. Chicago: Encyclopaedia Britannica, published annually since 1938.

Facts on File Yearbook. New York: Facts on File, published annually since 1940.

World Almanac and Book of Facts. New York: Newspaper Enterprise Association, published annually since 1868.

The Card Catalog

By this time you have accumulated several leads for finding material for your topic. You have read articles in the general and specialized encyclopedias and other reference works. You have looked over the bibliographies and lists of recommended readings in those reference works, noting on separate cards the titles of those that sounded helpful, following the style of the sample bibliographical cards on pages 247–48.

Now you are ready to go to the card catalog to find those books you have noted and to find other books on your subject.

The card catalog contains an alphabetical listing for every book in the library. Some libraries' card catalogs are now stored on computers, but most libraries still retain their paper catalog too. Libraries differ in what they include in the card catalog. For example, some list books and journals; others list books, journals, and phonograph records; and some list only books. Each book is listed on at least three separate cards: by its *author*, by its *title*, and by its *subject*. Each card contains the same information, except that the title card has the book title at the top and the subject card lists the subject at the top of the card. (See page 241 for examples of the three types of cards.)

Libraries that have "divided" catalogs place the author and title cards together alphabetically in one section and the subject cards in another. Libraries that have "dictionary" catalogs combine all three—author, title, and subject—into a single alphabet.

Author cards. Author cards are arranged alphabetically under the author's last name (Arendt, Hannah). If the author has written more than one book, the author cards are arranged alphabetically by title under the author's name.

Title cards. Title cards are arranged alphabetically under the first word of the title, except for articles (*A, An,* and *The*). Thus, *A History of Irish Literature* would go under *H* and *The Life of Marco Polo* would go under *L*.

Subject cards. The heading or top line of a subject card lists the subject

THREE LIBRARY CARDS

Author Card

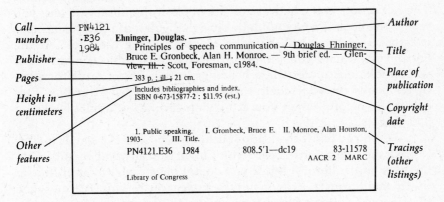

Title Card

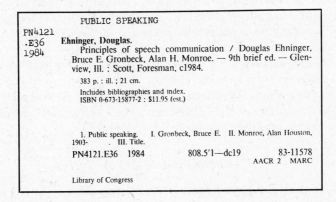

Subject Card

of the book. Subject cards are arranged alphabetically by the first word of the heading on the card.

Two kinds of information on the card are particularly important. The *call number* is the address of the book in the library; it tells you where the book can be found. Be sure that you write the call number exactly so that you will have no trouble finding the book. At the bottom of the card you will often see additional subjects mentioned; you should look under these headings in the subject cards for additional books on your topics. These listings, called "tracings," are extremely helpful when you are trying to find additional books on your subject.

When you know the title or author of a book, it is a simple matter to go to the title or author card, copy down the call number, and locate the book in the library. But if you do not have a particular author or title in mind, you have to consult the subject cards. This is a time when the *Library of Congress Subject Headings* can be very helpful. It gives the subject headings and subheadings in the card catalog, as well as cross-references. By listing every imaginable subject and then showing under what other subject the entry might be classified, this reference work can send you to additional books that you would probably have missed. For example, if you look up "Death Penalty" in your college library subject catalog but do not find any books, you can look up "Death Penalty" in the *LCSH*, which will send you to "Capital Punishment."

As you examine the cards in the catalog, you should make a note card for every book that looks helpful for your paper. Your job now is not to read them, but merely to select the most promising; you will examine them in detail later to determine their relevance to your subject.

In general, you should select the most recently published books on your topic. The reason is obvious: you will have up-to-date information. Imagine writing an article about corruption in American politics without consulting any books published after Watergate. Or imagine working on a paper about the Social Security system using only books written before 1980.

Another yardstick for determining whether or not to select a book is its relevance to your subject. Because titles are sometimes deceiving (one reader thought that *Animal Farm* was about raising pigs!), you should read the table of contents and preface carefully in order to decide whether a book will be helpful.

Periodical Indexes

The books that you have found will contain a great deal of material, but you will need articles for current information. Even if your topic is a war fought over a hundred years ago, you will want the most recent theories or findings on the subject. To find articles, you will need to consult the periodical indexes.

The steps for finding an article on your subject in a magazine or journal are simple:

1. Determine which periodical index you need. Almost every discipline or academic subject has its own index, and you should locate the one that lists articles on your topic.
2. Look under the subject headings for articles on your topic. The subject headings in indexes are similar to those in the subject card catalog.
3. Write down the author, title of the article, name of the periodical, volume number, date of the issue, and the pages on which the article is located. If you don't understand the abbreviations used in the entry, look in the front cover of the index for an explanation.
4. Find out whether your library has a copy of the periodical you want by looking in the Periodicals Catalog, usually located near the index tables. It contains a list of every periodical in the library and tells you where it may be found.

The Readers' Guide

If your topic has been treated in a popular magazine, you should start with the *Readers' Guide to Periodical Literature*, which indexes articles from more than 150 magazines of general interest: *Reader's Digest, Time, Cosmopolitan, Ebony, Esquire,* and so on. It is the most popular and widely used periodical index.

The *Readers' Guide* is published every two weeks and then gathered in large, cumulative volumes covering a year or more. To find an article on a particular subject, you should consult several of the most recent issues. Articles are listed twice: by author and under a subject heading. Like the subject card catalog, it will often refer you to another subject entry by printing *see* or *see also* before an entry.

Here is a sample entry from the *Readers' Guide*.

READER'S GUIDE

Subject heading—**John F. Kennedy Space Center**
    Status report—Kennedy Space Center. R. S. Wagner.
      Space World T-2-230:34 F '83
    Status report—KSC. R. S. Wagner. *Space World*
      T-1-229:31 Ja '83
    Wildlife abounds around the Cape [Merritt Island National
      Wildlife Refuge] R. S. Wagner. il *Space World*
      T-3-231:26 Mr '83
Subject heading—**John Jay French House (Beaumont, Tex.)** *See* Historic
    houses, sites, etc.—Texas

Subject heading —**John Paul II, Pope, 1920-**
about
The agenda for 1983. *America* 148:3 Ja 1-8 '83
Bishops' summit. F. O'Sullivan. *Commonweal* 110:37
Ja 28 '83
Cardinal Wyszynski's spirituality of work. R. Barta and
Subhead — W. Droel. *America* 148:11-12 Ja 1-8 '83
Assassination attempt, May 13, 1981
The Bulgarian connection. *America* 148:23 Ja 15 '83
The Bulgarian connection. S. Gilbert. il *Macleans* 96:21
Ja 17 '83
A cardinal sin to be atoned [KGB involvement] B. Amiel. — *Illustrated*
il *Macleans* 96:9 Ja 17 '83
The defector's tale [implicating KGB] F. Willey. il — *Name*
Newsweek 101:42 Ap 4 '83 *of magazine*
Kremlin papers. *Natl Rev* 35:15 Ja 21 '83
Title of article — New pieces for the puzzle. J. B. Kelly. il *Time* 121:36— *Page*
F 7 '83
Date of — New twists in the plot to kill the Pope. K. Rogal. *Newsweek* — *Volume number*
magazine 101:31-2 F 7 '83 *of magazine*
The plot sickens [possibility of Soviet involvement]
New Repub 188:7-8 Ja 24 '83
Pope's shooting: a global hot potato [Soviet involvement]
il por *U S News World Rep* 94:8 Ja 10 '83 — *Author*
The undiplomatic Bulgarian [alleged Soviet involvement
in attempted assassination of John Paul II; views of
I. Mantarov] J. Kelly. il *Time* 121:38-9 Ap 4 '83
Reporters and reporting
Counterattack [Soviet reaction to accusations of KGB
involvement] il *Time* 121:30 Ja 17 '83
Equal time [French communists protest anti-Soviet bias
in press coverage of KGB involvement in shooting
of John Paul II] *Time* 121:31 Ja 10 '83
Subhead — **Travel**
Globe-trotting Pope: what drives him? J. Mann. il por
Subhead — *U S News World Rep* 94:22 Mr 21 '83
Visit to Central America, 1983
Central American pietà. S. Christian. *New Repub* 188:12-14
Ap 4 '83
Dialogue in Central America. *America* 148:203 Mr 19
'83
Into the Central American volcano. R. N. Ostling. il
por map *Time* 121:52-4 Mr 7 '83
John Paul II's rescue mission. il por *U S News World
Rep* 94:9 Mr 14 '83
John Paul's blunt message. K. L. Woodward. il pors
Newsweek 101:81-2 Mr 21 '83
Papal perseverance. *Christ Century* 100:266 Mr 23-30
'83
The pontiff's turbulent pilgrimage. D. North. il por
Macleans 96:18-19 Mr 14 '83
The Pope & politics in Central America. *Commonweal*
110:163-4 Mr 25 '83
The Pope in Central America. *America* 148:163 Mr 5
'83
The Pope takes a stand in Central America. F. X. Maier.
il por *Bus Week* p50 Ap 11 '83

Specialized Indexes

For articles on specialized subjects, the *Readers' Guide* will not be adequate. You should consult the appropriate subject index. Each index
lists articles restricted to the topic implied in its title. The date in
parentheses indicates when the index began publication.

American Indian Index (1953–)
Applied Science and Technology Index (1958–)
Art Index (1929–)
Biography Index (1947–)
Biological and Agricultural Index (1947–)

Black Information Index (1970–)
Book Review Digest (1905–)
Business Periodicals Index (1958–)
Dramatic Index (1909–1949)
Education Index (1929–)
Film Literature Index (1973–)
General Science Index (1978–)
Humanities Index (1974–)
Index to Religious Periodical Literature (1954–)
International Index to Film Periodicals (1972–)
Monthly Catalog of United States Government Publications (1895–)
Music Index (1949–)
Poole's Index for Periodical Literature (1802–1907)
Psychological Abstracts (1975–)
Public Affairs Information Service Bulletin (1915–)
Social Sciences and Humanities Index (1965–1974)
Social Sciences Index (1974–)
Sociological Abstracts (1975–)
United Nations Documents Index (1950–)
Women's Studies Abstracts (1972–)

Current Events

For current subjects or events, the following reference guides are helpful:

Facts on File. This is a weekly digest of world news, with an annual index, that began in 1940.

The New York Times Index. This index enables you to locate stories published in *The Times* since 1913.

Newsbank. This unique reference work reproduces on microfiche selected articles on urban and public affairs from newspapers in 103 cities and indexes them under major subject areas.

Reading and Taking Notes

If you followed the strategy outlined in the preceding section, you are now faced with an imposing stack of books and articles. You will discover that not all of your material is usable, and you will continue to come across more leads as you continue to work on your paper. Right now, however, it's time to start reading and taking notes.

As you begin reading, you will need a stack of 4″ x 6″ cards to keep a record of the books and articles that you use and to record accurately and concisely the ideas and facts from your sources. You will compile two kinds of cards: *bibliography* cards and *subject* cards.

For every article or book that you consult, fill out a separate *bibliography* card. This means that if you use two works by the same author, you will need two separate cards. For each book or article, write on the card: *the full name of the author or editor, the full title of the publication,* and *the facts of the publication.* For books, write the call number in the top left corner of the card; this will save time if you have to refer to the book later. When arranged alphabetically, your bibliography cards will form the basis of the list of works at the end of your paper. Look on page 247 for an example of bibliography cards.

As you read each book or article, the notes that you take will be written on your *subject* cards. You will take three kinds of notes: *quotations, paraphrases,* and *summaries.*

Quotations are the actual words (including the spelling and punctuation) of the author. You should place quotation marks around them to remind yourself that they are from the original work, and write the page number(s) of the source where the quotation can be found. Quote the words of the original exactly, being certain not to change the meaning of the passage. If you omit words from the quotation, use ellipses (. . .); if you insert your own words in the quotation, use brackets ([]). See the handbook for a discussion of the use of ellipses and brackets.

Most of your subject cards will contain *paraphrases* and *summaries.* Use direct quotations only when the original words will create an impact or lend authority to the passage or when you intend to analyze it in detail. Paraphrased material is the author's ideas in your own words. Paraphrasing is useful because it keeps you from being too dependent on the words of the original, and it forces you to digest the ideas in the original in order to express them in your own words. Be certain that you don't distort or exaggerate the ideas in the original passage when rewriting them.

Summaries present the key ideas in a brief condensation of the original in your own words. In that sense, they are shorter versions of paraphrased passages. The difference is not too important; in both cases you are using your own words.

Here are a few suggestions for note cards:

1. Keep separate bibliography cards for each source. This will simplify alphabetizing the list of "Works Cited" at the end of your paper.
2. Write the call number of every book or bound magazine on its bibliography card so that you can find it later without too much trouble.
3. Limit each subject card to one idea; this will make it easier to arrange and rearrange your ideas when planning your paper. To adjust your plan, simply adjust your cards.

4. Work out a code or set of symbols so that you know where the quotations and ideas on each subject card come from. This will make it unnecessary to repeat all of the information on the bibliography card.
5. Supply page references for all quotations, summaries, and paraphrases.
6. Write in ink (pencil often smudges) and do *not* write on the back of a card (you may forget to turn it over).

Examples of bibliographical and subject cards follow.

R 726
M 28

Maguire, Daniel C.
Death by Choice
New York: Doubleday and Company
1974

Tipler, Frank. "We Are Alone."
Discover (March, 1983), pp. 56-60.

Tipler p. 56

"At least one intelligent species exists, namely the human race. I claim that we are probably the only intelligent species ever to exist in our galaxy, and quite possibly the only such species that has ever existed in the known universe."

Plagiarism

Plagiarism is presenting someone's ideas or words as your own without giving proper credit. It is stealing, and many colleges and universities discuss it in their catalogues or student codes.

To avoid plagiarism, document the following material from your reading:

1. *All directly quoted material.* Enclose all quoted passages within quotation marks and document them according to the guidelines on pages 254–55. An exception would be well-known proverbs, expressions, or famous lines from literature ("To be or not to be; that is the question").
2. *All paraphrased and summarized material.* Because the words are your own, you do not place quotation marks around them, but you have an obligation to cite your sources whenever you paraphrase or summarize another person's words or ideas.
3. *Information which is not generally known.* Facts not generally available or widely known should be documented. If you state, "Over 33,000 Turks and their allies were drowned in the Battle of Lepanto in the straits of the Gulf of Corinth," your reader has a right to ask, "Says who? How do you know that? What's your source?" On the other hand, facts that are common knowledge ("The sun rises in the east") do not have to be documented.

For the correct way to document your sources, see pages 255–260.

Most students know that when they copy another person's ideas word for word, they must acknowledge their source. Failure to do so is plagiarism. Some students, however, do not realize that when they paraphrase—when they restate or summarize information from a source in their own words—they still have an obligation to acknowledge that source.

These examples illustrate the difference between an unacceptable paraphrase (plagiarism) and an acceptable paraphrase.

Original Source

Frederick the Great, King of Prussia, came to power in 1740. Although he is remembered in history books mostly for his military astuteness, he was also devoted to the life of the mind and the spirit. His court in Potsdam was one of the great centers of intellectual activity in Europe in the eighteenth century. The celebrated mathematician Leonhard Euler spent twenty-five years there. Many other mathematicians and scientists came, as well as philosophers—including Voltaire and La Mettrie, who wrote some of their most influential works while there. (from Douglas R. Hofstadter, *Gödel, Escher, Bach: An Eternal Golden Braid*, p. 3)

Unacceptable Paraphrase (Plagiarism)

Although Frederick the Great, the King of Prussia, is remembered in history books for his military ability, he was devoted to activities of the mind and spirit. One of the great centers of intellectual activities in Europe during the eighteenth-century was his royal court at Potsdam. Among the famous mathematicians, scientists, and philosophers who were at his court were the celebrated mathematician Leonhard Euler, who spent twenty-five years there, and the philosophers Voltaire and La Mettrie, who wrote some of their most important works while there.

Comment: With the exceptions of a few word changes ("military ability" for "military astuteness," "activities of the mind" for "life of the mind," "most important works" for "most influential works") and a few slightly altered sentences, this passage has been copied from Hofstadter. By failing to credit the source or use quotation marks, the writer implies that the ideas and words are original.

Acceptable Paraphrase

As Douglas Hofstadter points out, Frederick the Great attracted some of the greatest thinkers of eighteenth-century Europe to his court at Potsdam. Despite his encouragement and patronage of many prominent mathematicians, scientists, and philosophers, however, "he is remembered in history books mostly for his military astuteness" (3).

Comment: Following the format in the 1984 edition of the *MLA Handbook*, the writer acknowledges indebtedness to the source by mentioning Hofstadter's name, placing quotation marks around the passage that has been used from the source, and identifying the page number in parentheses from which the quoted passage was taken. With the exception of the quoted passage, the paragraph is the student's.

Organizing and Outlining Your Paper

The best time to outline your paper is after you have completed most of your reading. When you have accumulated a sizeable stack of note cards, you can use them as the basis for organizing your paper. By sorting them into stacks by topics, you will develop the major headings of your paper. You will notice topics that are too thin and will require some development. You will also see that some ideas have bulged out and need pruning. Still others are off the subject, not supporting the thesis statement or contributing anything to the controlling idea of your paper. As painful as it may be, you should remove them from your collection of notes.

You can prepare a rough outline at this point by arranging your note cards in the order in which you want to present your ideas. (See Chapter 4 for examples of rough outlines.) As you develop more ideas and information, your outline will become increasingly detailed. Your instructor may want you to turn in a more detailed *formal outline*, written just before you write the final copy of your term paper. (See page 262 for an example of a formal outline for a term paper.)

If you have to write a formal outline, begin with your thesis statement. If it is sharply focused, it will contain key words that suggest ways to divide the outline into manageable parts or sections. Using those key words as guides, make a list of all the major ideas that develop the thesis. They are represented by Roman numerals (I, II, III, and so on). The minor ideas that support the major ideas are represented by uppercase letters (A, B, C, and so on). This system lets you see at a glance whether ideas are in the right place, whether less important ideas are given too much prominence, and whether your paper has gotten sidetracked by unimportant or trivial facts and ideas.

When you outline, you divide larger ideas or topics into smaller ones. This means that every idea or topic will be divided into at least two parts. If you have a Roman numeral I, you must have at least II; if you have an A, you must have a B, and so on. Your instructor may ask you to write either a *topic* or a *sentence* outline; the two types differ chiefly in the way they express each idea or thought.

In the *topic outline*, a phrase or even a single word serves to indicate an idea in the essay. In the *sentence outline* each thought or idea is stated in a complete sentence. Obviously, the topic outline is briefer and more general; it is convenient if you are concerned with facts more than with ideas. When writing a topic outline, be sure that you don't include sentences. Further, don't mix grammatical forms—that is, if Roman numeral I is a prepositional phrase, make sure that all of the other Roman numerals contain prepositional phrases; if A and B under I are nouns, the capital letters under the other major headings should also be nouns, and so on.

The *sentence outline* is more detailed and makes the writing of the essay easier. Unlike the topic outline, each major and minor idea is expressed in a sentence. The sentence outline is often used when the subject is complicated and when the relationships among the ideas are subtle. Regardless of the type you use, a good outline will give your term paper a sense of direction. It will also test the relevance of your notes, revealing the relationship of your ideas to your controlling idea or thesis statement.

Writing the First Draft

After you have arranged your cards in the order in which you wish to present your material and then written an outline to serve as a guide as you write, you should take another glance at your thesis statement. It should reflect precisely the point you want to make in your paper, the goal that all of your facts, ideas, impressions, and conclusions are aiming toward. By focusing your thesis statement sharply now, you have another way to test the relevance and relationship of your ideas.

As you write the first draft of your paper, you will continue to add, delete, and adjust. Therefore, leave abundant space at the top, bottom, and margins of each page. Don't try to include in your paper every note from every card merely because you hate to see it wasted. If it is irrelevant, it will stick out in your paper. On the other hand, if you see that more facts or ideas are needed in a particular section, make a note to remind yourself that you should go back to your books and articles for additional information.

As you write your first draft, mention the author's name, the title of the book or article, and the page number after each quotation that you incorporated in your paper. Detailed instructions for documenting your sources are on pages 255–60; for the time being, your goal is to make sure that you don't omit or lose this information while writing your first draft.

Revising and Editing Your Term Paper

After writing the first draft, set your term paper aside for a day or two before beginning your revision. This will allow you to return to it with a fresh perspective and to "see again" (the root meaning of revision) your paper from an objective distance. As pointed out in Chapter 6 ("Revising the Essay"), every piece of writing can profit by careful revision.

Before beginning your revision, look over the checklists on pages 104 and 112. Then read your paper aloud, listening for the flow of ideas, smooth sentences, and the right word choice. As you reconsider your paper, keep a pair of scissors and a roll of Scotch tape or a stapler handy so that you can cut, rearrange, delete, or add material. As Chapter 6 illustrates, there are different levels of revising. As you go through your paper the first time, make certain that you have enough material and that it is in the right order. Be sure that your paper makes a point—that it informs the reader clearly and without confusion, or that it offers a persuasive argument that is logical and fair.

An important part of the revising process is checking your paper for mistakes in spelling, grammar, or punctuation. Errors in these areas can detract from the overall impact of an otherwise excellent term paper. If you are uncertain about the spelling of a word, look it up in a dictionary. For problems or uncertainties in punctuation, consult the handbook.

After you have carefully reread your paper for its completeness, organization, smoothness, and mechanical correctness, you are ready to prepare your final copy.

Format

Unless your instructor specifies otherwise, your term paper should include the following parts:

1. *A title page.* The title page includes the title of your paper about a third of the way down the page, your name about two inches below the title, and starting about two inches below your name, the name of the course, the instructor, and the date.
2. *An outline.* If your instructor requests an outline, place it between the title page and the first page of the text. If it is

two or more pages long, number the pages with small Roman numerals (for example, "ii," "iii,") beginning with the second page of the outline, placing the numerals at the top right-hand corner of the page.

3. *The text of the paper.* The title of your paper should be typed two inches from the top of the first page of your text and separated from the first line of the text by four lines of space. The text should be double-spaced. Leave a margin of one inch at the top, bottom, and both sides of the text. Indent the first word of a paragraph five spaces from the left margin. Do not number the first page of the text; begin numbering with page 2.

4. *Content endnotes page.* The "Works Cited" page will list all of the books, magazines, and other sources used in your term paper. Occasionally, however, you may find it necessary to add a note of explanation or commentary that you cannot logically fit into the body of your paper. Examples of the kind of information typically included in a content endnote are suggestions for further reading, an explanation of a particular procedure or term, a comment about an apparent conflict between sources, or other matters not directly related to the text. Content endnotes should be placed on a separate page following the last page of your text. Label this page with the word "Notes" centered two inches from the top of the page. The first note should begin four spaces below this heading. Do not number the first page, but begin numbering subsequent pages according to the overall sequence of your paper. Using raised superscript numerals, number your notes in sequence so that they match those in your text. Double-space all entries and double-space between the entries. See page 257 for examples of endnotes.

5. *"Works Cited" page.* At the end of your term paper you should include a bibliography or list of all the source materials actually used in writing your paper, as well as those sources mentioned in your content endnotes. The items should be arranged alphabetically by the last name of the author, placing the first line of each entry flush with the left margin and indenting succeeding lines five spaces. Double-space each entry and double-space between entries. Place the title "Works Cited" two inches from the top of the page and leave four spaces between it and the first entry. Begin numbering the second page of the bibliography; page numbers should be placed in the upper right-hand corner of each page. See pages 257–59 for the correct format for books and other sources listed in the "Works Cited," and see page 271 for a sample "Works Cited" page.

How to Handle Quotations Within the Text of Your Paper

As you write your term paper, you will frequently incorporate quoted material directly into your text. A quotation should be introduced smoothly into the text so that it does not clash or conflict with the surrounding passage, yet it should contribute forcefully and convincingly to the the paper.

If a quotation takes up *no more than four lines* in your paper, place it in the body of your text and enclose it within quotation marks. If a quotation is *longer than four lines*, it should be indented ten spaces from the left margin and double-spaced, *without* quotation marks. See below for an example of the correct arrangement of a longer quotation.

Shorter quotations should be introduced by the name of the author, when possible, and a verb like *states, claims, declares, adds*, or similar words. If the quotation forms a grammatical part of the sentence in which it occurs, the first word of the quotation does not have to be capitalized, even though it might be capitalized in the original. Note the following example:

> Typical of the optimism expressed in recent weeks concerning the economic future is the statement of Richard Curtin who claims that "we are talking about a surge in consumer confidence that has never been seen before" (19).

If the quotation follows a formal introduction set off by a comma or colon, you should capitalize the first word as in the original:

> Typical of the optimism expressed in recent weeks concerning the economic future is the statement of Richard Curtin: "We are talking about a surge in consumer confidence that has never been seen before" (19).

Longer quotations should be introduced by the author's name, when possible, and by a colon or comma. The entire quoted passage should be double-spaced and set off from the rest of the text by triple-spacing. If the quoted material is a single paragraph, do not indent the first line. If two or more paragraphs are quoted consecutively, indent the first line of each an additional three spaces.

Below is an example of a quotation that exceeds four lines.

...undertook to determine whether the universe really was expanding. As Jastrow has pointed out, Hubble took a series of logical steps:

> Hubble's first step was to find out what the mysterious spiral "nebulas" were. Photographing these objects with the 100-inch

telescope, he found that they contained vast numbers of individual stars. Hubble's photographs convinced astronomers that spiral nebulas were true galaxies, or island universes.

Hubble's next step was to find out how far away the galaxies were. He proceeded to measure their distances, using, as a yardstick, a certain kind of star called a Cepheid, whose true brightness was known from studies of similar stars in our own galaxy. (491)

From the degree of faintness of Cepheid stars in other galaxies, Hubble was able to estimate the distance to these galaxies. His . . .

Parenthetical Documentation

With the exception of content endnotes (described on page 256), endnotes and footnotes are no longer necessary for identifying a source in a term paper. The new system set forth in the *MLA Handbook* (1984) specifies that the source for each quotation and paraphrase must be included within the text in parentheses by author, short title, and page. Any (or all) of these elements should be omitted if they are mentioned in the body of your paper. The title may be omitted if only one work by the author is cited. Because the "Works Cited" will list only general information about the books and articles you used, you must include within the text the specific page in the book or journal.

For quotations of four lines or less, the following examples illustrate this system. Notice that the parenthesis is placed after the closing quotation mark but before all punctuation marks.

> According to Alvin Toffler, "We develop a self-image by assuming the roles of others" (*Learning* 21).

The writer mentions Toffler's first name because this is the first reference to the author; subsequent references will dispense with the first name. Because there is more than one work by Toffler cited in the paper, the writer includes a shortened version of the title in question. Notice the page reference follows the title and is not separated by a comma.

> As Wills points out, "Revolution was a respectable term in eighteenth-century English" (52).

Because the writer has previously identified Gary Wills, he does not repeat his first name. Because only one work by Wills is cited in the paper, the writer does not include the title of the work he is quoting from.

Suzuki claims that Zen differs from all other philosophic and religious meditation practices (21).

The writer is presenting an indirect quotation from a book by Suzuki. The reader can turn to the list of "Works Cited" at the end of the term paper for further information, including the title, publisher, and date of publication.

To document longer quotations, omit quotation marks and indicate the page in parentheses after the final period. Below is an example of this style; notice that the writer has identified the author and title of the selection in the body of the term paper.

. . . and the relationship between style and art is pointed out by Susan Sontag in Against Interpretation:

> All works of art are founded on a certain distance from the lived reality which is represented. This "distance" is, by definition, inhuman or impersonal to a certain degree; for in order to appear to us as art, the work must restrict sentimental intervention and emotional participation, which are functions of "closeness." It is the degree and manipulating of this distance, the conventions of distance, which constitute the style of the work. In the final analysis, "style" is art. And art is nothing more or less than various modes of stylized, dehumanized representation. (39)

According to Sontag, style is the principle of decision in a work of art, the signature of the artist's will. And as the human will . . .

Notice that the page reference follows the final period and is not followed by another period.

The sample term paper on pages 260–272 contains additional examples of the new MLA documentation style.

Sample Content Endnotes

Content endnotes contain comments, explanations, and other information that you cannot fit into the text of your paper. They should be placed on a separate page following the last page of your text (see page 253 for detailed instructions for the arrangement of the "Notes" page). As in the case of your citations within the text of your paper, endnotes must be fully documented in your "Works Cited."

Here are some typical endnotes:

¹On this point see Highet (76) and Murray (191).

²For an opposing point of view, see Ogilvie (211).

³For the behaviorist response to Chomsky's theories, see Skinner (78–83).

Preparing Your "Works Cited" Page

The final section of your term paper, "Works Cited," is an alphabetical list of the source materials you used when writing your paper. If you have kept your bibliography cards up-to-date, it is an easy matter to arrange them alphabetically by author. Be sure to include those works mentioned in your content endnotes.

Entries are arranged alphabetically by the author's last name. If the work is anonymous or unsigned, its place is determined by the first word of the title (other than *A*, *An*, and *The*). The first line of each entry should be flush with the left margin, and succeeding lines should be indented five spaces. Double-space each entry and double-space between entries. See page 253 for further details concerning the format of the "Works Cited" page.

The new MLA system asks that you omit unnecessary items in your list of works cited. Abbreviations such as "p." and "pp." (for "page" and "pages") and "l." and "ll." (for "line" and "lines") should no longer be used; in their place use "page" or "pages" and "line" or "lines."

Bibliography Form: Books

A BOOK WITH ONE AUTHOR

Winzerling, Oscar W. *Acadian Odyssey*. Baton Rouge: Louisiana State University Press, 1955.

[If you used more than one work by an author, it is not necessary to repeat his or her name with each title. Insert a seven-dash line flush with the left margin, followed by a period, as in the following example.]

———————. *The Settling of Belize*. New York: Holt, 1981.

A BOOK WITH TWO OR THREE AUTHORS

Mead, Margaret, and Rhoda Metraux. *A Way of Seeing*. New York: William Morrow, 1968.

A BOOK WITH MORE THAN THREE AUTHORS

Turk, Amos, et al. *Environmental Science*. Philadelphia: W. B. Saunders, 1978.

A BOOK WITH A CORPORATE AUTHOR
The National Commission on Excellence in Education. *A Nation at Risk.*
Washington, D.C.: GPO, 1983.

AN EDITION AFTER THE FIRST
Coleman, James C., James N. Butcher, and Robert C. Carson. *Abnormal Psychology and Modern Life.* 6th ed. Glenview, Ill.: Scott, Foresman, 1980.

AN EDITED COLLECTION
Valdez, Luis, and Stan Steiner, eds. *Aztlan: An Anthology of Mexican American Literature.* New York: Alfred A. Knopf, 1972.

STORY OR ARTICLE FROM AN ANTHOLOGY
Spark, Muriel. "The Twins." In *Fiction 100: An Anthology of Short Stories.* Ed. James H. Pickering. New York: Macmillan, 1982.

A TRANSLATION
de Cervantes Saavedra, Miguel. *Don Quixote of La Mancha.* Trans. Walter Starkie. New York: Macmillan, 1957.

A WORK IN MORE THAN ONE VOLUME
Washburn, Wilcomb E. *The American Indian and the United States.* 2 vols. New York: Random House, 1973.

A MODERN REPRINT
Bury, J. B. *The Idea of Progress.* 1932; rpt. New York: Dover, 1955.

A BOOK WITH AN EDITOR AND AN AUTHOR
Newman, John Henry. *Apologia Pro Vita Sua.* Ed. David J. DeLaura. New York: Norton, 1968.

Bibliography Form: Periodicals

The entry for a periodical shares some similarities with the entry for a book, but it also contains some differences. The author's name should be placed flush against the left margin and succeeding lines should be indented five spaces. The last name is placed first, followed by a comma, the author's first name or initials, and a period. The title of the article should be placed within quotation marks followed by a period inside the closing quotation mark. The name of the journal or magazine from which the article is taken should be underlined, followed by a volume number, using arabic numerals, followed by the year of publication (within parentheses), a colon, and the page numbers for the entire article. Monthly or weekly magazines require only the date without a volume number.

Encyclopedias and Almanacs

A SIGNED ARTICLE IN AN ENCYCLOPEDIA
Ogilvie, R. M. "Livy." *Encyclopaedia Britannica: Macropaedia.* 1974 ed.

AN UNSIGNED ARTICLE IN AN ENCYCLOPEDIA
"Cyclone." *Encyclopedia Americana.* 1981 ed.

AN UNSIGNED ARTICLE IN AN ALMANAC
"Notable Sports Personalities." *World Almanac and Book of Facts.* 1981 ed.,
815–17.

Magazines and Newspapers

A SIGNED ARTICLE IN A WEEKLY MAGAZINE
Barber, Benjamin. "Beyond the Feminist Mystique." *The New Republic,*
11 July 1983, 26–32.

A SIGNED ARTICLE IN A MONTHLY MAGAZINE
Christian, Shirley. "El Salvador's Divided Military." *The Atlantic,* June
1983, 50–60.

A SIGNED ARTICLE IN A DAILY NEWSPAPER
Ostrow, Ronald J. "Cuban Refugees Get Due-Process Rights." *Los
Angeles Times,* 8 July 1983, A14, col. 1.

AN EDITORIAL
"Power Defined Is Not Power Lost." Editorial. *The New York Times,* 3
July 1983, D12, cols. 1–2.

**A SIGNED ARTICLE IN A JOURNAL WITH
CONTINUOUS PAGINATION**
O'Reilley, Mary Rose. "The Peaceable Classroom." *College English,* 46
(Feb. 1984): 103–112.

**A SIGNED ARTICLE IN A JOURNAL WITH
SEPARATE PAGINATION**
Kane, Declan F. "Irish Place Names." *Gaelic Studies,* 14 (1956): 29–33.

AN UNSIGNED ARTICLE
"London Express." *Time,* 6 June 1983, 45–46.
"British Doctors Report New Infant Disease." *The San Diego Union,* 9
July 1983, A10, col. 1.

Bulletins and Pamphlets

U.S. Department of Health, Education, and Welfare. *Ethical Issues in Health Services.* Washington, D.C.: GPO, 1970.

Proposed Changes in Rules and Regulations for Secondary School Teams. Southern California Soccer Referees' Association, 1983.

Unpublished Dissertations

Willis, Veronica. "An Investigation of the Use of the Documented Research Paper in College Courses." Diss. United States International University, 1970.

Television and Radio Programs

"A Town Like Alice." *Masterpiece Theatre.* PBS, 3 July 1983.

A Prairie Home Companion. KPBS, San Diego, 10 February 1984.

Films

Return of the Jedi. Twentieth-Century Fox, 1983.

Recordings

Fleetwood Mac. *Rumours.* Warner Bros., BSK 3010, 1977.

Interviews

Hogins, James B., and C. P. McAuliffe. Personal interview. San Diego, CA., 1 April 1983.

A Sample Term Paper

Here is a term paper that argues a thesis. As you read it, notice how the author incorporates her sources in her paper and follows the documentation style recommended in this chapter.

Euthanasia: The Right to Die

by
Roberta Demel

English 101
Mr. Kane
May 20, 1984

Outline

I. Introduction
   A. Problems posed by medical advances
   B. Definitions of euthanasia
II. Legal Questions
   A. Ambiguity of laws and court practices
   B. Hippocratic oath
III. Religious Questions
   A. Objections
      1. Traditional Judeo-Christian view
      2. "Sanctity of life" and other objections
   B. Recent changes in attitude
IV. Principles of euthanasia movement
   A. Dignity of life vs. value of life
   B. Physician's responsibility
   C. Right to be "at liberty"
   D. Equity of treatment
V. Conclusion

Euthanasia: The Right to Die

Two years ago two Los Angeles physicians unplugged a patient's respirator, cut off all his nourishment, and let him die. "Last August the Los Angeles district attorney's office filed murder charges against them, apparently the first time doctors have been criminally prosecuted for cutting off life-support systems" (Newsweek 76).

This case highlights the dilemma that doctors and society in general are facing today. In an amazingly short time, incredible biomedical gains have been made so that it is now possible to save lives that once were regarded as beyond help. Organ transplants, sophisticated diagnostic tools such as the CAT scanner, and dialysis machines have not only prolonged life but also sharply escalated the cost of health care, forcing hard choices about who should benefit from these limited resources. As the philosopher Joseph Fletcher observes:

> The question of human or medical initiatives in living and dying is therefore a problem caused by success, not by failure. Now we can preserve and prolong life beyond our grandfathers' rosiest dreams— so much so that we can at last see why prolonging life may paradoxically be prolonging dying. Along with the problem of how to save life comes the problem of when to stop it. (47)

Medical doctors, theologians, and legal scholars in recent years have devoted increasing attention to the question of who should live and who should die, a question made urgent by the ability of modern technology to keep a person alive indefinitely. The human "vegetable" was once a rare problem in terminal wards of hospitals, but now it is a common daily problem because of medical success. The loss of personal integrity now often occurs long before biological death. As Fletcher graphically describes the encounter, "Patients do not meet death any more; the end comes for them while comatose, betubed, aerated, glucosed, narcosed, sedated—not conscious, not even human anymore" (48).

Because of these advances in the art and science of medicine, one of the most frequent and difficult questions that arise in the context of terminal medical care is the question of euthanasia. The problem itself is an ancient one, rooted in the conflict between the duty to relieve suffering and the duty to preserve human life, but it has assumed new proportions in recent years. Decisions to determine the time and circumstances of one's own death have become more frequent and complex because of the ability of modern medical science to sustain biological life almost indefinitely by artificial means. The purpose of this paper is to examine the principal arguments for and against euthanasia and to argue for the legalization of voluntary euthanasia.

Originally the Greek word euthanasia meant painless, happy death. This meaning still appears as one definition of the term. However, a second meaning is now usually added that describes euthanasia as an act or method of causing death painlessly so as to end suffering. Increasingly, euthanasia has come to be equated with mercy killing.

An analysis of the debate on euthanasia, especially in newspaper and magazine articles, gives the reader the impression of a somewhat emotional and at times illogical public debate on the question. Specific cases of euthanasia generate reactions of approval and disapproval. Arguments for death with dignity inspired by instances of hopeless suffering are countered by arguments warning of the dangerous consequences of assuming the right to take life. Legislative proposals to sanction euthanasia are met with rebuttal by those who oppose it.

Most doctors, theologians, and lawyers recognize two types of euthanasia: passive and active. The withholding of surgery from an elderly hopelessly dying patient who begs to be left alone is an example of passive euthanasia. The injection of a massive dose of morphine to this same patient, producing death, would be considered active euthanasia. Both instances are illegal in the United States, as the case in Los Angeles cited above demonstrates.

The worldwide legal position of euthanasia varies greatly. Throughout most countries in South America, benevolent killing is a complete defense, while in the United States and Great Britain, it is murder. Other countries such as Switzerland, Norway, and Germany have adopted approaches similar to the South American for evaluating homicide. As Milton Heifetz points out, motivation is the main question:

> Although euthanasia is illegal, they weigh the three factors of premeditation, deliberation, and motivation involved in the act and, in reaching a decision, place the greatest emphasis on motivation. The fact that homicide may be premeditated and deliberate is of lesser importance. (103)

-3-

The emphasis on motivation permits the courts in those countries to develop a total understanding of the situation. As a result, sentences may be reduced or not imposed at all.

In the United States, on the other hand, motivation is not a significant factor according to law. Consent or request for euthanasia is not legally acceptable. It is not a defense in court, according to Kathy Fackelmann:

> Lawyers say existing laws about decisions to stop treatment are hopelessly ambiguous. While doctors are implicitly required to treat patients to the best of their ability, laws are unclear about the extent of treatment required. Morris B. Abram, commission chairman of an inquiry into the study of ethical problems in medicine and a New York attorney, says any attempt to rigidly legislate these decisions would probably make things worse. Each case brought before the court would result in a new precedent. Doctors, already unsure about their legal obligations, would be even more confused. Abram says he can imagine a future horror scene in which a dying patient looks up from his deathbed to see the doctor flipping through a thick docket of legal cases. (233)

The ambiguity of the present laws is demonstrated by a series of examples cited by Jerry Wilson (149-55). He describes a number of cases within the last several years in this country in which prosecutors and grand juries tended either not to indict or to give lenient sentences and probation to those who killed in order to relieve suffering or prevent prolonged unconscious existence when there was no hope of recovery.

The gap between theory and practice in the United States as it pertains to mercy killings is an embarrassment to American law. This gap should not be allowed to exist. Our laws should be modified and not surreptitiously bypassed. The legal arguments to support this view are plentiful. In the first place, "bad laws make hard cases," as the old expression states. The inconsistent and ad hoc judgments referred to by Wilson (above) do not establish legal precedents with which doctors can make and evaluate terminal medical decisions.

In the second place, these decisions have resulted from legal and extralegal maneuvers in the administration of the law. Each person should have the right to die with dignity, but under the present laws, only those for whom a doctor is willing to act at his own peril are permitted to exercise this right. The fact that the law has been lenient in other cases is no guarantee that a doctor would not be indicted, tried, and prosecuted for practicing euthanasia.

Finally, the failure to apply existing laws in some cases and the leniency with which they are applied in others undermines public confidence in the law. A parallel situation is the uneven prosecution of individuals in this country who are arrested for possession of marijuana and the wide variation in the disposition of their cases. The result, all too often, has been contempt for the courts.

An argument frequently cited by opponents of euthanasia is the Hippocratic oath. This oath, which has guided physicians for centuries, contains a passage relevant to euthanasia: "I will neither give a deadly drug to anybody, if asked for, nor will I make a suggestion to this effect." As Daniel Maguire points out, "It is to these words of the oath that many people repair when contradicting the right to death by choice" (341). As Maguire explains, the oath promises two things: first, to relieve suffering, and second, to prolong and protect life. When the patient is in the grip of an agonizing and fatal disease, these two promises are incompatible. Two duties come into conflict. To prolong life is to violate the promise to relieve pain. To relieve the pain is to violate the promise to prolong and protect life.

Maguire says that the oath can actually be used to justify euthanasia:

> One could maintain the utmost respect for human life and observe the laws of humanity by recognizing that the inducement of death when death is good and befitting is a reasonable and good service to human persons. The decision to do this, of course, would not be the doctor's, since he does not have the moral authority to make these decisions for anyone. His expertise does not in any way equip him to make moral decisions for his patients. He may be asked to administer the injection that causes death. In that case his conscience must guide his own response. The decision to initiate is not his; the decision to cooperate is. (343)

As evidence that most physicians agree with Maguire's interpretation of the oath, a 1970 survey published in the Journal of the American Medical Association revealed that "eighty-seven percent of doctors queried said they agreed with the principle of passive euthanasia. . . . Eighty percent said they practiced this type of euthanasia in varying degrees, and another fifteen percent said they favored actively ending certain [terminal] patients' lives" (Fackelmann 233). As one physician commented in a Newsweek interview, "There is a time and a place where prolonging suffering is not doing my job as a physician" (31 August 1981, 49).

The Judeo-Christian tradition in the past has been opposed to euthanasia. According to the theologian Richard Sullivan, this tradition is based to a great extent on sacred scripture: "Euthanasia is a reversal from culture to barbarism. The advocates of euthanasia must face the fact that they are opposing the traditional Christian teaching on the value of human life" (61).

In recent years, however, there has been general agreement that it is morally permissible to allow a person to die if therapy would not lead to recovery. Views diverge, however, when this principle is applied to specific situations, as a recent Time article points out:

> The Roman Catholic Church has the most explicit position. The Vatican's 1980 declaration on euthanasia clearly permits an end to treatment that would only "secure a precarious and burdensome prolongation of life" when death is imminent. Says Rabbi Seymour Siegel of New York's Jewish Theological Seminary: "It is the individual's duty to live as long as he can, but if a person is destined to die soon, there is no obligation to prevent that death from happening." (68)

Maguire contends that although most Catholics are not aware of this teaching, "The position favoring the possibility of moral mercy killing in certain circumstances is more probable by reason of its intrinsic reasons and the inadequacy of the opposing objections" (343).

Some religious opponents of euthanasia are not affected by these views. They strongly oppose any form of euthanasia on the basis of the sacredness of life. Yet there is a contradiction in this argument that should be obvious to others. The sanctity-of-life doctrine is readily discarded when it is convenient. For example, most religions approve of killing during war in defense of their religious principles, and as capital punishment. As Heifetz observes, "The history of religion is rampant with killing, death, and destruction as a result of religious maneuvering. At the same time, to grant merciful death to someone who needs it, begs for it to prevent further debasement of human qualities is considered abhorrent" (103).

Aside from the religious objections to euthanasia, there are those who oppose it because of the consequences and difficulties that would result, according to them, if euthanasia were legalized. They insist, for example, that it would be impossible to determine whether a patient whose mind is weakened by narcotics and pain really wants to die. They point out that such a patient would be unable to make an informed decision. They also argue that to permit euthanasia would require families to make life and death decisions when they are least able to do so emotionally.

Another opposing argument, called the "wedge" theory, is that to permit a single instance of the direct killing of an innocent person would be to admit a most dangerous wedge that might eventually put all life in a precarious position. Once a man is permitted on his own authority to kill an innocent person directly, according to this theory, there is no way to stop the advancement of that wedge. Once the exception has been admitted, it is too late; therefore, no exception should be allowed.

Still another argument is that euthanasia would lead to the horrors of the Nazis in World War II—the mass killing of innocent people. Those who invoke this argument claim that scientific experimentation and euthanasia were the preludes to such atrocities in Germany before they reached such horrible excesses.

The rebuttal to these arguments can be summarized easily. It is true that it would be impossible to determine whether a weakened patient really wants to die. But the obvious answer is what proponents of euthanasia call the "living will," a statement signed when one is well, or at least when one has not been treated with mind-numbing medicines and drugs. The will states that the signer does not want extreme or extraordinary life-prolonging measures applied when he or she is terminally ill. Such a will would also be a consolation to the family, who would be unable to make rational decisions at such a time.

The "wedge" theory is very appealing at first glance. But to argue that euthanasia would lead to misuse does not make it unique. That is the fate of any moral choice and power. It may be misused, even perverted from its true nature. As Eike-Henner Kluge observes, "... to argue that since euthanasia may be misused, therefore, it is morally unacceptable, is to argue invalidly—to commit a non sequitur" (151). In other words, the fact that something can be abused does not mean that it should not be used. Rather, the use should be promoted if it is good, and the abuse curtailed by every means available.

Finally, those who invoke the spectre of Nazi Germany to attack euthanasia forget that the Nazis never engaged in euthanasia or mercy killing; what they did was merciless killing, either genocidal or for ruthless experimental purposes. Those are not the goals of the advocates of euthanasia.

Proposals to sanction or legalize the practice of euthanasia are based on several principles. In the first place, the dignity of life is superior to the value of life per se. The belief that a person should have the right to die with dignity, just as he or she should have the right to live with dignity, is expressed in the "living wills" concept sponsored by pro-euthanasia organizations.

In the second place, the physician's responsibility to relieve suffering is more important than his or her responsibility to prolong life. Many would concur with Dr. Frank J. Ayd, who states that "when death is imminent and inevitable, it is neither scientific or humane to use artificial life-sustainers to protect the life of a patient. Instead, it is right to choose only ordinary means to sustain his life and to provide palliative care" (Wilson 54-55).

The right to be at liberty is a third value which is more important than the value of a life that is radically restricted. To prolong life uselessly, while the personal qualities of freedom, knowledge, self-possession, control, and responsibility are sacrificed, is to attack the moral status of a person and to deny his morality.

Finally, laws should be amended in fairness to suffering patients, because legal requirements tend to cause their suffering to be prolonged unnecessarily. While an easy death is secretly granted to some, it is denied to many others. Legalizing the practice of euthanasia would make it available for all.

The practice of voluntary, legal euthanasia would enhance the general welfare of human beings. Society has no genuine interest or need to preserve the terminally ill against their will. Above all else, the greatest good of euthanasia would be the comfort it could provide by replacing the agonizing dread of impending death felt by both patient and family with the anticipation of a "fair and easy passage."

Works Cited

"Debate on the Boundary of Life." Time, 11 April 1983, 68-70.

"Did the Patient Die—Or Was He Murdered?" Newsweek, 14 February 1983, 76.

Fackelmann, Kathy. "A Question of Life or Death." Science News, 9 Oct. 1982, 232-33.

Fletcher, Joseph. "The 'Rights' to Live and to Die." In Beneficent Euthanasia. Ed. Marvin Kohl. Buffalo: Prometheus Books, 1975.

Heifetz, Milton D. The Right to Die. New York: G. P. Putnam's Sons, 1975.

Kluge, Eike-Henner W. The Practice of Death. New Haven: Yale University Press, 1975.

Maguire, Daniel. "Deciding for Yourself." In From Ethical Issues in Death and Dying. Ed. Robert F. Weir. New York: Columbia University Press, 1977.

Sullivan, Joseph V. The Morality of Mercy Killing. Westminster, Md.: The Newman Press, 1950.

"When Doctors Play God." Newsweek, 31 August 1981, 48-54.

Wilson, Jerry B. Death by Decision. Philadelphia: The Westminster Press, 1975.

CHAPTER

12

Writing Essay Examinations, Business Letters, and Résumés

Some of the most important writing you will do in college will be essay examinations; some of the most important writing you will do *after* college will be writing business letters, including letters of application and résumés. These special kinds of writing require the same skills you have been developing writing expository and persuasive themes. They must be clear, well organized, and correct.

Writing Essay Examinations

Many of the examinations that you will take in college will require you to write an answer of several paragraphs. Your success or failure on the examination will often depend as much on your writing skills as on your mastery of the subject.

Writing an essay examination answer can best be done by dividing the task into manageable steps. You have seen that writing an essay is a process; so, too, is writing an essay exam. Here are the four steps comprising that process:

Step 1: Understanding what an essay examination requires
Step 2: Preparing for an essay examination
Step 3: Prewriting the essay examination
Step 4: Writing the essay examination

Steps 1 and 2 have to be done *before* you attend class the day of the examination; steps 3 and 4 are completed *in class* on the day of the examination.

Step 1: Understanding What an Essay Examination Requires

An essay written in response to an examination question is usually a discussion or an analysis of a topic. It is usually three or four paragraphs long and is written within a time limit. An instructor gives an essay exam to test your ability to recall certain facts. He or she may also want to test your ability to understand relationships, to organize the material in a new and different way, to separate the important from the unimportant, to solve problems, and to recognize new trends. In addition to all of these purposes, your instructor may ask you to make a judgment or draw a logical conclusion on the basis of the facts you present.

To accomplish all of these tasks, you have to provide more than a recitation of facts. Essay examinations measure your ability to assimilate, organize, and synthesize the material your instructor has presented. If you cram your head full of facts and just spill them all on the test paper, you will probably fail to answer the questions adequately.

Step 2: Preparing for an Essay Examination

When studying for an essay examination, take the following steps:

1. Review your lecture notes and the textual material carefully. Take notes as you read. Notice chapter headings and their subtopics. Try to discover relationships between ideas and headings. Recite the subtopics to yourself as a review.

2. There is no substitute for being able to quote names, dates, places, numbers, and events. This lends authenticity to your statements. Therefore, review your notes regularly and memorize the facts. If possible, review the material with another person. An active recitation can help both memorization and understanding.

3. Discover the patterns in your study material. Decide which facts are related to other facts, and thereby contribute to an overall design. Make sample questions and answer them. Posing your own questions will help you organize the material in new and different ways.

4. To clarify your understanding of the material, write outlines and summaries. This will help you organize and capsulate information. As a result, you will acquire an overview and control of the material.

5. Review the following "command" words. Remember, different commands require different procedures and responses. These command words are those most often used in essay examination questions.

To Compare means to give both the similarities and the differences; *To Contrast* means to give the differences.

> Compare a polyp and a medusa. (from a zoology course)
>
> Contrast Rembrandt's early etching of "Christ Presented to the People" with his later version of the same subject. (from an art history course)

To Define means to state accurately the meaning of a word or a concept and to include an example when possible.

> Define the term "personality" as it is used by psychologists. (from a psychology course)
>
> What is blank verse? (from a poetry course)

To Describe means to tell the qualities of a thing in such a way that your reader can visualize it.

> Describe the range of colors in the spectrum. (from a physics course)

Describe the effects on our economy if the proposed gold standard were enacted. (from an economics course)

To Discuss means to examine the subject in detail, giving as much information as you can in the time allotted. It may also include your reaction where appropriate.

Discuss the processes and stages of memory. (from a psychology course)

Discuss this statement: "Instruction to foreign-born students should be provided in their native language." (from a sociology course)

To Explain means to make clear by giving details, by giving reasons, or by showing cause and effect.

Explain the economic importance of angiosperms in the food chain. (from a biology course)

Explain the chemical reaction that occurs when an acid and a base are mixed. (from a chemistry course)

To Identify (or *To Define*) means to name, to classify, to give the *who, what, when, where,* and *why* of your subject. A brief description is also necessary.

Identify the six stages in Piaget's sensorimotor period of infancy. (from a psychology course)

Define the term *irony,* giving an example. (from a literature course)

To Illustrate means to give examples.

By referring to several novels, illustrate how the Western frontier has influenced American literature. (from a literature course)

Illustrate divergent, convergent, and parallel evolution. (from a biology course)

To Trace means to show the development of a subject or a process in time or space.

Trace the early history of the French settlers in the Mississippi Valley. (from a geography course)

Trace the steps necessary in setting up a profit and loss ledger for a small business. (from a bookkeeping course)

Step 3: Prewriting the Essay Examination

Here are four things to do when the examination begins:

1. As soon as you receive the examination, glance over the

entire set of questions. Notice how many questions are to be answered. Some instructors ask for only a certain number out of the total number of questions. For example, an instructor might ask you to respond to only three out of five questions. If no more credit is earned for answering five than for answering three, you should direct all of your time and effort toward those three only. If you answer more, you will have wasted valuable time.

Budget your time. Notice the number of points assigned to each question and the time limit (if any) for each. If a time limit is specified, it is a clue to what the instructor expects for a complete answer. A ten-minute limit is usually given for identification or short-answer questions. They can be answered with a single paragraph of five or six sentences. A twenty-minute time limit would indicate two or three paragraphs, and a thirty-minute time limit would require three or four paragraphs. Therefore, budget your time according to the questions you must answer. Remember, there is no additional time allowed for revising.

Notice which questions are easier and which are more difficult for you. Answer the easier ones first. This will encourage your self-confidence and also prod your recall of other related facts and information.

2. Read the question. Then read it a second time. Look for the "command" words. Notice the limiting phrases and clauses. For example:

"Compare the Port-a-Punch with the Optical Scanning Punch and determine which is more effective for use in physical inventories." (from a computer course)

The command word in this question is, of course, "compare." This means that you must give similarities and differences between the Port-a-Punch and the Optical Scanning Punch. Your answer will be made more specific by the words "determine" (meaning "to decide"), "effective" (in what respect), and "physical inventories" (what kinds of items or under what conditions). Be sure that you understand what the question calls for, and then plot your strategy for answering.

3. Jot notes for your essay answer on scratch paper. Jot key ideas (this is where your memorization of chapter headings and subheadings will help), specific terms, names of people and places, dates, events, and statistics. Don't panic if you see a question about which you think you know absolutely

nothing. If you attended all the classes, listened to the lectures, and read the assigned material, you are sure to be able to recall something about the topic. Leave it for the moment, and come back to it later. Answering the easier questions first will jog your memory for the difficult one.

4. Organize your main points (key ideas) into a brief outline for your essay answer. Then decide what specific details and examples you will include under each main point. Check the question again to see if you have included all the specific tasks required of you. If you simply write everything you know about the topic, you may still receive a low grade because you did not show that you saw relationships or recognized larger patterns in the course material. You might set up a relationship by showing cause and effect, contrast, example, analogy, or order of importance. These are not all inclusive, but they suggest some ways for developing an essay answer. Using transitional expressions such as "therefore," "on the other hand," "as a result of," and "in addition to," will emphasize connections and make your essay easier to read.

Step 4: Writing the Essay Examination

Begin your essay with a thesis statement (see Chapter 3). You will always have a beginning if you incorporate part of the question in your answer. To do this, begin your essay with key words of the question but turn them into a statement. For example:

Question:	How does the diesel engine differ from the gasoline engine?
Thesis statement:	The diesel engine differs from the gasoline engine in three important ways.

This technique assures your reader that you have a strategy for answering the question. Your thesis statement gives direction to your answer. Changes of direction confuse your reader. Therefore, know how you are going to answer the question before you begin to write. Having jotted down what came to mind and rearranged it in rough outline in your prewriting stage, you can now develop your answer in the same way that you would write a longer essay.

As you write, be sure to include supporting statements and specific details. Explain, expand, and clarify. Omitting an important point can lower your grade. On the other hand, don't pad. Your instructor will not be impressed with mere words. Write only what is relevant to your topic. If you want to add material after you have moved on to another section, use an asterisk and then write an addendum at the bottom of the page, or attach a second page with a note to indicate the proper place for the addition.

Finally, edit your paper *as you write* because there is no time for rewriting a final draft. Check for the mistakes you usually make in spelling, capitalization, and punctuation. For example, if you frequently confuse *it's* and *its*, *their* and *there*, *affect* and *effect*, or use *must of* for *must have*, check for these errors. Look for omissions such as the second set of quotation marks in a title or quotation. Cross out vague words and expressions like "kind of," "sort of," and "thing." A simple line through a word or phrase indicates to your reader that you want the item to be deleted.

Regardless of what students think, instructors do not grade examination papers capriciously. There is a reason for the grade you receive. When your instructor reads your paper, he or she is looking for particular facts and ideas, relationships and applications, judgments and conclusions—*not* wordiness, padding, and hot air.

Sample Questions and Answers

Here are several typical examination questions and sample answers. Read each and decide which is the better essay. Then read the accompanying discussion of each answer.

Sample Question "A": "Identify the three originators of Modern Art, and evaluate a major work of each."

Answer 1. The three originators of Modern Art were Goya, David, and Constable. Goya painted the *Maja Nude* which hangs in the Prado in Spain. It is the mate to another painting, the *Maja Clothed*, which I think I like better.

David painted the *Death of Marat* which I find startling but dreary because the entire upper half of the picture is empty. The dedication at the bottom of the picture, "To Marat," with "David" underneath it, strikes me as unnecessary.

Constable painted the *View at Stoke*. This is an oil sketch which seems to need more delineation as I can't make out a lot of what is in the picture except for a house to the left and an animal of some kind standing in front of it. The whole painting needs more elaboration.

Answer 2. The three originators of Modern Art were Francisco Goya of Spain (1746-1828), Jacques Louis David of France (1748-1825), and John Constable of England (1776-1837).

Goya represents the beginning of modern painting because he depicts man and society from the scientific viewpoint. For example, in the *Family of Charles IV*, painted in 1800, he conveys realistically the insanity of the king and the ambition of his queen. This rendition does not glorify the royal family, or even offer a humanizing treatment. However, it is Goya's strength that he painted his subjects as he knew them to be, not as they appeared to be. Therefore, his painting conveys a combination of psychological analysis and scientific dissection.

David's most famous painting is the *Oath of the Horatii*, which depicts a stern Roman father asking his sons to make a self-sacrificing pledge, probably for a military battle. The diagonal lines in the painting convey movement of legs, arms, and swords. This movement contrasts with the background of vertical columns and horizontal masonry. The women grieving at the right of the picture help to complete the artist's protest against war. There are large areas in the painting which seem to exist only to emphasize the main action, which is a departure from the usual formal aspects of balance and style. The painting, therefore, contributes a revolutionary theme of lines and shapes to nineteenth-century art.

John Constable, the third originator of modern art, is known for his paintings of the English landscape. His *The Leaping Horse* shows a deep reverence for nature. The child and his horse are communing with nature in an almost religious simplicity. Man and nature seem to be united, but this is only part of the picture. A large part of the scene is given to the rendition of light and clouds. In fact, if it were not for the sky, the horse and rider would not even be evident in the pastoral scene. It is the light from the heavens that focuses the viewer's attention on horse and rider. The light and clouds are an important part of this painting, not just a background. Therefore, *The Leaping Horse* introduces an important idea to modern landscape painting—concentration on the use of light.

Criticism of Answers.   Answer 2 is better for several reasons. First, it incorporates the key words of the question in the answer. Second, it acknowledges the meaning of the command words "identify" and "evaluate." Answer 2 immediately gives the *who, what, when,* and *where.* Through the use of classification it suggests an organizational pattern for the essay. Goya, David, and Constable will be discussed in order. The essay then proceeds to give both the strengths and the weaknesses of a specific work by each painter. Answer 2 was obviously the result of careful planning, because the main points and subpoints can be readily seen.

Answer 1 has a stab at organization, but it is superficial in its discussion of the paintings. The answer does not fulfill the task of identification. It answers the command word "identify" only superficially. The essay does not support the thesis statement with specific facts or information; it offers, instead, a series of subjective reactions and irrelevant information. For example, where the *Maja Nude* hangs is extraneous to the question, as is the fact that it has a mate. Vague generalities and asides follow each other in a haphazard order, creating the impression that the writer really hadn't looked at the paintings carefully. In short, the answer fails to give a specific evaluation of any major work as specified by the question.

Sample
Question "B": "Explain the difference between *attitudes* and *opinions*."

> *Answer 1.* Although people frequently use *attitudes* and *opinions* interchangeably, there are important differences between the two terms. Opinions are cognitive, that is, they are the result of a mental operation, not an emotional one. For example, it is my *opinion* that Chicago is less humid in August than St. Louis. If someone shows me meteorological records to the contrary, I will change my opinion. Opinions can be changed if irrefutable evidence is presented.
>
> Attitudes are based upon emotional reactions combined with cognitive and action components. For example, if a person has a positive attitude toward animals, then he has favorable opinions (the cognitive component) about them. He is happy to be around them (the emotional component), and he spends some time with them (the action component). Because attitudes are more complicated than opinions, they last longer and are usually more difficult to change.
>
> *Answer 2.* The difference between *attitudes* and *opinions* is not always easy to discover. For example, if a person holds the opinion that Chinese are shorter than Americans, this is not the same as a person calling all Mexicans shiftless and lazy.

Criticism of Answers. Answer 1 is better because it is specific. It tells what an opinion is and is not. It furnishes a simple, clear example. The term "attitude" receives a more specific treatment in accordance with its more complex nature. It is also accompanied by an example. Answer 2 is completely unsatisfactory. It has an inadequate thesis statement and gives no examples, definition, or explanation. It careens off into an illustration that is incorrect.

Sample
Question "C": "Identify the following terms: *acid, base,* and *salt*."

> *Answer 1.* An acid is a chemical compound that has a sharp, sour taste, will corrode metals, and will turn blue litmus red. Some examples are sulfuric, nitric, and hydrochloric acids.
>
> A base is a chemical compound sometimes called an alkali. It feels soapy to the touch and turns red litmus to blue. It can neutralize an acid when mixed with it, thereby forming a salt. Some examples are soda, lime, and ammonia.

A salt is a crystalline substance produced by mixing an acid and a base. A salt is soluble in water and has a salty taste. It has none of the characteristics of the acid or base from which it is formed. Some examples are alum, borax, and common table salt.

Answer 2. Acids, bases, and salts are all related. They react differently on litmus paper and all have a different taste. Mixing two of these together will result in the third. It's never a good idea to mix chemicals together without first reading the label.

Criticism of Answers. Answer 1 is better because it uses classification, description, and examples as it formulates its clear, organized response. An acid or a base is a "chemical compound"; a salt is a "chemical substance." Answer 1 follows this information with a description of how acids, bases, and salts work. Then the essay gives examples of each. Answer 2 attempts to explain too much at once. Before any relationship is made, the terms need to be identified. This answer, however, fails to show how acids, bases, and salts are all related, despite its thesis statement. The discussion of each item is vague, and the last sentence is irrelevant and unnecessary. All in all, it is a very unsatisfactory answer.

Some Final Words About Writing Essay Examinations

Writing an essay examination and writing an expository or persuasive essay for your English class share several steps. In both cases it is necessary to do some prewriting: gathering ideas, developing a thesis statement, and organizing the material. The wording of the essay examination question will usually dictate the method of development for the test essay, but the importance of coherence, unity, clarity, and correctness is identical in both assignments. Learning the "command" words and the unique requirements of each will be helpful to you, as will the other suggestions in this section.

Writing Business Letters

A business letter initiates or transacts business. It asks someone to do something for you: fill an order, handle a complaint, give you a job, furnish information, answer a claim, or correct a mistake. Regardless of its purpose, a business letter requires the same kind of exactness and clarity that all good writing does. It must be clear, well organized, interesting, and grammatically correct. And because a business letter is often sent to someone you don't know—someone who may judge you in part by the appearance of your letter—it must follow certain expected patterns or conventions.

Appearance and Format of the Business Letter

Business letters are typed on 8½" x 11" unlined white paper of good quality. Your letters should be single-spaced and limited, if possible, to a single page. If you write more than one page, number the pages. Double-space between paragraphs. Center the letter, leaving margins at least 1½" at the top and bottom and 1" on the sides. If your letter is brief, the top and bottom margins will be larger.

Most business letters follow either the *block style* or the *semi-block style*. In the block style, which is the most formal, all parts of the letter, including the first lines of paragraphs, are flush with the left margin. The letter on page 285 is written in block style.

The semi-block style, which is the format most widely used today in American business correspondence, is essentially the same as the block style except for the location of the heading, complimentary close, and signature, which are toward the right half of the page. All other parts of the letter are flush with the left margin. The letter on page 288 follows the semi-block style.

Regardless of its style, the business letter has six basic parts:

1. Heading
2. Inside address
3. Salutation or Greeting
4. Body
5. Complimentary Close
6. Signature

Heading.   If you are typing a letter on a letterhead which is preprinted with the name and address of the company or organization, type the date directly beneath the letterhead. If you are using plain white stationery, start 1½" from the top. The heading consists of your address (street, city, state, ZIP code) and the date. With the exception of the two-letter abbreviations approved by the postal service, do not use any abbreviations in the heading.

If you follow the block style and are using plain white stationery, all lines in the heading should be flush with the left margin (see page 285). If you are following the semi-block style, the longest line in the heading should be flush with the right margin (see page 287). In both cases you should not use end punctuation. Here is an example of a heading:

5730 Warren Avenue
Nashville, TN 37203
January 15, 1984

Inside Address.   The inside address gives the name and address of the company or person to whom you are writing. It contains the full name of the person or firm and the complete mailing address. Type the person's title, if appropriate (Mrs., Ms., Mr., Dr., and so on). It is always more effective to address a letter to a specific person than to a company. As in the case of the heading, do not use any other abbreviation except for the two-letter abbreviation for the state.

The location of the inside address is the same for the block style and the semi-block style. It should be even with the left margin and from two to four lines below the heading, as in the following example:

Miss Jacqueline Davis
Personnel Manager
Grunden Valve Company
9211 Orange Boulevard
Jacksonville, FL 32111

Salutation.   The salutation or greeting begins two spaces below the inside address and is followed by a colon. In both the block style and the semi-block style it is flush with the left margin.

If you have used the addressee's name in the inside address, use it in the salutation: "Dear Mr. Jones," "Dear Mrs. Edwards," and so on. If you are uncertain about the marital status of a woman, you may use "Ms.," which is widely accepted today. You may also use professional titles in your salutation: "Dear Dr. Ellis," "Dear Professor Dreyfus," and so on. If you do not know the name or sex of your addressee, you may use "Dear Sir or Madam."

The following forms are correct:

Dear Ms. Hogan:

Dear Professor McAvoy:

Dear Mrs. Manley:

Dear Dr. Lehane:

Body.   Begin the body of your letter two spaces below the salutation. In both the block style and semi-block style, all paragraphs begin flush with the left margin. Paragraphs should be single-spaced, with double spacing between paragraphs. The content of the body is discussed below.

Complimentary Close.   If you are following the block style, begin the complimentary close two or three lines below the last line of the body, typed flush with the left-hand margin (see page 286). In the semi-block style, it is typed to the right of the letter in alignment with the heading (see page 289).

The most common forms of the complimentary close are "Sincerely yours," "Yours truly," "Sincerely," and "Cordially." Capitalize only the first word and place a comma after the complimentary close.

Signature.   Type your name four to six spaces directly below the complimentary close. In the space above the typed signature, sign your name legibly in ink in longhand. When typing your name do not put a professional title in front of it (Dr., Rev., etc.) or degrees after it (M.A., Ph.D., etc.). Some medical doctors make an exception to this rule, placing "M.D." after their typed name. Beneath your typed signature you may indicate your official capacity (Chairman of the Board, Athletic Director, Sales Manager, etc.). A married woman uses her own first name, not that of her husband. A woman may indicate the title she prefers to be addressed by in her typed signature: (Miss) Joan Reiter; (Mrs.) Irene Farber; (Ms.) Rita Touhill.

General Guidelines for Effective Business Writing

In addition to arranging the parts of your letter according to the standard form, the grammar and style must also fulfill the recipient's expectations. Your reader expects your letter to be accurate, to the point, and clear. He or she must be able to grasp its contents immediately, without confusion or ambiguity. Misspellings, careless punctuation, or faulty grammar will keep your reader from taking you seriously. The tone of the letter should be appropriate to the subject and the situation. If the reader does not like the way you say it, your message will not be received favorably.

Your letters will be more effective if you follow these guidelines:

1. Write to express, not to impress. Present your ideas simply and directly. The writer who makes the best impression is the one who can express complex ideas in a simple way.
2. State the purpose of your letter in the first paragraph. Your reader is busy; don't keep him or her guessing. If you are applying for a job, name the position. By getting to the point, you will let the personnel manager know which position you are interested in.
3. Write in a natural, informal tone. Avoid business jargon. In particular, avoid such hackneyed phrases as "Enclosed please find," "I beg to acknowledge," "Contents noted," and so on.
4. Keep your sentences short. For easy reading, sentences should vary in length and structure, but reading is hard when sentences average more than twenty words.
5. Prefer the simple to the complex. Avoid words, phrases, and constructions that are too complicated. If there's a simpler way to say something, use it.
6. Avoid unnecessary words. Make every word in a business letter carry its own weight; get rid of any you don't need.
7. The tone of your letter should be courteous.

8. Put action in your verbs. The heaviness of much business writing comes from overworking passive verb forms. Active verbs put life into your writing.
9. Make it clear what you expect from your reader. Ask for an appointment or mention when you will be calling.
10. Read and re-read your letter, checking for errors in spelling, punctuation, and grammar.

Types of Business Letters

There are as many types of business letters as there are business situations. This section discusses three of the most common types: an order, a claim or letter of complaint, and a job application.

The Order Letter. An order letter is from a person who wants to buy something. The most important requirement in such a letter is that it state clearly and accurately (1) what is wanted, (2) how it will be paid for, and (3) how and where it is to be delivered.

Make sure that you describe the item that you want precisely and accurately. Give the name of the product, the model or stock number, and the quantity desired. If they apply, specify the color, size, finish, and weight.

Mention the price and the method of payment. If you have enclosed a check or money order, mention that fact. If the purchase is to be charged to your account or credit card, give the account number or name.

Tell where you want the item shipped and how you want it shipped (parcel post, air express, etc.). If you need it by a certain date, let the seller know.

An example of an order letter follows. Notice that it is written in the block style and is centered on the page.

Order Letter

4611 Avocado Drive
Santa Barbara, CA 93101
November 5, 1984

Mrs. Ann Remington, Manager
Remington's Luggage Mart
500 East Seventh Street
Los Angeles, CA 90017

Dear Mrs. Remington:

I would like to order the four-piece set of Skymate luggage advertised on page 14 in your 1984 catalogue. The four pieces include a tote, carry-on, pullman, and garment bag. I prefer the blue model; if it is unavailable, burgundy is acceptable.

The sales price specified in your catalogue for the set is $99.50. I have enclosed a personal check for $108.45, which includes shipping charges of $8.95. Because I would like to use the luggage for a trip during the Christmas holiday, I would appreciate receiving the set at the above address by December 10.

Sincerely yours,

Charles J. Nowotny

Charles J. Nowotny

E X E R C I S E 1

Write a letter to a company in another city ordering a part for your car, an accessory for your computer, or a tool for your workshop. Be sure that you include all of the information listed on page 285.

The Claim or Letter of Complaint.   The purpose of a claim or complaint letter is to correct a situation. It usually arises from what the buyer regards as an error on the part of the merchant: an overcharge, the wrong size, style, or color, a delayed or missent shipment, or similar complaints. Regardless of the problem, the writer's immediate reaction usually is to fire off an angry letter "telling off" the merchant. Although such a letter might make the writer feel better, it's not likely to correct the situation. In fact, it will probably make the merchant unsympathetic to the buyer's complaint.

Claim letters and complaints that follow these guidelines will usually accomplish the writer's goal:

1. Describe the transaction completely; give identifying information such as the date, model and serial numbers, style, color, brand name, price, your check number, and so on.
2. Explain the problem in detail. Write in a calm, courteous, and factual style.
3. Tell the recipient of the letter how you think the situation

should be corrected. If you want a replacement or a refund, state your reasons.
4. Above all, avoid sarcasm, threats, and name-calling. Most companies want to be fair.

The following letter was the first version of a complaint written by Michael Anderson, a student who had ordered a telescope by mail from a catalogue. As you read it, imagine that you are the recipient of the letter. What would your reaction be to Michael's complaint? If you were to give him advice on rewriting his letter, what suggestions would you give?

Draft Letter of Complaint

7250 Artillery Drive
Dallas, TX 75201
December 4, 1984

Prentiss Corporation
1640 Lincoln Road
Portland, OR 97208

To Whom It May Concern:

I want my money back on a telescope I order from your catalog. If I had know that it was damaged, I would never had ordered the thing. You're ad says that it has "a specialy coated 30 mm objective lens to guarantee 30-power magnification." The only thing I can see out of it is a big scratch that one of your employes obviously put on it out of stupidity or ingorance. I sent you a check in full payment for this shabby merchandise, and if I do not receive a full refund immediately I will take this to the proper authorities. I'd like to know how many other suckers you have sold these to. I would like to hear from you at once on this matter.

Yours truly,

Michael Anderson

Michael Anderson

You probably noticed several weaknesses in Michael's letter that were guaranteed to irritate the recipient of his complaint. The most obvious (and most serious) is the sarcasm and anger that almost smothers the letter. Such a tone would put the reader on the defensive and make him unsympathetic to Michael's problem. Another problem with the letter is the series of spelling and grammatical errors ("If I had know," "I would never had ordered," "You're ad says," and so on). Finally, his letter loses its impact because it is not directed to anyone specifically; "To Whom It May Concern" is such a vague greeting that no one would feel personally responsible for the sender's complaint.

Luckily, Michael showed the draft of his letter to a couple of friends who suggested some changes. One suggestion was to learn the name of the manager or owner so that Michael could address his letter to a specific person. Another idea was to adopt a calmer, more reasonable tone and to propose the specific adjustment that he wanted. Another suggestion was to follow a more conventional form for his letter (you may have noticed that his letter was a mixture of the block and semi-block styles). After Michael thought about these ideas, he rewrote his letter.

As you read his revised letter, compare your reaction to it with your reaction to his earlier version. Which letter is more likely to get the desired results?

Letter of Complaint

7250 Artillery Drive
Dallas, TX 75201
December 4, 1984

Mr. Harry T. Prentiss, Manager
Prentiss Corporation
1640 Lincoln Road
Portland, OR 97208

Dear Mr. Prentiss:

Last Monday I received by parcel post a telescope that I had ordered from your 1984 catalogue. The telescope is the Fidelity Model 4 as pictured on page 15 of the catalogue.

Upon unpacking the telescope I was disappointed to find that the lens is deeply scratched across its entire width, making the telescope impossible to use. I would like a replacement for this telescope at your earliest convenience. If a telescope of identical quality and power is not available, I wish a complete refund. A photocopy of my check for $23.10 is enclosed.

I would appreciate your prompt response to this letter.

Yours truly,

Michael Anderson

Michael Anderson

E X E R C I S E 2

Write a letter to a local utility company in which you complain about a mistake in your bill. Before writing, review the guidelines on page 286–87.

The Letter of Application. One of the most important business letters that you will ever write is the letter of application. It will accompany your résumé, a list of your experiences and qualifications for a job. Although the résumé is very important, it is the covering letter of application that your prospective employer will see first. The application follows the format already described for the business letter. But because it has a unique purpose, it follows additional guidelines.

Guidelines for the Letter of Application
1. Be specific about the position for which you are applying. Begin your letter by mentioning the person or advertisement that informed you of the job opening.
2. Emphasize your experience that is relevant to the job. You can be brief, because your résumé will provide details. Nevertheless, point out any practical experience that you have.
3. Mention your interest in the company; show that you are familiar with its products or its reputation. Explain how your experience and education can help the company.
4. Keep in mind that your letter will be your introduction to its reader. Be certain that it is neat, readable, concise, and correct.
5. Ask for an interview. Tell your prospective employer when you can be reached and when you are available for an interview.

On the next pages are two letters of application for the same position. Which person would you hire, based only on the letters?

Letter of Application

1911 Odell Drive
Carleton, IL 62237
May 15, 1984

Miss Arlene Ruggiero
Director of Personnel
Illinois Chemical Company
10631 East O'Fallon Street
Belleville, IL 62224

Dear Miss Ruggiero:

I would be interested in applying for the position of a management trainee at your company. I believe that I have the qualifications for the job. I attended Southern Illinois University for two years but had to quit because of personal problems. While I was there I took courses in business that prepared me for the world of finance. I enjoyed my classes very much, and I made many good friends while I was at college. I played in the marching band (flute) and was active in the homecoming activities.

I can type about sixty words a minute and took a class in computers at a local business college. I am anxious to find a position with a company that will give me a chance to advance so that I can reach my goal in the world of business. I think that I have had many experiences and kinds of training that would your company could use.

Feel free to call me for an interview. I am looking forward to hearing from you soon. While I don't know very much about Illinois Chemical Company, I know that chemicals are very important in our daily lives, and that your company is probably doing its best to make this a better place in which to live.

Yours,

Doris Campbell

Doris Campbell (Miss)

The Résumé

The résumé is a one- or two-page list of your achievements and qualifications. Its purpose is to give your prospective employer enough

Letter of Application

320 Hawksbury Drive
Belleville, IL 62221
May 16, 1984

Ms. Arlene Ruggiero
Director of Personnel
Illinois Chemical Company
10631 East O'Fallon Street
Belleville, IL 62224

Dear Ms. Ruggiero:

Your classified advertisement in last Sunday's <u>News-Democrat</u> indicates that there is an opening on your staff for a management trainee in your payroll department. I would like to apply for that position.

As the accompanying résumé demonstrates, I have extensive academic and professional experience that would qualify me for this position. Next month I will receive an Associate in Arts degree from Belleville College, with a major in accounting. In addition, I have had practical work experience in a variety of part-time positions for local companies.

I have admired Illinois Chemical's participation in such community activities as the United Way and the Youth Symphony, as well as its support of strict environmental regulations. For these reasons, I believe that I would be an enthusiastic and competent employee of Illinois Chemical Company.

If I can provide information not specified on the résumé, I shall be glad to do so. I am available for an interview at your convenience.

Sincerely yours,

Jennifer L. Woodward

Jennifer L. Woodward

---

information about your background to help him or her determine your potential as an employee. The most qualified people don't always get the job. It goes to the person who presents himself or herself most persuasively in person and on paper. That is why it is very important that your résumé and letter of application be carefully written.

Résumés vary in their content and format, but most of them present the following information: personal data, job objective, education, work experience, extra-curricular activities, and references. The résumés on pages 293 and 294 follow the most popular formats.

Information in the Résumé

Personal information. Federal guidelines prevent your being hired on the basis of your race, religion, national origin, or sex. Many applicants, however, include this information on their résumés; in any event, you should include your name, address, and telephone number. Other items commonly listed in this section are height, weight, marital status, and condition of health.

Job objective. List either the actual position you are seeking or your long-range objective. If you name the latter, your covering letter of application should specify the position you are applying for.

Education. Begin by giving the date of attendance at the college you are currently enrolled in and work backwards to the high school from which you graduated. Mention the degree or certificate you received, your major, and the name and location of each institution. Mention your grade-point average (GPA) if it was high.

Work experience. List in reverse chronological order—most recent first—your full-time and part-time jobs. Tell when you held the job and list your former employers' names and addresses. If one of the jobs was similar to the job you are applying for, describe your duties.

Extra-curricular activities. This section gives you a chance to list any related hobbies, memberships in organizations, and skills that might be useful in the job you are applying for. If you have been active in community activities or civic organizations that have given you experience in leadership, mention them. If you are a recent graduate and do not have much work experience, mention any campus clubs and organizations you belonged to, offices you held, and awards you received. Do not list political or religious affiliations; they are irrelevant in the hiring process.

References. In this section you have a choice: you can simply state, "References on request," or you can list from three to five people who know you. These can be of several kinds. You can list former or present employers, coworkers, prominent people in your community who know you, or instructors. In each case, list the name, title, address, and telephone number. Make certain that you obtain permission to use a person's name before listing it in your résumé.

Some Reminders When Writing the Résumé

1. The appearance of your résumé is very important. It should be attractive, organized, and readable. It should have no spelling or grammatical mistakes or erasures.
2. Your résumé should be easy to read. Type on white paper, using wide margins and lots of white space between sections. Never send a carbon copy; photocopies are acceptable, however.
3. Underline or capitalize headings to make them stand out on the page. Don't use complete sentences; phrases and clauses are satisfactory and require less room.
4. As mentioned above, list your education and work experience in reverse order.
5. Don't pad your résumé with inflated language; keep your writing style simple.

Study the following résumés; they follow the suggestions in this chapter.

RÉSUMÉ FOR POSITION OF PETROLEUM REFINERY OPERATOR

Arthur L. Cardenas

1951 Oleander Drive
Tulsa, OK 74101
(918) 555-1240

Education

1973-75: Winchester Community College, Winchester, Oklahoma. Received A. S. degree in Petroleum Engineering.

1965-69: Jackson High School, Claremore, Oklahoma. Took vocational and technical courses.

Military Experience

1969-73: United States Navy. Received honorable discharge June 1973 with rank of 3rd Class Petty Officer (PO-3). Served on oil tanker as pumper and main propulsion assistant.

Work Experience

1975-77: Challenge Oil Laboratory, Inc., Del Mar, Oklahoma. Duties included maintenance and operation of reactors and stabilizers; performed chemical and physical tests of earth samples in the field and laboratory to determine extent of hydrocarbons or other components; drew samples of petroleum products from various parts of refinery for laboratory analysis.

1977-
present: Big Sky Petroleum Refinery, Big Sky, Oklahoma. Duties include operation of batch treating equipment to process petroleum products, remove impurities and to improve color, stability, and odor according to specifications. Maintain and check distillation operations, read processing schedules, operating logs, test results of oil samples. Familiar with exchangers, quenchers, fractionators, and other distillation process equipment.

Personal

Age: 32; Height: 5′ 11″; Weight: 178 pounds; Health: excellent

References

Available upon request

RÉSUMÉ

Jennifer L. Woodward
320 Hawksbury Drive
Belleville, Illinois 62221
(618) 555-3820

Job Objective   Management trainee in payroll department

Education

    1982-84   Belleville College, Belleville, Illinois
Degree: Associate of Arts (expected in June, 1984)
Major: Accounting

    1978-82   Belleville High School, Belleville, Illinois
Graduated with honors in June, 1982

Work Experience

    Sept. 1983   Payroll clerk (part-time), Memorial Hospital
to present   Caseyville, Illinois

Summer 1983	Typist, North American Life Insurance Company St. Louis, Missouri
Sept. 1982–June 1983	File clerk (part-time), Associated Credit Bureau Belleville, Illinois
Extracurricular Activities	President of Business Club, Belleville College (1983) Chairman of Junior Achievement Program, Belleville High School (1981-82)
References	Mr. Gerald Dee, Business Manager Memorial Hospital Caseyville, Illinois (618) 555-1992

Ms. Patricia Martin, Comptroller
North American Life Insurance Company
1200 Locust Street
St. Louis, Missouri
(314) 490-1568

Mrs. Margaret Massey, Chairperson
Business Department
Belleville College
Belleville, Illinois
(618) 555-3948

E X E R C I S E 3

Write a résumé for yourself that includes the information listed on page 292. Then write a letter of application to accompany your résumé.

A Handbook
of Grammar
and Graphics:
Usage
and Punctuation

A Guide to Editing: Usage and Punctuation

To be an effective writer, you will have to follow certain principles of *standard written English*, the kind of writing used in practically all public communication. In conversation, of course, many of these principles can be ignored. "I be going" and "He stay," for example, are perfectly acceptable to speakers of Black American English. *Written* English, however, is more standardized and conservative; it follows certain predictable guidelines that often conflict with your own speaking dialect.

If your sentences—including your punctuation—do not follow or conform to these guidelines or standards, there is a good chance they will not be read. If read, there is a likelihood that they will confuse or mislead your reader. In either case, you have failed in your effort to communicate.

Many of the guidelines that regulate written English deal with sentence structure and punctuation. This handbook deals with major problems that you are going to encounter in those areas as you revise and edit your papers. The emphasis is on recognizing the problems and then learning how to correct them.

Common Problems with Sentences

Surveys of employers, research by scholars, and the day-to-day experience of your instructors support the notion that most writers have the following problems in their writing: incomplete sentences (or fragments), comma splices, run-on sentences, lack of subject-verb agreement, misplaced modifiers, faulty pronoun usage, and shifts in tense, voice, and person. This is not a complete list of all the possible errors, but it includes the most serious. We will examine each of these errors in turn.

Sentence Fragments

A *sentence* is a group of words containing at least one independent clause and conveying a certain sense of completeness. In other words, it has a subject and a verb and is capable of standing alone. A *sentence fragment* is a group of words that lacks an independent clause—it looks like a sentence because it begins with a capital letter and ends with a period or other end punctuation, but it leaves the reader "hanging," waiting for more to follow.

Notice the sense of "incompleteness" in the following italicized fragments:

Larry told a joke. *Which embarrassed everyone.*

Many of Shakespeare's plays have been made into films. *Such as Romeo and Juliet.*

Although he should have known better. Con tried to jump over the glass coffee table.

Fragments are common in speech, particularly in informal conversations when they serve as responses to what someone else has said or as additions to something we have just said.

The use of fragments in writing can sometimes be justified by an experienced writer when their meaning is clear and when the writer is striving for a particular effect or purpose. In general, however, fragments should be avoided in writing. They imply that the writer is careless or ignorant (or both). They distract readers and create confusion in their minds.

There are two types of fragments: *dependent clauses* and *phrases.* Dependent clauses have subjects and verbs, but they cannot stand alone—they depend on independent clauses to complete their meaning. Dependent clauses can be spotted by the kinds of words that introduce them, making them dependent. The technical terms for these introducing words are *subordinating conjunctions* and *relative pronouns.* In the following fragments, notice that each begins with such a word:

When the ceasefire was announced.
Before the first guest arrived at the party.
Which was enough to do the job.

If you read each fragment aloud, you will detect its sense of incompleteness.

The following list contains the most common dependent clause introducing words. Whenever a clause begins with one of them (unless it is a question), it is a *dependent clause* and cannot stand alone.

after	in order that	where, wherever
although	since	whether
as, as if	that	which, whichever
because	unless	while
before	until	who, whose
how	what, whatever	whom
if	when, whenever	

Notice what happens to the following independent clause when words from the above list are placed in front of it:

We studied for our finals.

After we studied for our finals. *(fragment)*
Although we studied for our finals. *(fragment)*
As we studied for our finals. *(fragment)*
Because we studied for our finals. *(fragment)*

Before we studied for our finals. *(fragment)*
If we studied for our finals. *(fragment)*
Unless we studied for our finals. *(fragment)*

As you can see, the independent clause has been changed into a series of dependent clauses. Each dependent clause is a fragment, even though it is punctuated like a sentence. To correct this kind of fragment, simply add an independent clause:

After we studied for our finals, *we ate pizza.*
Although we studied for our finals, *we were still nervous.*
As we studied for our finals, *we listened to the radio.*
Because we studied for our finals, *we felt prepared.*

Here are some examples of dependent clause fragments along with their corrections.

- *Dependent clause:*
  Although the price had been lowered. *(fragment)*
- *Revised:*
  Although the price had been lowered, the house remained unsold.

- *Dependent clause:*
  While they were watching the movie. *(fragment)*
- *Revised:*
  Their car was stolen while they were watching the movie.

- *Dependent clause:*
  After a lifetime in public office. *(fragment)*
- *Revised:*
  After a lifetime in public office, she retired to her farm.

The other kind of sentence fragment is the *phrase.* The phrase fragment is a group of words that is missing a subject or a verb or both, and therefore does not make sense by itself. Here are some examples of phrase fragments:

Quebec, the oldest city in Canada and the capital city of the province of Quebec. *(fragment)*
Attracted by the tales of adventures and the rumors of gold. *(fragment)*
Soaring above the crowd. *(fragment)*
The fans in the stands. *(fragment)*

Phrase fragments can be corrected in two ways:

- By supplying the missing part:

  Quebec, the oldest city in Canada, *is* the capital city of the province of Quebec. *(adding a verb)*

The miners were attracted by the tales of adventures and the rumors of gold. *(adding a subject and verb)*

• By tying the fragment to a complete sentence:

Soaring above the crowd, the dirigible relayed the radio signal.
He waved to his teammates, to the cameras, and to the fans in the stands.

Sentence fragments can usually be detected when they are read aloud, because they convey a sense of incompleteness—you are left waiting for more to follow. Don't rely on your ear, however. When revising your writing, make certain that every sentence contains at least one independent clause.

Comma Splices and Run-on Sentences

A *comma splice* results when two independent clauses are mistakenly connected ("spliced") with a comma instead of being separated into two sentences or joined with a conjunction or a semicolon. (See page 320 for a complete discussion of this use of the semicolon.) If the independent clauses are just run together without a conjunction or punctuation, the result is a *run-on* sentence.

Here are examples of both errors:

• *Comma splice:*

Synthetic furs are widely used for winter coats, they are gradually replacing genuine animal pelts.

• *Run-on sentence:*

Synthetic furs are widely used for winter coats they are gradually replacing genuine animal pelts.

You should avoid comma splices and run-on sentences in your writing for the same reasons that you should avoid sentence fragments: they are hard to read, they confuse your reader, they suggest that you are careless, and they indicate that you do not know what a sentence is. Perhaps equally important is the fact that English instructors rarely regard them as indications of your creativity.

Comma splices and run-on sentences can be corrected in four ways:

1. By using a period between the independent clauses, making them two sentences.

   Synthetic furs are widely used for winter coats. They are gradually replacing genuine animal pelts.

2. By inserting a semicolon between the independent clauses.

   Synthetic furs are widely used for winter coats; they are gradually replacing genuine animal pelts.

3. By placing a comma and a coordinating conjunction *(and, but, for, or, yet, so)* between the independent clauses.

   Synthetic furs are widely used for winter coats, **and** they are gradually replacing genuine animal pelts.

4. By using one of the dependent words (or subordinating conjunctions) from the list on page 298, making one of the clauses dependent.

   Because synthetic furs are widely used for winter coats, they are gradually replacing genuine animal pelts.

E X E R C I S E 1

The word groups below contain sentence fragments, comma splices, and run-on sentences. Following the suggestions already given, correct the errors. If a sentence is correct, mark it "C."

1. Some fans believe that Bill Russell is the greatest basketball player of all time, others would name Bill Walton.
2. A city in Illinois passed a law banning ownership of guns a city in Georgia passed a law requiring ownership of guns.
3. Although the Dead Sea, despite its name, is actually a lake.
4. Because most of the vitamins in rice are concentrated in the husk, and ninety-five percent of the world crop is grown in the Orient.
5. Each camper was asked to bring food and supplies to last for four days some, however, were obviously prepared to be gone for a month.
6. A toothbrush, some paper clips, and a book of matches, disappointing to those who had hoped to find more in the safe.
7. As language grows and adds new words, it drops other words no longer used.
8. Mel thought he had returned the library book, however, he found it in the trunk of his car.
9. The price of gasoline has decreased within the last few months this is due in part to the popularity of small cars.
10. Eating balanced meals, sleeping eight hours a night, exercising regularly, and drinking in moderation throughout his long, boring life.
11. Groucho Marx had been an entertainer for almost seventy years, he died when he was eighty-six.

12. As the sun sank in the west and the mosquitos' buzz grew louder and more persistent, until we decided to go back into the house.
13. He told us that a truce had been declared.
14. Many schools now have computer terminals in their libraries, some of them have been donated by computer manufacturers.
15. Mrs. Sheehan gave a lecture on the history of the calendar, I was surprised to learn of its changes throughout the ages.
16. Clare works for a printer who specializes in restaurant menus.
17. Ben smiled sheepishly. As if he were caught with his hand in the cookie jar.
18. She had read the works of Gandhi and seen the movie of his life, now she wanted to visit India.
19. His blood pressure went down it was because of his salt-free diet.
20. The rain, dripping slowly from the leak in the porch roof and onto the porch swing.

Subject-Verb Agreement

Mistakes in subject-verb agreement are among the most common writing errors, and they are particularly irritating to readers. They are often the result of carelessness. Sometimes, however, they are caused by the writer's confusion concerning the subject and the verb.

Subjects and verbs must agree in two important ways: in *number* and in *person*. To help you understand the distinction, here are two rules:

Rule 1: The subject and the verb must agree in number.
• A singular subject takes a singular verb.

The muffler rattles when the car goes over forty miles per hour.

• A plural subject takes a plural verb.

The sparkplugs are expensive but they make the engine more efficient.

Rule 2: The subject and the verb must agree in person.
• First person:

I stay [not *stays*] with my uncle when I visit [not *visits*] Baltimore.
We stay [not *stays*] away from strange-looking weeds because we are [not *is*] afraid of poison ivy.

- Second person:

  You are [not *be* or *is*] one of the most helpful friends I
  have.
  You throw [not *throws*] the ball just like your sister.

- Third person:

  Judith and Dick decided to get married next month.
  They are [not *is*] very excited.
  Maggie is enrolled in a Chinese class. She enjoys [not
  enjoy] practicing the vocabulary drills.

To help you apply these rules, study the following suggestions:

1. A verb must agree with the subject—not with any words or
   phrases that follow the subject but are not part of it. These
   include terms like *along with, together with, including, as well as,*
   and *in addition to.*

   Anita, as well as the other members of her family, is [not *are*]
   looking forward to the trip.
   I, together with Earl and Dave, am [not *are*] going to give a
   party for the custodian.

2. The verb must agree with the subject—not with words that
   rename it in the sentence.

   My favorite memory of the reunion was [not *were*] the hours
   spent talking to my newly-found relatives.
   Customers who want to exchange their purchases without a
   receipt are [not *is*] the biggest problem.

3. Don't be confused by sentences that are out of the usual
   subject-verb pattern.

   Under the desk were [not *was*] the missing folders.
   Beyond the hills was [not *were*] the cottage.

4. Two or more subjects connected by "and" require a plural
   verb.

   His loud voice and bizarre behavior make [not *makes*] him
   unpopular.

   Note: When the compound subject consists of two words of
   closely related meaning or of two nouns that name the same
   person, a singular verb is often used:

   Her wit and humor *is* known to everyone.
   The best athlete and scholar in the class *is* Mario.

5. Singular pronouns require singular verbs. The following pronouns are singular: *another, anybody, anyone, anything, each, either, everybody, everyone, everything, neither, nobody, no one, nothing, one, somebody, someone, something.*

> No one *was* able to solve the puzzle.
> Everybody *wants* to be the first in line.
> Something *tells* me I should study harder.

6. Some pronouns may be singular or plural in meaning. This means that verbs used with them depend on the noun or pronoun they refer to. Such pronouns include the following: *all, any, more, most, none, some, that, which,* and *who.*

> All of the tools *were* missing.
> All of the ice *was* melted.

> Most of the speakers *were* interesting.
> Most of the ice cream *was* eaten.

> None of the students *were* in their seats.
> None of this candy *is* any good.

7. When subjects are connected by "either-or" or "neither-nor," the verb agrees with the subject that is closer to it.

> Neither the driver nor the passengers *were* able to tell what happened.
> Either the passengers or the driver *is* to blame.

8. Some nouns plural in form but singular in meaning require a singular verb. These include *economics, news, mathematics, physics, politics, headquarters, electronics.*

> The news from the lab *was* encouraging.
> Physics *is* a required course for premed students.

9. Subjects that indicate distance, measure, money, or time require a singular verb.

> Six miles *was* the longest race he had ever run.
> Four quarts of oil *is* the capacity of the motor.
> To a child, fifty cents *seems* like a fortune.
> Four minutes *is* a long time to wait for a taxi.

10. A collective noun (a word singular in form but referring to a group of people or things) takes a singular verb when the group is regarded as a unit, and a plural verb when the individuals of the group are regarded separately. Some common collective nouns are *army, assembly, committee, company, couple, crowd, faculty, family, flock, group, herd, jury, pair, squad,* and *team.*

The couple *was* seated at the head table.
The couple *were* unable to agree on the wine to order with
their meal.

The faculty *was* given a raise.
The faculty *were* assigned their parking spaces.

11. Subjects plural in form that indicate a quantity or number
take a singular verb if the subject is considered a unit but a
plural verb if the individuals of the subject are regarded
separately.

Three-fourths of the earth's surface *is* covered with water.
Three-fourths of the words in the spelling list *were* of Latin or
Greek origin.

12. When *a number* is used as the subject, it requires a plural verb.
The number is always singular.

A number of tourists *are* always surprised by the size of the
Grand Canyon.
The number of tourists visiting the Grand Canyon *is* quite
large.

E X E R C I S E 2

Find the subject in each of the following sentences and determine
whether it is singular or plural. Then select the correct verb.

1. One of the best places for taking pictures (are, is) Niagara
   Falls.
2. Under the eaves (was, were) a nest of hornets.
3. The coach, as well as the players, (was, were) disappointed at
   the score.
4. A student's grade point average, as well as his extracurricular
   activities, (determine, determines) his eligibility for the Hon-
   or Society.
5. In this bed (has, have) slept several famous presidents.
6. An attorney from one of the most distinguished law firms in
   the city (represent, represents) the suspect.
7. Lane, like hundreds of other students, (want, wants) a
   summer job to pay for her school expenses.
8. Among the many surprises (was, were) a visit from his
   daughter in England.
9. Muhammad Ali, no longer slugging opponents, (appear,
   appears) in television commercials.
10. A sheet of directions accompanying the snow chains (explain,
    explains) how to install them.

11. Drowning out the boos (was, were) the applause of her admirers.
12. In contrast to the urgings of her friends (was, were) the cautions of her family.
13. Their company, along with hundreds of other companies, (publish, publishes) an annual stock report.
14. Two members of the exploration party (has, have) been commended for bravery.
15. Each participant, as well as the members of his family, (receive, receives) bonus points that can be applied to the next drawing.

E X E R C I S E 3

Select the correct verb in the following sentences.

1. All of the visitors (agree, agrees) that they were unprepared for the extreme heat.
2. A couple from Iowa (has, have) won the jackpot.
3. The president and spokesman of the club (has, have) been asked to give his views.
4. An engraved certificate, as well as other gifts, (are, is) given to the Father of the Year.
5. None of the winners of the Ugly Man on Campus contest (want, wants) their names announced.
6. A group of dissatisfied customers (is, are) suing the utility company.
7. The psychologist said that most of the anxiety experienced by the children (is, are) caused by their parents' absence.
8. Professor Carman stated that anyone in the class who (turn, turns) in a late paper will fail.
9. Although her father is a politician, Lois claims that politics (bore, bores) her.
10. Most of the food on the tiny neighboring islands (contain, contains) high levels of starch and carbohydrates.
11. Neither the tornadoes nor the flood (has, have) succeeded in destroying the spirits of the townspeople.
12. Chili powder and cayenne pepper (provide, provides) the tang in my chili.
13. None of the candidates (want, wants) to talk to the reporters.
14. All of the appreciation expressed by the survivors (was, were) directed to their guide.
15. Neither the telegram nor the letters (has, have) mentioned the news of his marriage.

Misplaced and Dangling Modifiers

Modifiers are words that describe other words in a sentence. They may be single words or groups of words, and they may come before the word they modify, or they may follow it. In either case, the modifier should appear *near* the word it modifies so that there will be no confusion about which word it modifies.

A *misplaced modifier* is one that is separated from the word it modifies and as a result modifies the wrong word. Sentences with misplaced modifiers are usually confusing and often humorous because of the unintended meaning. Read carefully the following examples of sentences containing misplaced modifiers:

> Craig bought a motorcycle for his wife with an electric starter.
> The pizza was served by an unsmiling waiter covered with anchovies, tomato sauce, and mushrooms.

By placing the modifier next to the word it modifies or by rewording the sentence, we can make the meaning of such sentences clear to the reader:

• *Revised:*

> Craig bought a motorcycle with an electric starter for his wife.

• *Revised:*

> The pizza, covered with anchovies, tomato sauce, and mushrooms, was served by an unsmiling waiter.

A *dangling modifier* is a word or group of words that does not modify the proper word in the sentence. The result is uncertainty, as in the following:

> Planning for months and reading about the countries to be visited, Bob's vacation was unforgettable.

> Frightened and alone, our walk through the cemetery was terrifying.

Sentences with dangling modifiers can be corrected by inserting the missing word to be modified, or by rewriting the sentence, making sure that each modifier is close to the word it should modify.

• *Revised:*

> Because we had planned for months and read about the countries to be visited, our vacation was unforgettable.

• *Revised:*

> Frightened and alone, we were terrified as we walked through the cemetery.

Faulty Pronoun Reference

Pronouns are words that stand for (or refer to) other words, called their *antecedents*. A pronoun must agree with its antecedent in number. This means that a singular antecedent should have a singular pronoun, and a plural antecedent should have a plural pronoun.

- *Singular antecedent and pronoun:*

Steve Garvey set *his* record in 1983.

- *Plural antecedent and pronoun:*

The players put on *their* uniforms before *they* left for the stadium.

If you follow these rules, your pronouns will agree with their antecedents:

1. The antecedent should be specific rather than implied. The pronouns *that, this, it,* and *which* are often used to refer to an idea never mentioned in the sentence but only vaguely implied. In such cases give the pronoun a specific antecedent to refer to.

   - *Vague:*

   My childhood hero was a chemist, which inspired me to major in it.

   - *Revised:*

   My childhood hero was a chemist who inspired me to major in chemistry.

   - *Vague:*

   She arrived early at the surprise party, which was not her fault.

   - *Revised:*

   Her early arrival at the surprise party was not her fault.

2. Rewrite sentences in which there are two possible antecedents for a pronoun.

   - *Confusing:*

   Sylvia told Arlene that she had been mistaken.

   - *Revised:*

   Sylvia admitted to Arlene that she had been mistaken.
   Sylvia told Arlene, "I have been mistaken."
   Sylvia told Arlene, "You have been mistaken."

3. Use the correct pronoun when referring to animals, people, and things.

    • Use *which* only for animals and things:

    The German shepherd, *which* is a good watchdog, can be trained easily.
    A fire *which* had started in the cellar destroyed the home.

    • Use *who* and *whom* only for people:

    A person *who* does not smoke often receives a discount when applying for life insurance.
    Charles Lindbergh was a hero *whom* everyone admired.

    • Use *that* for animals, people, and things:

    Dogs, children over five, and large containers *that* occupy a separate seat must have tickets.

Masculine pronouns *(he, him, his)* are often used when the gender of the antecedent is not specified, as in the following sentence:

A student should turn in *his* work on time if *he* wants credit for it.

Many writers and readers object to the exclusive use of masculine pronouns, and prefer the following form:

A student should turn in *his or her* work on time if *he or she* wants credit for it.

Some writers and readers, while trying to avoid using only masculine pronouns, believe that the preceding sentence is awkward. Their suggestion is to rewrite the sentence by making the antecedent plural:

Students should turn in *their* work on time if *they* want credit for it.

Problems with Personal Pronouns

Problems often arise in the use of pronouns because many of them have different forms, depending on their use in the sentence. When you are not certain how a pronoun is used, you will be uncertain which form to use.

The *subject* pronouns are used as the subject of a sentence or a clause and as a subject complement. (A *subject complement* is a noun, adjective, or pronoun used after a linking verb. After a linking verb, use only the subject form of a pronoun.)

• *As a subject:*

Marty and I [not *me*] stayed until the game was over.
Who [not *Whom*] is going to pay for this?

• *As s subject complement:*

It was they [not *them*] who ordered the new posters.
That was he [not *him*] yelling at the dog.

Note: Some exceptions to this rule are allowed in informal speech and writing. "It is me," "That's him," and "It was her," for example, are widely accepted in such situations. Careful speakers and writers, however, continue to use the subject form in more formal situations.

The *object* pronouns are used as direct objects, indirect objects, and objects of prepositions.

• *As a direct object:*

Rita suspected George and me [not *I*] of dropping the balloons
   filled with water.
Whom [not *Who*] do you want?

• *As an indirect object:*

When we were children, our parents gave my brothers and me
   [not *I*] an electric train.

• *As the object of a preposition:*

The damage to the car was a surprise to Reggie and her [not *she*].
To whom [not *who*] do you wish to speak?

The *possessive* form of a pronoun is usually used immediately before a noun ending in *-ing* (such nouns are called *gerunds*, and they are formed by adding *-ing* to verbs).

My friends laughed at my [not *me*] singing.
He resents your [not *you*] being taller than he is.

The possessive forms of *it, who,* and *you* cause problems for many writers. Remember that the apostrophe in *it's, who's,* and *you're* indicates that these forms are contractions, not possessive forms.

I am fascinated by the history of Mexico and its [not *it's*] culture.
Any applicant whose [not *who's*] record includes a serious traffic
   violation will be disqualified.
You will always remember your [not *you're*] twenty-first birthday.

Shifts in Tense, Voice, and Person

Your reader follows your ideas in your sentences much like someone follows you along an unfamiliar path. If you suddenly shift or head in a new direction without warning, you will confuse or lose your reader. Three kinds of unnecessary shifts in a sentence are particularly distracting: shifts in *tense,* in *voice,* and in *person.*

Shifts in Tense.   You tell your reader when an action takes place—in the past, at present, or in the future—by the tenses of your verbs. The first verb in a sentence usually affects all of the other verbs in the sentence or paragraph because it lays down a track or sequence for the events being described. A sentence that begins, "After I *bought* my ticket, I . . ." signals the reader that the incident will be told in the past tense because *bought* is a past tense verb. If, however, the sentence were to switch to the present tense, the result would be chaos: "After I bought my ticket, I *enter* the stadium and *try* to find my seat." Is the writer telling about a particular instance when he bought a ticket and tried to find his seat? Or is he describing his usual procedure: he buys a ticket, enters the stadium, and then tries to find the right seat? We don't know, because the writer has switched tenses. When relating an incident, keep in mind the tense forms you are using.

The most common kind of unnecessary shift—going from past to present and back again—usually happens when telling something that becomes so real that it seems to be happening to the narrator *now*. Notice what happens in the following paragraph when the writer forgets when the events took place.

> Because it *was* a beautiful day yesterday, I *decided* to wash my car. I no sooner *get* it washed off than it *begins* to rain. But this *isn't* the first time this *happened* to me. Last Monday evening, when I *was* watering the lawn, it *begins* to drizzle.

To avoid unnecessary shifts and to express your ideas more precisely, you should review the following summary of the six common tenses in English.

Present	I live (am living)
Past	I lived (was living)
Future	I will* live (will be living)
Present Perfect	I have lived (have been living)
Past Perfect	I had lived (had been living)
Future Perfect	I will* have lived (will have been living)

Each tense has a specific use and should not be confused with any other tense.

The *present tense* is used in the following situations:

- To express an action or condition that is going on or exists now:
  That music *is* too loud.
  The cream *tastes* sour.

- To express action that is habitual:
  Ed *plays* poker every Saturday night.
  He *strikes* out more often than any other player on the team.

Shall is often substituted for *will* in the future and future perfect tenses.

• To express universal truths or ideas that are always true:

> The sun *sets* in the West.
> Silence *is* golden.

The *past tense* is used to express an action or condition completed in the past.

> Sam *divorced* her in 1959.
> President Truman's election in 1948 *was* a surprise.

The *future tense* is used to express an action that will take place in the future.

> We *will arrive* in Denver tomorrow night.
> The band *will be playing* four engagements next week.

The future may also be expressed by using the present tense and an adverb or adverb phrase.

> I *am going* to start my paper *tomorrow*.
> *Next Monday* we *leave* for Detroit.

The *present perfect tense* expresses an action or condition that started in the past and has been completed at some indefinite time or is still going on.

> Gwen *has seen* the Acropolis in Athens.
> George *has kept* the secret to himself for many years.

The *past perfect tense* expresses an action that was completed before another action in the past occurred.

> Before she accepted the job, she *had investigated* the responsibilities
>   and duties of the position.
> Mary *had saved* her money for several years before she bought her
>   new car.

Note: The simple past tense is sometimes used for the past perfect: Before she accepted the job, she *investigated* the responsibilities and duties of the position. Mary *saved* her money for several years before she bought her new car.

The *future perfect tense* indicates an action that will be complete before a particular time in the future.

> We will have lived here six years next June.

Here are a few additional suggestions for using the correct tense.

• Don't use the past tense of a verb when it should be present.

> Last summer he visited New Orleans. He said that the old French
>   section *was* interesting and picturesque. [*Incorrect*. The second

sentence implies that the old French section has been destroyed. The correct verb is "is."]

• Use the present infinitive *(to leave, to bring, to remember,* and so on) unless the action referred to was completed before the time expressed in the governing verb.

I wanted to talk [not *to have talked*] to her about it.
We are happy to have had [not *to have*] you stay with us.

• When a narrative in the past tense is interrupted by a reference to a preceding event, use the past perfect tense.

Rachel repaired the bicycle that she *had broken.*
His letter stated that his father *had died.*

Shift in Voice.   A sentence written in *active voice* contains a subject which performs an action expressed by an *active verb:*

The composer *wrote* the song as a tribute to his wife.

A sentence is in the *passive voice* when the subject is acted on by a *passive verb,* consisting of a form of *be* plus the past participle:

The song *was written* by the composer as a tribute to his wife.

As you saw in Chapter 9 (page 201), passive voice constructions often lead to weak and wordy sentences. Another trap to avoid is shifting from one voice to another in the same sentence:

• *Shift:*

The jury returned to the courtroom after their verdict had been reached. *(Confusing; it sounds as though the verdict were reached by someone else.)*

• *Revised:*

The jury returned to the courtroom after they had reached their verdict.

A shift in the voice usually creates a confusing or irritating shift in the subject:

• *Shift:*

When you look up into the night sky, a falling star is sometimes seen.

• *Revised:*

When you look up into the night sky, you can sometimes see a falling star.

Shift in Person.   Shifts in person occur when the writer shifts from one point of view to another. They happen because the writer forgets the subject of the sentence. The most common faulty shifts are from second person *(you)* to third *(he, she, they)* and from third person to second.

Here are some examples of confusing shifts in person:

• *Shift:*

A *person* should look both ways when *you* cross the street.

• *Revised:*

A *person* should look both ways when *he* crosses the street.

• *Shift:*

As *you* leave the freeway and enter the main business district, a *person* can see the damage caused by the twister.

• *Revised:*

As *you* leave the freeway and enter the main business district, *you* can see the damage caused by the twister.

These shifts in person occur within the same sentence. It is equally important that you avoid unnecessary shifts in person from one sentence to another, and from paragraph to paragraph. The best way to avoid such shifts is to decide in advance whom you are talking about—and stick with that point of view.

E X E R C I S E 4

Correct any mistakes in the following sentences. If a sentence is correct, mark it "C."

1. A student in a word processing course has a good chance of employment when they graduate.
2. The drivers' licenses in some states are color-coded for drivers of automobiles that wear eyeglasses.
3. A course in statistics is required for psychology majors, but they will not offer the course next semester.
4. Astrologers and clairvoyants are consulted by some people before they make an important decision.
5. My history prof said that if a person wants to understand the present, you should read about the past.
6. Although most pizza has a thin crust, pizza is preferred by some people with a thick crust.

7. Tom's favorite music is of the Big Band era because they remind him of his youth.
8. All candidates reported the amount of campaign contributions they receive.
9. Trucks have been rumbling through the streets all day with dirt and rock.
10. Wailing and demanding its bottle, the sermon was interrupted.
11. Vince bites his fingernails, and he is trying to stop it.
12. Ignoring the rain, the mail was delivered on time.
13. Beverly admires her father, who is an architect, and that is the profession she plans to follow.
14. I thought the movie last night was the funniest comedy anyone has ever seen.
15. Last Monday was the deadline to register to vote in the primary election.
16. Fran wore an outfit to her martial arts lesson with a black belt.
17. The restaurant was famous for their steaks and barbecue.
18. Urban-cowboy fashions were popular for several months, but it is not as common now.
19. Many performers which have experienced success early in life cannot face failure later.
20. Julie and her mother are very close, although she lives in Europe.
21. The freshmen students last year had the highest scores on entrance tests, according to counselors, but their reasons are not certain.
22. The jet landed safely at the airport with landing gear problems.
23. Acid rain has been studied by scientists which are unable to link it to any single cause.
24. Any animal who is caught without a license will be held in the animal pound.
25. As we entered the room, you could smell the fresh paint.

A Guide to Punctuation and Capitalization

The purpose of punctuation and capitalization is to make your meaning clear to readers. Every mark of punctuation carries some meaning and gives hints about how to read written English. The capitalization of words, too, helps the reader and serves as a guide to meaning.

The wrong punctuation mark or incorrect capitalization can often change the meaning of a sentence; at the very least, it diverts the reader's attention from what you are saying and suggests that you are careless.

Learning to punctuate and capitalize correctly is not hard. It does, however, require a little effort. In this section we will look at the most common situations in written English that require punctuation and capitalization.

Punctuation

The Period

1. Use the period at the end of a declarative sentence, a mild command, and an indirect question.

   - *Declarative sentence:*

     The Japanese consume more fish per capita than Americans do.

   - *Mild command:*

     Please write in ink.

   - *Indirect question:*

     I wonder where I put my wallet.

   - *But:*

     Where is my wallet?

2. Use the period after most abbreviations.

Mr.	St.	Nov.	p.m.	Weds.

   Periods do not usually follow abbreviations of organizations and governmental agencies.

AFL	USA	CBS	UN	FBI

The Question Mark

1. Use a question mark after a direct question.

   Are these your socks?

2. Use a question mark to indicate uncertainty about the accuracy of a date, word, or phrase.

   Hubert van Eyck (1366?–1426) was a founder of the Flemish School of painting.

The Exclamation Point

Use an exclamation mark after a strong interjection or an expression of very strong feeling.

> Help!
> Darn it!

Don't overdo the use of exclamation points. Excessive use dulls their impact.

The Comma

The comma is the punctuation mark most frequently used inside the sentence. It also offers the widest range of individual choice. Do not use a comma unless you have a definite reason for doing so. The following rules will help you avoid cluttering your sentences with unnecessary commas while at the same time making certain you use commas to make your meaning clear.

1. Use a comma to separate independent clauses joined by *and, but, for, nor, or, so,* and *yet.*

   She worked and saved for her children, but they did not appreciate it.
   The centennial of the village was approaching, and everyone was contributing ideas for the celebration.

   If the independent clauses are short, the comma may be omitted.

   I stayed but he left.

2. Use a comma to separate an introductory dependent clause from the main part of the sentence.

   Because Pete was only three when he left Vienna, he does not remember the city.

3. Use a comma to separate a long introductory prepositional phrase.

   Despite an exhausting and often confusing overnight journey, Randy volunteered to work at the picnic.

4. Use a comma to set off an introductory phrase containing a past or present participle or infinitive.

   Wanting to be remembered for his contribution to the arts, Mr. Crow named the symphony as the major recipient of his estate.

To be so confident and yet to appear concerned, the actor pretended to be nervous.

5. Use a comma to set off items in a series.

To be a successful salesman, you must have enthusiasm, confidence in your product, and a knowledge of psychology.

6. Use a comma to set off interrupting elements (also called parenthetical elements) like the following: *as a matter of fact, at any rate, it appears, for instance, nevertheless, of course, however,* and *therefore.*

7. Use commas to set off *nonessential* elements in a sentence. Nonessential elements are modifiers and appositives that are unnecessary to identify the term they refer to. They should be set off on both sides by commas, unless they come at the beginning or end of a sentence. Do *not* set off essential modifiers and appositives with commas. Notice the following examples:

Abraham Lincoln, *the sixteenth President,* was a complex and often contradictory person. (The nonessential appositive merely gives additional information; the subject is identified by his name. Because the appositive is nonessential, it is set off.)

The poet *Wordsworth* is famous for his descriptions of nature. (The appositive is essential; if it were omitted, we would not know the poet referred to. Therefore, it is not set off with commas.)

New Orleans, *which is known for its jazz,* is a city I have always wanted to visit. (The clause is nonessential because the subject is fully identified; therefore, it is set off with commas.)

A city *that I have always wanted to visit* is New Orleans. (The clause is essential and therefore is not set off with commas.)

8. Use a comma to set off coordinate adjectives. Adjectives are coordinate if *and* can be placed between them.

It was a long, boring novel. (You can say "long *and* boring.")
But note:
It was a long detective novel. (No comma: you would not say, "a long *and* detective novel.")

9. Use a comma to set off contrasted elements.

I ordered a steak, not oysters.

10. Use a comma to set off quoted material.

    In a clear voice she announced, "I am resigning."

11. Use a comma in direct address.

    Eddie, when are you leaving for Des Moines?

12. Use a comma in dates if the month is given first.

    September 28, 1929

    If the date is followed by the rest of the sentence, the year should also be followed by a comma.

    December 7, 1941, is a day that will live in infamy.

13. Use a comma to separate the elements in an address.

    United Nations Plaza, Riverside Drive, New York, New York

    Within a sentence, place a comma after the final element in an address.

    His office at the United Nations Plaza on Riverside Drive,
       New York, is his headquarters.

14. Titles and degrees are set off by commas on both sides.

    James L. Tierney, Ph.D., was the graduation speaker.

15. Use a comma to prevent misreading.

    Although angry, Tim shook hands with his opponent.

Misusing Commas.   The comma is misused more than any other punctuation mark. Too many commas can slow down the thought or confuse the meaning. The following list presents some of the frequent situations that might tempt you to use the comma.

1. Do not use a comma to separate the subject from its verb.

   • *Incorrect:*

     A valid driver's license or credit card, is required.

   • *Revised:*

     A valid driver's license or credit card is required.

2. Do not use a comma after the last item in a series of adjectives preceding the noun.

   • *Incorrect:*

     She was a creative, imaginative, dedicated, dancer.

- *Revised:*

  She was a creative, imaginative, dedicated dancer.

3. Do not use a comma before indirect quotations.

- *Incorrect:*

  He said, that his favorite singer was Placido Domingo.

- *Revised:*

  He said that his favorite singer was Placido Domingo.

4. Do not use a comma between two words or phrases joined by a coordinator.

- *Incorrect:*

  Every applicant was asked to bring a résumé, and a photograph.

- *Revised:*

  Every applicant was asked to bring a résumé and a photograph.

5. Do not use a comma to separate a verb from a *that* clause.

- *Incorrect:*

  He often claimed, that he was a member of the royal family.

- *Revised:*

  He often claimed that he was a member of the royal family.

6. Do not use a comma to separate independent clauses.

- *Incorrect:*

  The average price of a personal computer is declining, more people are buying them for home use.

- *Revised:*

  The average price of a personal computer is declining; more people are buying them for home use. (There are several ways to correct this comma splice; the use of a semicolon is only one. See page 300 for others.)

The Semicolon

1. Use a semicolon to separate two closely related independent clauses when there is no coordinating conjunction to join them.

You do not have to be a brute to hit a tennis ball a long distance; a flick of the wrist will do it.

2. Use a semicolon to separate items in a series if the items contain commas.

The winners of the raffle were Joe Brady, a watch maker from Miami, Florida; Joyce Martin, a salesperson from Toledo, Ohio; Marino Garcia, a wrestling coach from St. Louis, Missouri; and Bill Hubbard, a butcher from Spokane, Washington.

The Colon

1. Use a colon before a list of items introduced by an independent clause.

She had articles published in three popular magazines: *TV Guide, Reader's Digest,* and *Woman's Day.*

Do not place a colon between a verb and its objects or complements or between a preposition and its objects.

- *Incorrect:*

  The three magazines she has published in are: *TV Guide, Reader's Digest, and Woman's Day.*

- *Incorrect:*

  While in Washington we saw: the Vietnam War Memorial, the White House, and the Washington Monument.

- *Incorrect:*

  As a source of energy, coal has been partially replaced by: nuclear energy, solar energy, and oil.

2. Use a colon between two complete thoughts when the second explains the first.

He told me what I wanted to hear: my application had been accepted.

Parentheses

Use parentheses to enclose unimportant information or comments that are not an essential part of the passage.

Some majors in college (English, for instance) require two years of a foreign language.

Two warnings: Never place a comma before a parenthesis. Always use parentheses in pairs.

Dashes

1. Use a dash to mark an abrupt change in the thought or structure of a sentence.

   Last night I went to—but do you really want to hear about it?

2. Use dashes to make explanatory matter more prominent.

   T. S. Eliot—a native of the United States—was one of England's greatest modern poets.

   Dashes are used to make explanatory matter *stand out;* parentheses are used to bury it in the sentence.

3. Use a dash to set off an introductory series.

   Chinese, English, Hindu, Spanish, and Russian—these are the major world languages.

Brackets

1. Use brackets to set off your own words that you have inserted into a quotation.

   "My favorite actors," the aging producer said, "are Ronnie [Reagan] and Helmut [Dantine]."

2. Use brackets to set off words and phrases that you have added for the purposes of explanation or identification.

   "Next year the G.N.P. [Gross National Product] will exceed our expectations," reported the Secretary of the Treasury.

Quotation Marks

1. Use quotation marks around the exact words of a speaker.

   "I will be happy to give you a tour of the museum," she said.

   Do not use quotation marks for indirect quotations.

   She said that she would be happy to give us a tour of the museum.

2. Use quotation marks to call attention to words that are being used in an unusual sense and in definitions.

   Many people mispronounce "mischievous."

   Note: Some people prefer to italicize (underline) words when used in this way.

3. Use quotation marks to enclose titles of short poems, paintings, magazine articles, television programs, short stories, songs, and any selection from a longer work.

> Dorothy's favorite poem is "Trees," by Joyce Kilmer.
> My uncle watches "General Hospital" on television every afternoon.
> "Stardust" is probably the most frequently recorded song in history.

Italics

When words that would be italicized when printed are handwritten or typed, they should be underlined.

1. Italicize titles of books, plays, magazines, movies, and newspapers.

   Death Comes for the Archbishop
   Hamlet
   Time
   Detroit Free Press
   Casablanca

2. Italicize foreign words and phrases that have not yet been adopted as English expressions. If you are not certain about the status of a particular word or phrase, check a good dictionary.

   por favor
   C'est la guerre

3. Use italics when referring to letters, numbers, and words.

   > The professor gave only two *A*'s all year.
   > All of the *9*'s were removed from the deck of cards.
   > He always mispronounces *discipline*. (As noted under quotation marks, some writers prefer to enclose words used like this in quotes.)

4. Use italics for special emphasis.

   > I know what I *should* do, but I don't *want* to do it.

Ellipsis

Use an ellipsis (three periods) to indicate an omission of unnecessary or irrelevant material from a quotation. If the ellipsis occurs at the end of a sentence, use four periods.

> The treaty stated, "The terms of this document . . . will be observed by both parties effective midnight . . . ."

The Hyphen

The hyphen is used to set off certain prefixes, to separate certain compound words, and to show that a word is to be carried over to the next line.

1. After *ex-*, *self-*, and *all-* when they are prefixes.

   ex-wife
   self-hatred
   all-knowing

2. After prefixes that precede a proper noun or adjective.

   pro-Democratic
   un-American
   anti-Semitic

3. Between compound descriptions serving as a single adjective before a noun.

   dark-green water
   a hard-bitten sheriff
   a slow-starting pace

4. Between fractions and compound numbers from twenty-one through ninety-nine.

   five-eighths
   three-fourths
   fifty-two
   eighty-four

5. Between syllables for words at the end of a line. Never divide a one-syllable word. When you are uncertain about the use of the hyphen in the syllabication of a word or in compound words, consult a collegiate-level dictionary.

The Apostrophe

The apostrophe is used for the possessive case (except for personal pronouns), to indicate an omitted letter or number, and to form the plural of numbers, specific words, and letters.

1. Use the apostrophe to form the possessive case.

   • To form the possessive case of a singular person, thing, or indefinite pronoun, add *'s:*

   Lou's parking space
   the girl's job

the owl's hooting
anyone's duty

- If a proper name already ends in *s* in its singular form and the adding of *'s* would make the pronunciation difficult, it is best to use the apostrophe only:

  Jesus' teachings *(Jesus's* would be difficult to pronounce but is acceptable)
  Charles' telephone number *(Charles's* is acceptable)

- To form the possessive case of a plural noun ending in *s*, add an apostrophe only:

  the Smiths' new home
  the birds' song

- To form the possessive of a plural noun *not* ending in *s*, add *'s:*

  the children's program
  men's obligations

- To form the possessives of compound words, use the apostrophe according to the meaning of the construction:

  Sears and Roebuck's new stores (the new stores of Sears and Roebuck)
  J. C. Penney's and Montgomery Ward's stores (the stores of J. C. Penney and of Montgomery Ward)
  Her brother and sister's home (the home of her brother and sister)

2. Use an apostrophe to indicate an omitted letter or number.

   isn't
   the '80s

3. Use an apostrophe to form the plurals of letters, specific words, and numbers.

   Her *1*'s and *e*'s look the same to me. (Notice that they are italicized or underlined as well.)
   I counted forty *aye*'s and sixteen *nay*'s.
   Anyone who received a score in the *90*'s did not have to take the unit test.

   Note: An apostrophe is not necessary for the plural of a year.
   Example: The 1980s were a time of economic hardship for many.

4. The apostrophe should *not* be used with the possessive forms of personal and relative pronouns.

- Incorrect:

    it's, her's, your's, our's, who's (to show possession)

- Revised:

    its, hers, yours, ours, whose (possessive form)

Notice, however, that indefinite pronouns form the possessive case by adding *'s: one's, anyone's, someone's, everyone's,* and so on.

Numbers

1. If a number requires no more than two words, it should be spelled out.

    seven hours   eleven million dollars   two hundred workers

    If a number requires more than two words, use figures.

    125 pounds   4¼ ounces   1016 pages

2. Always write out a number beginning a sentence.

    - Incorrect:

        47 passengers were injured in a train crash this afternoon.

    - Revised:

        Forty-seven passengers were injured in a train crash this afternoon.

    If the number is a long one and spelling it would be awkward, figure out a way to reword the sentence so that the number comes later, in which case it can be stated as a figure.

    - Incorrect:

        Three hundred sixty four thousand nine hundred forty-one voters had gone to the polls by ten o'clock this morning.

    - Revised:

        By ten o'clock this morning 364,941 voters had gone to the polls.

3. Use figures when they are followed by A.M. or P.M.; write out whole hours.

    7 A.M., 12 A.M., 4:30 P.M.
    twelve midnight, nine o'clock

4. Figures can be made plural in either of two ways: by adding *-s*, or by adding *-'s*. The latter *(-'s)* is preferred by most writers. writers.

several *3*'s, four *10*'s

Notice that figures used in this sense are also italicized (underlined).

Do not use an apostrophe when writing out a number in the plural.

• Incorrect:

several three's and ten's

• Revised:

several threes and tens

Capitalization

The rules for capitalization are based, in general, on the following principle: the names of *specific* persons, places, and things *(proper* nouns) are capitalized; the names of *general* persons, places, and things *(common* nouns) are not capitalized.

1. Capitalize the first word in any sentence, including direct quotations that are complete sentences.

   The waiter approached our table and asked, "Is Doctor Marshall with this group?"

2. Capitalize the first and last words in a title and all other words except *a, an, the,* and unimportant words with fewer than five letters.

   One of the required texts in the course is titled *A Guide to the Principles of Ornithology.* I want to read *A Good Man Is Hard to Find.*

3. Capitalize the titles of relatives and professions only when they come before the person's name, or when they take the place of the person's name.

   I'll see you next week, Aunt Bea. *But:* Her aunt lived in Buenos Aires.
   The recruits reported to Corporal Trujillo.
   The corporal welcomed the recruits to the base.
   Is your mother home?
   Here's the magazine I was telling you about, Mother.

4. Capitalize the names of people, political, religious, and ethnic groups, languages, and nationalities, as well as adjectives derived from them.

Republicans	French	Mexican food
Mormons	Quakers	German wines
Chicanos	Chinese	Polish names

5. Capitalize the names of particular streets, buildings, bridges, rivers, cities, states, nations, specific geographical features, schools, and other institutions.

Wilshire Boulevard	Ireland
Merchandise Mart	Monks' Mounds
Eads Bridge	Julliard School of Music
Fox River	the United States Senate
Philadelphia	the Alps

6. Capitalize directions only when they refer to specific regions.

People who live in the West have language differences from those who live in the East.
But: The plane turned north.

7. Capitalize the days of the week, months of the year, and names of holidays.

The Fourth of July was observed on the first Monday of the month this year.

8. Capitalize the names of particular historical events and eras.

the First World War
the Roaring Twenties
the Age of Reason

9. Capitalize the names of school subjects only if they are proper nouns or if they are followed by a course number.

a biology course	Economics 102
Biology 215	French
the economics professor	English

E X E R C I S E 5

The paragraph below lacks correct punctuation and capitalization. Copy it, making the necessary corrections.

The american indian has had to endure bad housing lack of jobs dismal health conditions and poor education the present plight of the red man is in contrast to his condition four hundred and fifty years ago at first the newly discovered indians were respected and admired christopher columbus sir walter raleigh and the french philosopher michel de montaigne spoke highly of them the puritans in new england however regarded indians as stubborn animals that refused to acknowledge the obvious blessings of white civilization in 1637 a group of puritans surrounded the pequot indian village and set fire to it about 500 indians were burned to death or shot when the puritan preacher cotton mather heard about the raid he wrote in his diary on this day we have sent six hundred heathen souls to hell after the war of 1812 the conditions of the indians declined rapidly pressures increased to get the indians off the lands the whites had appropriated from them almost all of the indians were cleared from the east the experience of the indians west of the mississippi was only a sad duplication of what had happened east of it warfare broken treaties expropriation of land rebellion and ultimately defeat as president cleveland remarked the hunger and thirst of the white man for the indians land is almost equal to his hunger and thirst after righteousness the indian problem still nags at the american conscience in the 1980s indians exist as the most manipulated people on earth and yet our indian policy has produced only failure after failure.

E X E R C I S E   6

Add any missing commas and delete those that are unnecessary in the following sentences. If a sentence is punctuated correctly, mark it "C."

1. Miami, which has a large Cuban population is on the east coast of Florida.
2. Lacking the confidence to sing in public and believing that everyone was ridiculing him the tenor abandoned his career, and returned to Casper Wyoming.
3. Every morning while shaving Reggie thought of the breakfast of juice cereal, and toast that his sister Wilma, was preparing for him.
4. If you handle the ceramic jars before they are dry they will crack, when they are fired in the kiln.
5. According to Abraham Maslow one of the giants of modern psychology, productive individuals share certain common traits.
6. Because of migraine headaches and attacks of nausea, Ruth decided that she was allergic to eggplant.
7. The technology needed to make atom bombs is available to

almost any country or terrorist and some critics fear eventual nuclear blackmail.

8. According to Isaac Asimov science fiction is the only literature, that is based firmly on scientific thought.
9. Many people want to sound educated but they don't want to go to the trouble of becoming educated.
10. Some parishioners wanted a modernistic design for the new church however, others preferred a traditional plan.
11. Natural biological evolution in man is slow, cultural evolution has accelerated at a dizzy rate.
12. The Cuyahoga River in Ohio was so terribly polluted, that it actually caught fire.
13. A city that has a large ethnic population usually has a variety of ethnic restaurants.
14. Foreigners often have a difficult time understanding baseball, most Americans don't understand the English game of cricket.
15. Children on an Israeli kibbutz do not live with their parents, they are raised in groups.

E X E R C I S E 7

Some of the apostrophes in the following sentences are unnecessary, and some are missing. Make the necessary corrections.

1. Although its difficult to verify, the attitude's of today's college students toward alcohol have changed in recent year's.
2. Everyones' chances of winning were increased because of the low attendance.
3. We were surprised to learn that the mens' team was eliminated in the first round, but the women's team went to the semi-finals.
4. The McLaughlins' St. Patricks' Day parties always attract many people who are not Irish.
5. I recognized your cat by it's diamond-studded collar.
6. The professors' students remarked that she was a brilliant lecturer but somewhat reluctant to answer anyone's questions after class.
7. Americans who remember the '30s often refer to the Depression and to those who's fortunes were wiped out.
8. The chefs winning recipe had been in his family for generations.
9. Gloria Steinem is an eloquent speaker for womens' rights.
10. Biblical archeologists do not know the location of Moses' grave.

E X E R C I S E 8

The sentences below require capital letters and quotation marks and additional punctuation.

1. George Eliot born Mary Anne Evans is the author of the novel Adam Bede.
2. Tony has travelled to every state except three Alaska Florida and Hawaii.
3. The emotional responses evoked by Bach's music are different from those triggered by Chuck Berry's song Maybelline.
4. Shakespeare, the author of the play Hamlet wrote a sonnet which begins Shall I compare thee to a summers day.
5. One of the great philosophers of the middle ages was saint Thomas Aquinas.
6. After living in the west since the beginning of world war II, aunt Marilyn longed for the sights and sounds of the east particularly the lovely New Jersey cities of fort Lee and Secaucus.
7. My favorite movie is gone with the wind and my favorite song is as time goes by.
8. Sam had taken professor Barclay's economics 101 course so many times that he could mouth the lectures before professor Barclay said them.
9. The speaker concluded by saying I will conclude my remarks with the words of Gandhi unjust laws and practices survive because men obey them and conform to them.
10. The average American moves 14 times in his lifetime and the rate is increasing according to a columnist in the Louisville Courier.

A

A Glossary

of Usage

Here is a list of words that are often confused by college writers. If you want to know more about these (or other) words, consult one of the collegiate dictionaries recommended in Chapter 1, or Webster's Third *New International Dictionary.*

accept, except	*Accept* is a verb meaning "to receive," and *except* is a preposition meaning "but," or a verb meaning "to exclude."
	"We wanted to *accept* his offer, but we were unable to."
	"All of the countries *except* Peru were represented."
	"The committee decided to *except* the officers from the meeting."
adapt, adopt	To *adapt* something is to change it for a purpose; to *adopt* something is to control or possess it.
	"She *adapted* the words of the song to her own meaning."
	"She *adopted* the words of the song as her philosophy."
advice, advise	*Advice* is an opinion you offer; *advise* means to recommend.
	"The coach's *advice* was ignored."
	"My teacher can *advise* you of the best novel to read."
affect, effect	To *affect* is to change or modify; to *effect* is to bring about or cause something; an *effect* is a result.
	"The fog will *affect* traffic conditions."
	"The doctor will try to *effect* a change in his patient's condition."
	"The *effect* of the treatment was not noticeable."
aggravate, annoy	To *aggravate* is to make a condition worse; to *annoy* is to irritate.
	"The treatment only *aggravated* his condition."
	"The ticking clock *annoyed* Dean as he read."
ain't	*Ain't* is a nonstandard word never used by educated or careful speakers or writers except to achieve a deliberate humorous effect. Avoid the word.
all ready, already	*All ready* shows preparedness; *already* is an adverb meaning "before or by the time mentioned."
	"The troops were *all ready* for inspection."
	"It was *already* six o'clock when darkness came."
all right, alright	*All right* is the correct form; do not use *alright*, which is nonstandard.
all together, altogether	*All together* means "all at once or at the same time." *Altogether* means "completely" or "entirely."

"The family are *all together* in the living room."
"You are *altogether* correct."

allusion,
illusion

An *allusion* is an indirect reference to something. An *illusion* is a false image or impression.

"He made an *allusion* to his parents' wealth."
"It is an *illusion* to think that I will be a millionaire."

among, between

Use *among* when referring to more than two items and *between* when referring to two.

"Sandy was *among* the four finalists."
"Sid can't decide *between* a green or a blue shirt."

amount,
number

Amount refers to a quantity or to things in the aggregate; *number* refers to objects that you can count.

"A large *amount* of work remains to be done."
"A *number* of jobs are still unfilled."

anyone,
any one

Anyone means "any person at all," and *any one* means any single person.

"I will talk to *anyone* who answers the phone."
"*Any one* of these players can teach you the game in minutes."

anyways,
anywheres

These are nonstandard forms for *anyway* and *anywhere*, and they should be avoided.

bad, badly

Bad is an adjective, and *badly* is an adverb.

"Her pride was hurt *badly* (not *bad*)."
"She feels *bad* (not *badly*)."

being as,
being that

These are nonstandard terms and should be avoided. Use *since* or *because*.

beside, besides

Beside is a preposition meaning "by the side of." *Besides* may be a preposition or an adverb meaning "in addition to" or "also."

"The doctor sat *beside* the bed talking to the patient."
"*Besides* my homework, I have some letters to write."

burst, bursted,
bust, busted

Burst remains the same in past, present, and past participle forms. *Bursted* and *busted* are nonstandard forms. *Bust* as a verb meaning "break" or "arrest" is slang.

can, may

Can refers to ability, and *may* refers to permission.

"Henry *may* go with us if he wants to."
"Henry *can* go with us now that he feels better."

can't hardly,
barely

These are double negatives and are to be avoided. Use *can hardly* and *can barely* or *can't*.

complement, *compliment*   To *complement* is to balance or complete; to *compliment* is to flatter.

"Her new shoes *complement* her outfit."
"He *complimented* her for her ability to yodel."

conscience, *conscious*   A *conscience* is a sense of right or wrong. To be *conscious* is to be aware.

"His *conscience* wouldn't allow him to cheat on the test."
"I was not *conscious* of the noise in the background."

continual, *continuous*   *Continual* means "repeated frequently," and *continuous* "without interruption."

"We heard a series of *continual* beeps in the background."
"I was lulled to sleep by the *continuous* hum of the motor below deck."

could of   This is a nonstandard form. Use *could have.*

council, counsel   A *council* is a body of people; *counsel* refers to an advisor or to advice.

"The city *council* voted itself a pay hike."
"The trial was interrupted by her *counsel's* sudden illness."
"Her lawyer gave her excellent *counsel.*"

disinterested, *uninterested*   To be *disinterested* is to be impartial. *Uninterested* means "not interested."

"The losing team thought that the referee was not *disinterested.*"
"It was easy to tell by his falling asleep that he was *uninterested.*"

enormity, *enormousness*   *Enormity* means "atrociousness"; *enormousness* means "of great size."

"The *enormity* of the crime staggered the sheriff."
"Because of the *enormousness* of his feet, it was impossible to fit him with shoes."

farther, further   Use *farther* for physical distance and *further* for degree or quantity.

"They live *farther* from the center of town than we do."
"Their proposal was a *further* attempt to reach an agreement."

fewer, less   Although these words are often used interchangeably, careful speakers and writers still use *fewer* to refer to things that are readily distinguishable or in the plural *(fewer jobs, calories, hairpins)* and *less* to things that are singular or are not ordinarily capable of being separated *(less energy, money, freedom).*

"*Fewer* [not *less*] accidents were reported because of the
new stop sign."

"*Less* [not *fewer*] traffic congestion has been one of the effects
of the new stop sign."

flaunt, flout	To *flaunt* is to show off; to *flout* is to defy.

"He *flaunted* his knowledge of several languages."
"The tourists *flouted* the local laws."

good, well	*Good* is an adjective, never an adverb. *Well* is an adverb and an adjective; as an adjective it means "in a state of good health."

"She performs *well* (not *good*) in that role."
"I am *well* now, although last week I didn't feel very *good*."

hanged, hung	Criminals are *hanged* for their crimes; pictures are *hung*.

imply, infer	To *imply* means "to hint strongly"; to *infer* means "to derive the meaning by induction." You *infer* the meaning of a passage when you read or hear it; the writer or speaker *implies* it.

"He *implied* that he was only thirty-nine."
"We *inferred* from his remarks that he would not change his
mind."

irregardless	Nonstandard. Use *regardless*.

its, it's	*Its* is the possessive form; *it's* is a contraction for *it is* or *it has*.

"What was *its* price before it went on sale?"
"*It's* going to be a long day at the rate we're going."
"*It's* been a long day."

lie, lay	You *lay* or set something down; yesterday you *laid* it down. You *lie* down or rest; yesterday you *lay* down; you have *lain* down for an hour.

loose, lose	To *loose* means "to untie or unfasten;"; to *lose* is "to misplace." *Loose* as an adjective means "unfastened" or "unattached."

"His necktie was *loose*."
"Did he *lose* his necktie?"

maybe, may be	*Maybe* means "perhaps"; *may be* is a verb phrase.

"*Maybe* he'll come tomorrow."
"We *may be* surprised at the results."

myself	Correct when used as a reflexive: "I hurt *myself*," "I helped *myself*," etc. Colloquial when used as a substitute for *I* or *me* as in the following:

"My sister and *myself* were raised in Wisconsin."
"He spoke to my sister and *myself.*"

precede, proceed To *precede* means "to go before or in front of"; to *proceed* is "to continue moving ahead."

"Poverty and hunger often *precede* revolutions."
"They *proceeded* down the aisle as if nothing had happened."

principal, principle *Principal* has two meanings: "The administrator of a school," and "most important." *Principle* means "rule or theory."

"Mr. Lewis is the *principal* of our high school."
"The *principal* reason I can't swim is that I'm afraid of the water."
"The *principles* of geometry are too subtle for me."

set, sit To *sit* means "to occupy a seat"; the past tense is *sat* and the past participle is also *sat*. The present participle is *sitting*. To *set* means "to place something somewhere," and its principal parts are *set*, *set*, and *setting*.

"Please *sit* down and have a cup of coffee."
"He *sat* here for an hour waiting for you."
"Please *set* the box on the desk."
"She *set* her packages on the kitchen table when she came home."

their, there, they're Note carefully the following sentences:

"They were shocked to find *their* house on fire."
"Please stay *there* while I make a phone call."
"It looks as though *they're* going to be late."

these kind, those kind Both expressions are nonstandard. Use "that kind," "this kind," "those kinds," and "these kinds."

who's, whose *Who's* is a contraction meaning "who is" or "who has"; *whose* is the possessive form of *who*.

"Who's going with me?"
"Who's been eating my porridge?"
"Whose book is this?"

your, you're Similar to the preceding pair. *Your* is the possessive form of *you; you're* is a contraction for *you are*.

"Are these *your* gloves?"
"*You're* going to get a sunburn if you stay out much longer."

B

250

Writing Topics

When asked to select their own writing topics, some students panic. If you are one of them, this list may help. It contains 250 topics—some general, others more specific—that you may want to write about or that may trigger, through association, another idea that you can develop into an essay.

blind dates
recycling
exotic places
my church
a death in the family
parapsychology
a secret prejudice
pets
famous monuments
childhood dreams
diets
games
self-help books
acting
television
dissent
pollution
being a stranger
being organized
autistic children
lies
Playboy
classical music
scientific
   experiments
rejection
high school cliques
Elvis Presley
the CIA
car mechanics
fancy cooking
graffiti
the Civil War
magazines
cosmetics
weightlifting
the beach
pay raises

a surprise party
teachers' grading
   standards
making a cake
hunting without a
   gun
saving a life
skiing
writing music
astrology
birth control
Judaism
my first kiss
archaeology
my boss
affirmative action
prostitution
student rights
prisons
motorcycles
insurance
family history
veterinarians
forests
bartending
child support
Chinese food
nonsmokers
competition
airplanes
gangsters
astronomy
Zionism
Ernie Lombardi
addictions
life on other planets
living alone
Peanuts

perfume ads
science fiction
song lyrics
town characters
humor
clothing styles
cheating
old cars
hobbies for profit
painting
yoga
whales
model airplanes
funerals
breaking the law
making movies
memories
patriotism
on being
   handicapped
campus slang
computers
the exercise
   epidemic
black athletes
the "thin" craze
sexism in language
heroes
John Lennon
life after death
nuclear freeze
creationism
step-fathers
amusement parks
welfare cheaters
waiting tables
local elections
news anchormen

the nation

foreign customs

surveys

weddings

leaving home

swimming suits

dictators

objectionable
    commercials

a change in religion

labor unions

sex education

back-packing

our court system

being a worry-wart

the Equal Rights
    Amendment

vegetarianism

Ronald Reagan

stress

Woody Allen

automation

cats versus dogs

collecting antiques

large families

country living

job interviews

draft registration

phonies

first love

dirty movies

waitresses

ethnic customs

smoking

gay liberation

violence in America

a bore I know

Miss America

condominiums

doublespeak

libraries

Shakespeare

rhythm and blues

conservatives

athletes and grades

blue jeans

prayer

the American Indian

the "Me" generation

drive-in movies

Star Trek

the space shuttle

inflation

cable tv

electronic music

teenage drinking

witchcraft

shopping malls

foreign travels

bigotry

terminal illness

phobias

in-laws

capital punishment

dreams

genetic engineering

Viet Nam

an objectionable
    roommate

flying saucers

embarrassing
    moments

privacy vs. security

gun control

censorship on
    campus

doping in sports

the population
    explosion

radioactive waste

airports

foreign trade

euthanasia

sociobiology

subliminal
    advertising

movie starlets

scandal magazines

punk rock

Groucho Marx

gambling

hobbies

second marriages

I.Q. tests

adoption

terrorism

migrant workers

the Third World

newspapers

parking regulations

photography

race problems

Social Security

insurance men

Howard Cossell

living together

brain-washing

clones

local politicians

cults

night people

jogging

cafeteria food

small cars

Christmas

disco

parents

fear of math

swimming lessons

fathers and sons

the English language

nursery rhymes

the metric system

modern novelists

phrenology

opera singers

boycotts

a high school teacher

a favorite author

people-watching
the life of the party
best friend
worthless cures
being shy
suicide
reincarnation

the Super Bowl
anti-vivisection
the Bible
car dealers
birthdays
shock therapy
famous hoaxes

holy shrines
a threatening
    situation
my secret ambition
the pleasures of my
    youth
the joy of cooking

Index